CHAD

Nations of the Modern World: Africa

Larry W. Bowman, *Series Editor*

Chad: A Nation in Search of Its Future,
Mario J. Azevedo and Emmanuel U. Nnadozie

Angola: Struggle for Peace and Reconstruction, Inge Tvedten

Burkina Faso: Unsteady Statehood in West Africa, Pierre Englebert

Senegal: An African Nation Between Islam and the West,
Second Edition, Sheldon Gellar

Uganda: Tarnished Pearl of Africa, Thomas P. Ofcansky

Cape Verde: Crioulo Colony to Independent Nations, Richard A. Lobban, Jr.

Madagascar: Conflicts of Authority in the Great Island, Philip M. Allen

Kenya: The Quest for Prosperity, Second Edition,
Norman Miller and Rodger Yeager

Zaire: Continuity and Political Change in an Oppressive State,
Winsome J. Leslie

Gabon: Beyond the Colonial Legacy, James F. Barnes

Guinea-Bissau: Power, Conflict, and Renewal in a West African Nation,
Joshua B. Forrest

Namibia: The Nation After Independence,
Donald L. Sparks and December Green

Zimbabwe: The Terrain of Contradictory Development,
Christine Sylvester

Mauritius: Democracy and Development in the Indian Ocean,
Larry W. Bowman

Niger: Personal Rule and Survival in the Sahel, Robert B. Charlick

Equatorial Guinea: Colonialism, State Terror, and the Search for Stability,
Ibrahim K. Sundiata

Mali: A Search for Direction, Pascal James Imperato

CHAD

A Nation in Search of Its Future

MARIO J. AZEVEDO

AND

EMMANUEL U. NNADOZIE

WestviewPress

A Division of HarperCollinsPublishers

Nations of the Modern World: Africa

Copyright © 1998 by Westview Press, A Division of HarperCollins Publishers, Inc.

Published in 1998 in the United States of America by Westview Press, 5500 Central Avenue, Boulder,
Colorado 80301-2877, and in the United Kingdom by Westview Press, 12 Hid's Copse Road, Cumnor
Hill, Oxford OX2 9JJ

Library of Congress Cataloging-in-Publication Data
Azevedo, Mario Joaquim.
   Chad : a nation in search of its future / Mario J. Azevedo and
Emmanuel U. Nnadozie.
      p.   cm.—(Nations of the modern world. Africa)
   Includes bibliographical references (p.) and index.
   ISBN 0-8133-8677-2
   1. Chad—Politics and government—1960–   2. Chad—Economic
conditions.   3. Chad—Social conditions.   I. Nnadozie, Emmanuel U.
II. Title.   III. Series.
DT546.48.A97   1998
967.43—dc21
                                                                        97-15097
                                                                        CIP

The paper used in this publication meets the requirements of the American National Standard for
Permanence of Paper for Printed Library Materials Z39.48-1984.

10   9   8   7   6   5   4   3   2   1

We dedicate this book to
the late Gerald Hartwig, Duke University;
to Martin O. Ijere, University of Nigeria;
and to Marcel Mazoyer,
University of Paris, Sorbonne.

Contents

INTRODUCTION

1 CHAD: GEOGRAPHICAL SETTING

Physical and Human Geography, 5
Conclusion, 11
Notes, 11

2 CHAD'S HISTORY

Northern Kingdoms and Southern Stateless Societies, 13
Conquest of Chad and Colonial Administration, 17
Colonial Government, 18
The Colonial Cotton-Based Economy, 28
Migration, Violence, and Criminal Justice, 32
Post–World War II Political Reforms, 35
Conclusion, 40
Notes, 41

3 POLITICAL EVOLUTION AND THE CIVIL WAR IN CHAD

The Postcolonial Era, 45
The Stage for Civil War, 52
Gukuni and Habre: The Battles for N'Djamena, 54
Habre, the Desert Fox, 57

4   THE ECONOMY   67

5   SOCIETY AND CULTURE   91

6   INTERNATIONAL RELATIONS   114

7   CHAD: FACING THE FUTURE   136

Tables and Figures

Tables

Figures

Acknowledgments

We wish to thank the editors, particularly acquisitions editor Barbara Ellington and series editor Larry Bowman, for their assistance, as well as Tom William, U.S. Army, who assisted us with the editing of the section on the combat strategy that assured Habre his final victory over the Libyans in 1986–1987. We also wish to invoke the memory of the late Dr. Gerald Hartwig of Duke University's Department of History. It was Professor Hartwig who instilled in Mario J. Azevedo the idea of linking the fate of his career to Chad, a country visited by Azevedo in 1974, 1981, 1984, and 1995. In one sense, this book is a realization of Hartwig's vision and a tribute to his genuine concern for the plight of, to use Hartwig's words, "the wretched of the earth."

Our expression of gratitude goes as well to the late Dr. Steven Polgar, former director of the Population Center at Chapel Hill, and to Dr. N. O. Addo, former director of the Population Dynamics Programme at the University of Ghana, Legon, both of whom were instrumental in securing funds for research in Chad in 1974. Christian Bouquet and Nga Ngakoutou, director of the Chadian National Institute for Human Sciences (INTSH), and his Haitian secretary, General M. Mathieu, opened the archives in N'Djamena in 1974; they deserve many thanks. Sara interpreter-assistant Riongar Ngarambaye and chauffeur N. Jean indefatigably traveled with us through southern Chad.

We acknowledge the contributions of the key figures in Chad scholarship, including Bernard Lanne, Christian Bouquet, Jean Cabot, René Lemarchand, Gayo Kogongar, Jean Chapelle, Robert Buijtenhuijs, Virginia Thompson and Richard Adloff, Samuel Decalo, Dennis Cordell, William Foltz, Harold Nelson, and others; and more recently, Thomas Collelo, whose research and findings were generously incorporated into our present volume.

We wish to express special appreciation to Lisa Smith of the English Department at the University of North Carolina at Charlotte; to Vicki Dennington, Sue Sayre, Dr. Oswald Uwakweh, and Dr. Seymour Patterson for their critical reviews and comments; and to Jo Anne Moritz, Paula Presley, David Mitchell, Makima Spencer, Tracey Simmons, Janaki Jayawardena, Tracey Lantz, Evas Dusabe, and Erin Jacobs for their assistance in the preparation of the manuscript. We are also grateful to Sheila Swafford of Pickler Memorial Library at Truman State University for obtaining various Chadian government documents as well as information and statistical data of the Banque des États de l'Afrique Centrale (BEAC) from various sources outside the United States.

Finally, we could not overlook the invaluable assistance of Monsignor Paul Dalmais, archbishop of N'Djamena; the Jesuit community at Moissala and Koumra, especially Father Corti; and the Capuchins at Doba, particularly Fathers Raoul and René of Bodo for their touching hospitality and the rare sources and insights they provided. Above all, we thank the Chadian people for their hospitality and the data they freely provided and our staff and our families for their support and patience during the preparation of the manuscript.

Mario J. Azevedo
Emmanuel U. Nnadozie

Selected Acronyms

ADS	Action Démocratique et Sociale
AEF	Afrique Équatoriale Française
AFRICARE	Africa Cooperative for American Relief Everywhere
ANL	Armée Nationale de Libération
AST	Action Sociale Tchadienne
BADEA	Banque Arabe Pour le Développement Économique en Afrique
BCEAC	Banque Centrale des États de l'Afrique Équatoriale et du Cameroun
BDEAC	Banque de Développement des États d'Afrique Centrale
BDT	Banque de Développement du Tchad
BEAC	Banque des États de l'Afrique Centrale
BGT	Boissons et Glacières du Tchad
BET	Borkou-Ennedi-Tibesti
BICIT	Banque International pour le Commerce et l'Industrie du Tchad
BOP	balance of payments
BTCD	Banque Tchadienne de Crédit et de Dépôts
BTDT	Bloc des Travailleurs Démocrates Tchadiens
CAR	Central African Republic
CCCE	Caisse Centrale de Coopération Économique
CCFAN	Conseil de Commandement des Forces Armées du Nord
CDR	Conseil Démocratique de la Révolution
CFA	Communauté Financière Africaine
CIA	Central Intelligence Agency
COTONFRAN	Société Cotonnière Franco-Tchadienne
COTONTCHAD	Société Cotonnière du Tchad
CSM	Conseil Supérieur Militaire
DAC	Development Assistance Committee (of the OECD)
EC	European Community
EDF	European Development Fund
EIB	European Investment Bank
FAC	Fund for Aid and Cooperation
FAC	Front d'Action Commune
FAD	Fonds d'Aide et de Développement

FACP	Front d'Action Commune Provisoire
FAN	Forces Armées du Nord
FANT	Forces Armées Nationales Tchadiennes
FAO	Forces Armées Occidentales
FAP	Forces Armées Populaires
FAT	Forces Armées Tchadiennes
FIDES	Fonds d'Investissement pour le Développement Économique et Social des Territories d'Outre Mer
FLT	Front de Libération du Tchad
FPL	Forces Populaires de Libération
FPLT	Front Populaire de Libération du Tchad
FROLINAT	Front de Libération Nationale
GIRT	Groupement des Indépendants et Ruraux Tchadiens
GUNT	Gouvernement d'Union Nationale de Transition
IDA	International Development Association
IMF	International Monetary Fund
INTSH	Institut National Tchadien pour les Sciences Humaines
IRCT	Institut Français de Recherche sur le Coton
l'OCRS	l'Organisation Commune des Régions Sahariennes
MAGAVET	Magasin d'Approvisionnement en Produits et Matériels Veterinaires
MCT	Manufacture des Cigarettes du Tchad
MDRT	Mouvement Démocratique de la Rénovation Tchadienne
MDT	Mouvement Démocratique Tchadien
MNC	multinational corporation
MNLT	Mouvement National de Libération du Tchad
MNRCS	Mouvement National pour la Révolution Culturelle et Sociale
MPLT	Mouvement Populaire pour la Libération du Tchad
MSNT	Mouvement pour le Salut National du Tchad
MRA	Mission de Réforme Administrative
MSA	Mouvement Socialiste Africain
OAU	Oganization of African Unity
NGO	nongovernmental organization
OCAMM	Organisation Commune Africaine, Malgache et Mauritanienne
ODA	Official Development Assistance
OECD	Organization for Economic Cooperation and Development
ONHPV	Office National d'Hydraulique Villageoise et Pastorale
OPEC	Organization of Petroleum Exporting Countries
PNA	Parti National Africain
PPT	Parti Progressiste Tchadien
RDA	Rassemblement Démocratique Africain
SDR	special drawing rights

SONAPA	Société Nationale de Production Animale
SONASUT	Société Nationale Sucrière du Tchad
SOTERA	Société Tchadienne d'Exploitation des Resources Animales
STEE	Société Tchadienne d'Énergie Électrique
STT	Société Textile du Tchad
TNC	transnational corporation
UDEAC	Union Douanière et Économique d'Afrique Centrale
UDIT	Union Démocratique Indépendante du Tchad
UDSR	Union Démocratique et Socialiste de la Résistance
UDT	Union Démocratique du Tchad
UEAC	Union des États de l'Afrique Centrale
UNDP	United Nations Development Program
USAID	United States Agency for International Development
UNIR	Union Nationale pour l'Indépendence et la Révolution
UST	Union Socialiste Tchadienne

INTRODUCTION

Chad, the fifth largest country in Africa, has experienced one of the most difficult social and political evolutions on the continent. This difficult evolution began in the 1890s, when the French attempted to unite peoples of widely disparate cultural, geographic, economic, social, and political backgrounds: Muslims, traditionalists, and Christians; nomads, agriculturalists, herders, and permanent pilgrims; Europeans, expatriates from the French Antilles, and peoples with state and stateless traditions. In its brief forty-year formal colonial presence in Chad, however, France found it impossible to create a unified colony out of so diverse a population. As late as 1960, on the very eve of political emancipation, the potential for national conflict was apparent. This conflict was signaled by the continued French military presence in the northern prefecture of Biltine-Ennedi-Tibesti as late as five years after Chad gained independence. In 1965, the retreat of French forces from northern Chad unleashed a wave of dormant resentment against the government of President François Tombalbaye—a resentment that led to armed insurrection for the next two and a half decades. Despite this turbulent history and regardless of the spotlight into which it was cast briefly in the 1980s and 1990s, Chad has been neglected and understudied by the scholarly community.

The early neglect of Chad by statesmen and diplomats, by Africanist scholars and educators, and by the general public is understandable when one recalls its past. Even the French, who created Chad, showed little interest in their colony compared with other equatorial African territories such as Congo, Gabon, Oubangui-Chari, and Cameroon after 1919. Long labeled the Cinderella of the French Empire, Chad was an accidental creation of explorers, military adventurers, intrepid frontiersmen, and rugged administrators who, left alone, tried to make the best out of isolation. Chad was little more than a military territory carved out of Oubangui-Chari and Niger. Its landlocked position, difficult environment, and hostile social climate deterred many would-be colonizers and humanitarians, causing several civil service posts to remain unfilled up to the 1920s.

France applied colonial policy unevenly in the North, or *le pays des sultans,* and the South, or *le Tchad-utile,* giving the North greater autonomy. This division complicated matters for the future and undoubtedly contributed to Chad's pres-

1

ent political turmoil. As the reader will easily discern throughout this book, one of our underlying themes is the role played by France in the development of Chad over the past century. Although we do not fail to note the shortcomings of the Chadian leaders and regimes that have shaped the fate of Chad since the mid-1960s, certainly foreign interference in Chad's internal affairs has heightened the tension and the confusion in this large country located in the very heart of the African continent.

Chad's contradictions have the potential for drawing its neighbors—Libya, Sudan, Cameroon, and Nigeria, in particular—and to some degree France and the United States into its conflicts. As noted, Chad occupied center stage in international discourse during the 1980s and 1990s, mostly because of the implications of its war with Libya. The controversy surrounding the war inside Chad threatened the stability of the Organization of African Unity (OAU), forced the United States to reverse its policy from neutrality to active involvement, and caused France one of its worst foreign policy embarrassments. This is why it is important for scholars and statesmen to study the events and the drama unfolding in Chad. Could the country be a sleeping giant? What would be the regional impact of Libya's annexation of Chad? Has France played a generally positive role in Chad? What are the feelings of the Chadian people in this protracted conflict? Are the northern leaders simply warlords, or are they committed nationalists? What role can a politically stable and prosperous Chad play in Africa and the world?

Our objective is to explore the country's complexities in order to provide an understanding of contemporary Chad and to demythologize the events that have taken place since the mid-1960s. In Chapter 1 we introduce Chad's physical environment, which has suffered tremendous transformation and degradation as a result of agricultural production and other human activities. Chapter 2 examines the historical factors that are partly responsible for the present situation: the characteristics of the precolonial state and stateless societies; the nature of French conquest and pacification, including the consequences of the inconsistent colonial policies in the North and the South; the impact of the slave trade; and the political effects of the constitutional reforms that eventually led the territory to independence. Chapter 3 focuses on the evolution of Chadian politics in the postcolonial period. It highlights the changes that led to a single-party state under southern president François Tombalbaye's leadership and the roots of the present conflict in Chad.

In Chapter 4 we provide the background to Chad's current economic conditions. In this chapter, we also analyze the country's potential in mineral and agricultural resources, offer a glimpse of the economic achievements of the pre- and post-Malloum periods, examine the economic impact of the Chadian war, and look finally at the economic viability of the country with or without massive international assistance. Cultural and social issues such as ethnicity and language, religion, health, and education are the focus of Chapter 5. Also explored in Chapter 5 is the extent to which Chad's diverse social patterns and cultural traditions make the effort toward national integration more difficult than in other parts of Africa. This chapter asks whether Chad's political and social conflict is unresolvable, as some scholars have hinted. The final chapter reviews Chad's relations with the rest of the world and assesses the behavior of its leaders in their search for military and economic assistance. It examines the motives for external involvement on the part of various nations, particularly France, Libya, Sudan, Nigeria, Cameroon, and the United States, and examines the attitudes of such international organizations as the Organization of African Unity (OAU) and the United Nations (UN).

A note about the spelling of Chadian words and names: We have attempted to use the commonly accepted English spelling of words such as Wadai and Gukuni Wedei (rather than Ouaddai and Goukouni Oueddei, the French spellings). As for place names that have changed (e.g., from Fort-Lamy to N'Djamena and from Fort-Archambault to Sarh), we use the old names to alert the reader that events being referred to occurred at the time when the former designation was in use.

We have employed both primary and secondary sources of information in this book. We used oral data collected during the 1970s and archival material gathered in the country and in France to ensure that the long-neglected voices of the common people, particularly from the South, are heard.

1

CHAD: GEOGRAPHICAL SETTING

The Republic of Chad is landlocked at the crossroads of Central Africa. Chad (whose total area is 495,755 square miles; 1,284,000 sq km) is bordered on the north by Libya, on the south by the Central African Republic, on the east by Sudan, and on the west and south by Niger, Nigeria, and Cameroon. The country's fragile ecosystem and harsh terrain make for a difficult environment; nevertheless, there are reasonable prospects of economic growth and development. Over the past century, natural phenomena and human activity have combined to transform the environment, population distribution, social structure, economic conditions, and future prospects of this sparsely populated country.

Physical and Human Geography

Two seasons are clearly distinguishable in Chad: a rainy season that extends from June to October (peaking in August) and a dry season that begins in November and ends in May. The two seasons result from the convergence of trade winds that establish an intertropical front. As Figure 1.2 shows, Chad has four major rainfall-based climate zones, which extend south to north: (1) the Humid Tropical Zone, also called the Wet Zone; (2) the Tropical, or Sudanese, Zone; (3) the Sahelian Zone; and (4) the Desert, or Saharan, Zone.

The southernmost climatic area, the Humid Tropical Zone, has the most rainfall, between 900 and 1,200 mm annually. At the border with eastern Cameroon and the northwestern part of the Central African Republic, a small portion of Chad's southern tip falls into the Humid Tropical Zone, which has a rainy season lasting six to nine months and high temperatures year-round. This zone, encom-

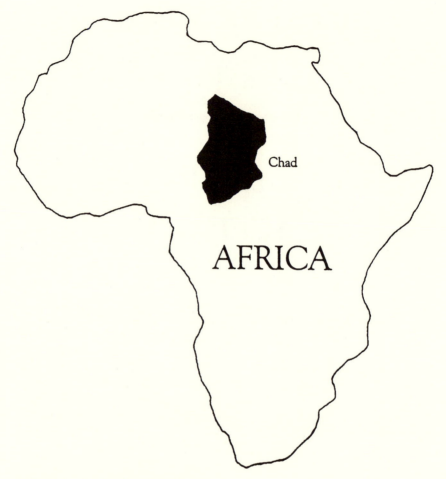

FIGURE 1.1   The Republic of Chad in Africa

passing some areas of the Mayo-Kebbi, Logone, and Moyen-Chari, is a transitional climate between the equatorial and tropical zones.

The Sudanese, or Tropical, Zone covers a substantial portion of Chad. It has a long dry season, the length of which (six to nine months) increases from south to north, and an annual average rainfall of 500 to 900 mm.

Immediately north of the Sudanese Zone is the Sahelian Zone, which covers the middle portion of Chad. This typically subdesert zone forms the transition between the tropical and desert climates. Here, rainfall is less than in the tropical zones (200 to 500 mm per year) and uneven from year to year, and average temperatures are higher.

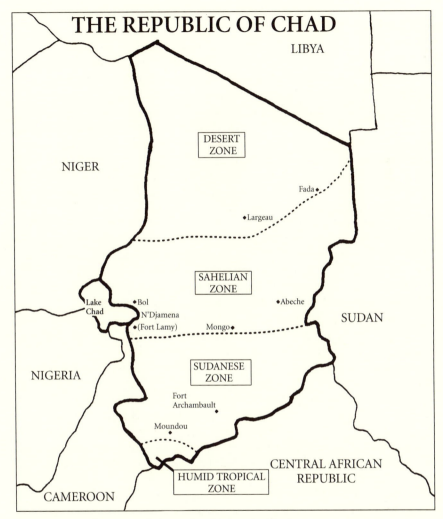

FIGURE 1.2   Climatic and Vegetational Zones in Chad

The northernmost zone, the Saharan, has a desert climate with less than 200 mm of annual rainfall. The extremes in temperature and the dry air combine to create significant temperature fluctuations between night and day. Because this region suffers from such low rainfall, it is unsuitable for human habitation.[1]

The irregularity, shortage, or absence of rainfall and the frequent dry spells interspersed with rainy years have a considerable impact on Chad's rain-fed crop production and animal husbandry. Areas of low rainfall support little or no agriculture.

Rainfall-Based Vegetational Regions

Chad has three main rainfall-based vegetational regions. From south to north, they are (1) the tropical wet-and-dry region, (2) the tropical semiarid (Sahel) region, and (3) the hot, arid desert region. The tropical wet-and-dry region is characterized by savanna with scattered trees or bushes. Wild animals thrive in this region, since it has grassland vegetation interspersed with trees. The Sahel region, found in the Sahelian Zone, is a savanna that gradually gives way to thornbushes and open grassland in the North. This is also a subdesert region with a discontinuous grassy carpet. There are, however, hot arid segments made up of dunes and plateaus where vegetation is scarce except for occasional oases. The third and northernmost region is desert steppe and arid barren land interspersed with oases and oasis vegetation.

Chad's vegetational regions are almost evenly divided between the two tropical regions and the desert region. In the desert areas, there is hardly any vegetation except in the oases, where grains and dates are grown and market garden production is practiced. Vegetation in the oases adapts to extended periods of dryness.[2] In the desertland, no farming is undertaken; rather, pastoral nomadism in which sheep, goats, and camels are reared predominates. Agricultural production in the savannas consists of mixed cropping of sorghum, peanuts, and manioc as well as commercial crops such as cotton and rice. The main livestock are cattle, sheep, goats, and horses. The savanna grassland products are millet, sorghum, and peanuts. Improved polders (reclaimed low or underwater land) support the production of wheat around the Lake Chad area, where fishing also occurs.

Chad experienced large annual rainfall variations, extended periods of drought interspersed with periods of good weather, and a prolonged downward trend in rainfall from the 1950s to the 1970s. These adverse climatic conditions have been exacerbated by human activities. For example, the growth and development of plant and animal life have suffered not only because of reduced rainfall and desertification, in this case a southward shift of the Sahara, but also because of overuse of the drylands. As F. Kenneth Hare and others argue, recent desertification involves the interaction of natural and temporary desiccation with the increase in population and extension of agricultural activities. Although desertification is reversible, the process renders the ecosystem more vulnerable to adverse climatic factors, leading to deteriorating health conditions for the growing population. Decreased productivity cannot support a growing population; thus migration ensues.[3]

In Chad's rain-fed agricultural production system, droughts and desert encroachment have caused crop failure. The adverse climatic conditions contribute to the gradual depletion of Lake Chad, a vital source of fish for many Chadians, and cause serious loss of livestock and reduction in agricultural output such as cotton. In addition, the recurrent drought has caused massive southward migration of herders, acceleration of deforestation, reinforcement of desertification (eolian regeneration), and disruption of harvests.

Topography

Chad's topography includes both flat and undulated-relief terrain. The plains that constitute the flat topography in the central area give way to plateaus in the South and other undulations in the territorial fringes. Chad is also a mountainous country: In northernmost Chad stands the volcanic Tibesti Massif, in the Northeast is the Ennedi Plateau, in the East are the crystalline rock mountains of the Wadai region, and in the South is the Oubangui Plateau.[4] The Tibesti Massif has peaks attaining heights of 11,152 feet (3,400 meters) and several interlocking craters characterized by large deposits of ash, basalt, and lava. In the central basin are the oases of Borkou. The Wadai highlands are located on the eastern boundary with Sudan. In central Chad stands its highest point, the Guera Massif, rising 4,900 feet (1,500 meters). In southwestern Chad, at the border with Cameroon, are the Mandara Mountains.

Soils

Most of the soil in Chad is either sandy (desert areas) or rocky (mountainous regions) and therefore unsuitable for farming.[5] The area surrounding Lake Chad (the polder) is mainly clay, however, and the seasonally flooded areas around the Chari and Logone Rivers and the Salamat Wadi have wet soils. The upland slopes of the Wadai region consist of tropical soils. To the north of Lake Chad, in the Kanem region, however, the soil is mainly subarid, although wet land in which salinization occurs is sometimes present.[6] Whereas a large portion of Chad is desert soil, other soils can be found in the North, such as the reddish-brown, brown, and grayish-brown soils of the subdesert areas. The reddish-brown soil of the dry tropical areas exists mostly in the South. Alluvial soil and reddish-brown bottomland are found southwest of N'Djamena in a southeasterly direction, that is, from the Lake Chad area toward the valleys of the Chari and Logone Rivers. These are areas with agricultural value where multiple cropping can occur in one year. Thus the main agricultural soils are found in the center and in the South.

Hydrographic Features

Perhaps Chad's most important hydrographic feature is the shallow lake from which it derives its name. The lake's size varies from 3,861 to 9,653 square miles.[7] It is progressively drying, however, as some rivers, such as the Bahr-el Ghazal, disappear under pressure from human activity and environmental change. The main rivers that feed the lake are the Chari and the Logone. The Chari and Logone flow north into Lake Chad from the Sudanese Zone, where rainfall is up to 36 inches (900 mm) yearly.

In south-central Chad, 25 miles (40 kilometers) southwest of Ati, is the shallow, reed-filled Lake Fittri (1,352 square kilometers). On the northeast and west of Lake Fittri are soils of the Quaternary geological period and important water tables: Batha, Kanem, and Chari-Baguirmi. East from the center of Lake Fittri are several underwater pockets that are restricted and localized in the valleys and interrupt the granitic massifs. The region to the west has neither notable relief nor underground water, and the eastern region comprising Wadai in the east and Guera in the center has a meager water supply.[8] The eastern region is characterized by high relief, granitic soil, and the absence of water tables. The southern half of the country is submerged under water during the rainy season; the northern half has hardly any surface running water except during certain periods of heavy rainfall.

Human Geography

Chad's regional geographical variations create differences in economic activities among its rapidly growing population. The North is populated by herders, the central area by farmers and semisedentary herders, and the South by sedentary farmers with some livestock. Population estimates vary due to lack of reliable demographic data:[9] Estimates for 1990 ranged from 5 to 6 million.[10] The population grew at an average rate of 2.1 percent in the years 1975 to 1980, 2.3 percent in 1980 to 1985, and 2.5 percent in 1986 to 1990.[11]

Figure 1.3 shows that Chad's population, which more than doubled between 1950 and 1990, reached 6,000,000 in 1994 and will reach 13,250,000 by 2025. As expected, the Desert Zone is the least populated with a density of 0.5 per square kilometer, or 2 percent of the population, followed by the Sahelian Zone with seven people per square kilometer. The Sudanese Zone has the highest population density with about 13 people per square kilometer.[12] Approximately one-half of the population lives in an area of this zone that composes 10 percent of the country.[13] Thus Chad's population density varies from 2 percent in the prefecture of Borkou-Ennedi-Tibesti (BET) to 42 percent in the Western Logone Prefecture.

According to United Nations Development Program and World Bank's *African Development Indicator* of 1992, the population age distribution has remained practically unchanged. Those occupying the age group 15 to 64 represented 55.7 percent in 1980, 56.8 percent in 1985, and 56.1 percent in 1989. The age group 0 to 14 represented a substantial proportion during the same periods—40.6 percent in 1980, 39.6 percent in 1985, and 40.2 percent in 1988; the age group 65 and over represented 3.7 percent. As a percentage of total population, females represented 50.8 percent in 1980 and 50.7 percent in 1985 and 1989.

When the population is viewed in terms of three major characteristics, several interesting features emerge. A comparison of the statistics from three periods—1980, 1985, 1990—shows that urban population as a percentage of total population increased 20 percent in 1980, 27 percent in 1985, and 33 percent in 1990. Life expectancy at birth was 42 years in 1980, 44 years in 1985, and 47 years in 1990. Infant mortality rate per thousand decreased from 174 in 1980 to 136 in 1985 and 125 in 1990. The rapid population growth combined with rapid urbanization

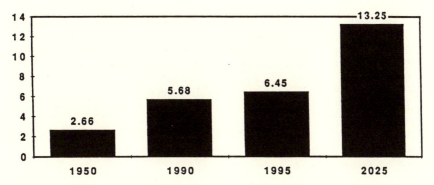

FIGURE 1.3   Actual and Projected Population Figures for Chad (millions)

should concern policymakers because a growing urban population will increase demands on limited urban resources. Such shortages often result in overcrowding and squalid living conditions, which in turn can lead to social instability and societal disintegration (see Chapter 3).

Conclusion

Chad's geographical location as an enclave precludes easy solutions to the country's difficulties. For example, Chad's lack of access to the seas imposes restrictions on trade and resource flows, causing high transportation costs that are passed on to consumers who are already suffering from environmental constraints on their agrarian economy. The extent to which Chad can use its human and capital resources to improve the welfare and standard of living of its citizens will depend mainly on its ability to remove or at least reduce these constraints. Chapters 2 and 4 provide more insight into the impact of geography on the political, social, and economic life of Chad.

Notes

1. Regine van Chi-Bonnardel, *The Atlas of Africa* (New York: Free Press, 1973), 34–35.
2. Ibid., 37–39.
3. F. Kenneth Hare, Robert W. Kates, and Andrew Warren, "The Making of Deserts: Climate, Ecology, and Society," *Economic Geography* 53 (October 1977): 332-346.
4. *The New Encyclopedia Britannica* (Chicago: Encyclopedia Britannica, 1992), 836.
5. Jean Cabot and Christian Bouquet, *Le Tchad* (Paris: Presses Universitaires de France, 1973), 19–20.
6. *New Encyclopedia Britannica*, 836.
7. George Thomas Kurian, *Encyclopedia of the Third World* (New York: Facts on File, 1992), 349.
8. Jean Chapelle, *Le peuple tchadien* (Paris: Harmattan, 1980), 8–22.

9. Much of the population and population-related data are based on 1964 and 1968 partial studies by the French Institut National des Études Statistiques et Économiques.

10. World Bank, *Trends in Developing Economies, 1992* (Washington, D.C.: World Bank, 1992), 106, estimated the population to have been 5.7 million in 1990; The World Bank, *World Development Report 1992: Development and the Environment* (Oxford: Oxford University Press, 1992), 268, estimates it to have been 6 million.

11. UN and World Bank, *African Development Indicators* (Washington, D.C.: World Bank, 1992), 317.

12. Dennis Cordell, "The Society and Its Environment," in Thomas Collelo, ed., *Chad: A Country Study* (Washington, D.C.: U.S. Government Printing Office, 1990), 43.

13. *Encyclopedia of the Third World,* 351.

2

CHAD'S HISTORY

One of Chad's most striking features, especially in the precolonial context, is the complexity of its history. For centuries, the hundreds of scattered ethnic groups lived a nomadic life. Over time, foreign conquerors, missionaries, contraband merchants, and slave traders came together in Chad, resulting in a multiplicity of languages, customs, and religious traditions and in uneven demographic distribution. Then came the French, who through their regionally uneven colonial policies complicated the situation further.

Northern Kingdoms and Southern Stateless Societies

The most well known state-level societies in precolonial Chad were the kingdoms of Kanem-Bornu, Wadai, and Baguirmi. In the 1960s, archaeologists led by Jean-Paul Lebeuf and A.M.D. Lebeuf uncovered southeast of Lake Chad an ancient civilization developed by the Sao people. The Sao civilization is identified by its use of stone and bone implements and construction of walled cities. With the exception of the Sao people, the history of societies in the area that predate colonialism is relatively well documented by Arab chroniclers, European explorers, ethnographers, and archaeologists and has been enriched by oral traditions.

Kanem-Bornu

Kanem, which emerged northeast of Lake Chad around A.D. 800 as a viable principality seems to have been established by the nomadic Zaghawa. When the Zaghawa began to settle in the central Sudanic region, they found the Tubu people already well established there. Apparently the Tubu joined the Zaghawa to form a new political entity that later became one of the most memorable states in central Sudan. However, the rule of the Beni Sefi seems to have ended during the second half of the eleventh century, when the Sefuwa dynasty, led by a mythic Yemeni Arab called Sayf Ibn Dhi Yazan, began; its rule in Kanem ended in 1814. Scholars are still debating whether the Sefuwa were of local origin or were outsiders and whether they took the throne following an internal struggle. Some accounts identify Hummay (and not Sayf Yazan) as the first Sefuwa *mai*, or king; he ruled from 1075 to 1180. Historians suggest that he was a Berber who came from "a profoundly Islamized community."[1]

Two major factors were responsible for Kanem's s survival as a contending force in Central Africa: its strategic location at the crossroads of trade for West, North, and Central Africa and its ties with North Africa through the Sahara Desert. Kanem flourished as a result of its ability to firmly control this trans-Saharan trade in salt, horses, glass, muskets, cloth, gold, copper, kola nuts, ostrich feathers, ivory, cotton, hides, slaves, jewelry, perfume, and wax. To protect its lucrative trade, Kanem's rulers—the Sefuwa as well as the Shehu dynasty—strove to keep the trade routes safe. In fact, they were so successful in this endeavor that it was said that "a lone woman clad in gold might walk with none to fear but God."[2]

The introduction of Islam into the region, through the travels and activities of Arabs and Berbers from the East and the North during the tenth century and the subsequent conversion of Mai Ulmme Jelne, allowed Kanem to establish long-distance contacts that reached as far as Saudi Arabia. An impressive assemblage of scholars and traders from the Muslim world constantly held religious events and pursued economic activities in Kanem. Kanem became so successful at state-building that during the reign of Mai Dunama Dabbalemi (1221–1259), the kingdom exerted political and economic control over what now constitutes north-western Chad, Wadai, and the Adamawa Plateau. In the late fourteenth century, however, internal strife over dynastic succession almost thwarted the political experiment of the Sefuwa dynasty. The Bulala people succeeded in pushing Mai Umar Ibni Idris (1384–1388), his entourage, and his family out of the capital to Bornu.

About a century later, the Sefuwa dynasty revived and its army was reorganized, which allowed the Muslim sultan Idris Katakarnabi (1504–1526) to reconquer the former kingdom, thus creating the Kanem-Bornu nexus. The kingdom, or sultanate, was further expanded under Mai Idris Alooma (1580–1619), allowing Kanem to reach its zenith, gain hegemony in Central Africa, and exact tribute from peoples and kingdoms as far east as the powerful sultanates of Wadai and Darfur. During his reign, Mai Alooma, a devout Muslim, built several brick mosques; he introduced and strictly enforced Kuranic teachings and laws in an effort to "purify" Kanuri and Kanembu social and religious traditions. To ensure that his personal power remained undisputed, Alooma established what are called "fixed walled military camps" and housed "armored horse riders and Berber cavalry, Kotoko boatmen, and iron-helmeted musketeers," likely trained by Turkish military advisers who employed "permanent sieges" and "scorched earth tactics, burning everything in their path."[3]

Over time the precariousness of the internal political situation was exacerbated by several factors, including constant raids and devastation of the kingdom by Fulani and Tuareg nomads and a temporary but successful invasion of the South by the Tunjur in 1611 together with debilitating periodic famines (particularly those of the seventeenth and eighteenth centuries). Finally, in 1808, the Fulani besieged and ravaged the capital. In 1814, the misfortunes that had beset the Sefuwa dynasty culminated in its forcible overthrow and its being replaced by the local Shehu family. In 1846, civil war broke out, and the Shehus were eventually dethroned by an ambitious Muslim leader, Umar al-Kanemi (1837–1853). Four decades later, in 1893, the famous Arab slave trader and conqueror Rabah (Zubair) Fadlallah drove the royal family permanently out of the capital.

Under Umar al-Kanemi, the Kanembu society was structured hierarchically and the military played a major role in state affairs. Livelihood depended on limited agriculture, slave labor, the export of slaves from the South, and trans-Saharan trade. It seems ironic that a "predatory state" that depended on slaves "not only for the purposes of defense but also for the enforcement of executive decisions" could itself engage in a slave trade executed by its own slaves. [4]

Wadai

During the sixteenth century, the Arabic-speaking Tunjur people established the kingdom of Wadai in eastern Chad. In 1611 or 1635 (the date is unclear), the Muslim *kolak*, or king, Abdel-el-Kerim II, conquered Baguirmi with the assistance of the Maba (presumably the first inhabitants of the area). The *kolaks* are usually described as absolute rulers (although S. P. Reyna disputes this claim) who used Islam to reinforce their power over their subjects' lives. The most well known *kolaks* are Ali (1858–1874) and Yusuf (1874–1898), remembered for having strengthened the kingdom militarily. They are also known for their use of force to ensure that Wadai exploited its strategic commercial location along two important trade routes. One route ran from east to west and linked the Upper Nile region with Darfur; the other, a trans-Saharan passage opened in 1810, established a profitable link between Abeche and Benghazi.

Like Kanem-Bornu, Wadai experienced constant internal strife while the ambitious *kolaks* devastated the surrounding areas in their efforts to expand their territory and to achieve control of the profitable slave market. In fact, replete with predatory activities, the role of slavery was prominent in reinforcing the power of the sultanate. The sultanate profitably exported thousands of captives each year to its North and East while using thousands of others in various capacities internally, including in the army. On the one hand, Wadai's incursions into other parts of Central Africa allowed the kingdom to expand and benefit economically from the tribute exacted from the conquered populations; on the other hand, the raids could only contribute to chaos in the region and cause resentment and rebellion among the societies thus subjugated by Wadai.

Baguirmi

In the sixteenth century, Baguirmi, a creation of the Barma, emerged to the south-east of Lake Chad, establishing its capital at Chad's present Massenya. Before reaching its height in the eighteenth century (1719–1786), the kingdom of Baguirmi adopted Islam following the conversion of the sultan, or *mbang,* Abdulla IV (1568–1598). Thereafter, it entered a period of decline stemming from a series of invasions from Wadai.[5] One such invasion was carried out under the pretext of restoring Islam and punishing Abdel Rahman Gaurang I (1784–1786) for his alleged incestuous marriage to a sister. Baguirmi was so severely beaten that some twenty thousand people were made prisoners and sold as slaves by Wadai, and practically the entire royal family was wiped out. In December 1870, Massenya was once again invaded by Wadai's Sultan Ali, who captured some thirty thousand Baguirmi and took the sacred Barma relic (a royal family *assegaye*) with him to Abeche, along with a host of "weavers, dyers, tailors, saddlers, princes, and princesses," among them the young Gaurang II. [6]

In 1893, Massenya was burned by the infamous Rabah (Zubair) Fadlallah, a former slave who rose to military prominence in Zubair Rahama Mansur al-Abbasi's army. However, Baguirmi stumbled on an unexpected ally, the French. Accordingly, in October 1897, Mbang Abdar Rahman Gaurang II sought French protection against Rabah, but at a cost to his sovereignty. He was forced to disclaim all lands on the left bank of the Chari River and to stop trading in slaves. He was, however, allowed to continue collecting taxes within the former kingdom while receiving a subsidy from the French colonial government.

Baguirmi society was feudal and hierarchical; its state was based on the concept of divine kingship, which justified unlimited territorial expansion through the use of force. It became renowned in Africa and the Middle East for its slaves (who had been forcibly captured, particularly from among the Sara in Central Africa) and because it was "specialized as an exporter of eunuchs."[7] S. P. Reyna notes that Barma society was predatory. To support the state and its military bureaucracy, composed of thousands of officials who performed little or no work, Baguirmi regularly carried out warring, raiding, kidnapping, and expansionism.[8]

Other Societies

Apart from the roles played respectively by the *kolaks* and *mbangs* in Wadai and Baguirmi, there were other political actors that significantly transformed other parts of Chad. The Sanussiya Brotherhood, or *tariq*, which originated in Algeria in 1835, deserves mention here because of the religious and political impact it had on precolonial northern and eastern Chad. In 1899, the *tariq* established its head-quarters at Gouro in the North, and in spite of its claim of being strictly a religious order, it became a warring theocracy of lodges that exacted tribute from its surrounding population while trading in slaves.[9] The Sanussiya *marabouts*

(Muslim clerics) exerted a great deal of influence over the leaders of the northern and eastern Muslim states, and they sent carefully selected envoys to Muhamad al-Sunni of Kanem to join their brotherhood and organize wars against the intruding French from 1890 to 1913. Pitched battles ensued; in 1913, the French expeditionary forces, particularly those operating under Colonel Emmanuel Largeau, conquered Gouro on November 14, Borkou on November 17, and Faya on December 3 and forced the order to retreat to Kufra.

Elsewhere, the reality was quite different from that in the North. Foremost, people in the South and the Southwest were not as politically organized. Societies there were generally organized into villages, some under chiefs. Whereas powerful theocratic predatory and full-time warring states dominated the North, the center, and the East of Chad, the South enjoyed a sedentary agricultural life that provided most of the necessities and ensured comfortable living. Although the North was spiritually united by Islam, it was fragmented politically because its people were ethnically divided. The South—decentralized, dispersed, disunited, and weak—remained the "milking cow" of rapacious kingdoms, traders, and enslaving proselytizers.

One of the worst historical legacies for modern Chad is the memory of the enslavement of the South by the North. This legacy has created hatred among Chadians. Violent raids into the South often depopulated entire villages and regions. After 1800, for example, the sultan of Baguirmi had a virtual slave trade monopoly over Sara land and Oubangui-Chari besides receiving at least two thousand slaves a year from Lai for his personal use.[10] The wars against the "white infidels," therefore, were waged not simply to safeguard the sovereignty of Kanem-Bornu, Wadai, and Baguirmi but as an excuse to maintain a servile system that had become a way of life in the North.

Conquest of Chad and Colonial Administration

The French came to Chad through the South, which explains why by 1900 most of the southern region, including Oubangui-Chari, had been annexed without major battles. The North, in contrast, turned out to be a real challenge for the French, but in 1897 a Franco-Baguirmi alliance helped eliminate Rabah Fadlallah. Several Anglo-French treaties made between 1899 and 1900 had theoretically ceded Kanem, Baguirmi, and Tibesti to the French, but only the use of force would allow the French to occupy and pacify the region that Rabah was now claiming as his domain. To displace Rabah, the French assembled three expeditionary forces that were eventually entrusted to Commander François Lamy: one from Algiers, one from Niger, and a third from the Moyen Congo. These were joined by Sultan Gaurang's troops on April 21, 1900. The four forces launched an assault on Rabah's troops the next morning at Kousseri (Cameroon) on the banks of the Chari River. The French won the battle, but both Lamy and Rabah lost their lives.

Rabah (Zubair) Fadlallah (1840–1900) was a former slave who rose to military prominence in the armies of Zubair Rahma Mansur al-Abbasi. He has been hailed by some as the greatest slave trader of all times; by others he is revered as a great pan-Africanist. He appeared in southeast Wadai in 1880 with five thousand men, known in Arabic as *bezinguer* (slave troops), who carried three thousand firearms and forty-four pieces of artillery. In 1886, supported by the powerful force of the *bezinguer* and a thousand horses, Rabah entered Sara country and executed chiefs who refused to submit or to provide slaves to his rising empire. In 1890, Rabah and his forces conquered Dar Kuti and placed Rabah's friend Muhamad al-Sanussi on the throne. A year later, in 1891, Rabah harassed the French exploratory mission under Lieutenant Paul Crampel (who was killed by Sultan al Sanussi of Dar Kuti in 1893). In 1893, Rabah and his men burned Massenya. He continued his forays into Korbol and besieged Mandjafa, where Sultan Gaurang of Baguirmi had sought refuge. He entered Kousseri and Kuka victoriously in 1894 and established his own capital at Dikwa, south of Lake Chad. By 1896, Rabah had taken total control of Bornu, coining for himself the title Emir of the Faithful.

It was during Rabah's expeditions in the late 1800s that the French began their conquest of the North at the cost of hundreds of African and European soldiers' lives. After intense fighting, Kanem was subdued by the French in 1905. On June 13, 1909, Abeche, the capital of Wadai, fell to the French, who installed Acyl, a member of the royal family who collaborated, as sultan, with the French; Acyl held this sultanate from 1909 to 1912. Yet effective occupation of the sultanate did not occur until 1912. Borkou and Faya-Largeau were not occupied permanently until November 13, 1913; the Teda, under the Turkish banner, continued to pose a threat to the French. However, Fada was overrun in 1914, Bardai in 1915, and Zouar in 1917. Finally, in 1920, the *derdei* (spiritual leader) of the Tubu submitted to French rule. That year, the French installed a civilian government in Chad for the first time. Earlier, on April 12, 1916, Chad had become separated from Oubangui-Chari and made an autonomous colony. Likewise, Tibesti was detached from Niger, French West Africa, and made a part of Chad on November 11, 1929.

Chad was, therefore, the last French territory to be occupied in Africa, the last to be developed, and the last to be given a civilian government. For many years Chad remained part of Oubangui-Chari, known as Oubangui-Chari-Chad, because it was a low priority in the French colonial enterprise. Since France had been humiliated at Sedan in 1870 and during the so-called Fashoda incident of 1898, it was now willing to settle for any lands in Africa. Thus by 1900 its claim to the "riverlands of the Oubangui and Congo and a pastoral and desert area in Chad"[11] became recognized internationally.

Colonial Government

The final conquest and sustained pacification of the French equatorial colonial empire at the turn of the century proved to be a difficult task, continuing to re-

TABLE 2.1   Recruitment for Military Service, 1922–1938

Year	Number of Recruits	Place of Origin
1922	1,350	Chad
1923	1,000	Chad
1924	1,000	Moyen-Chari alone
1926	600	Moyen-Chari alone
1927	800	Moyen-Chari alone
1928	7,000[a]	Moyen-Chari alone
1930	300	Moyen-Chari alone
1931	300	Moyen-Chari alone
1938	1,500	Chad

[a]including veterans

SOURCES: Musée du Tchad, W90, 1–10, 1940, 1–17, Jean Malval, *Essai de chronologie tchadienne (1707–1940)* (Paris: CNRS, 1974), 106.

quire a steady supply of men and a military force recruited mainly from among the Africans themselves. The French colonial army became very mobile in the sense that contingents from one colony often fought for the pacification of another, as exemplified by the use of Senegalese and Dahomean troops along with Sara recruits in the conquest of Chad.

Recruitment of soldiers in Chad often required the use of some force. Chiefs were to provide certain quotas of men to serve for a minimum of three years. Invariably, most of the recruits came from among the general population of the Sara (or *du pays sara,* as the French called the South). In fact, Sara army recruits became synonymous with the *tirailleurs sénégalais* of Chad (Chadian African shooters or skirmishers). Table 2.1 presents information on recruitment for military service from 1922 to 1938. From Table 2.1, it is evident that the Moyen-Chari region supplied a substantial proportion of recruits for the colonial military service.

Guardsmen paid frequent visits to the villages in search of healthy men. Recruitment tactics elicited two major forms of resistance—migration and violence. Archival materials stored before the 1979 civil wars at the Musée National du Tchad, in N'Djamena, give details of the resistance against military recruitment that occurred between 1918 and 1940, recorded by four French administrators of Chad, Isambert, Latrille, Herse, and Christian.[12] The following incident, recorded about Sara Goulaye, is an example of the information in the archives:

For the first time in 1918, several Sara Goulaye who were distressed by the recruitment of servicemen escaped across the river Barh Salamat. Others from Nabia, the subdivision of Kyabe in Moyen-Chari, and from the villages of Boi, Bekono, Moule, Koume-Sali-Aouni, and Kaouhabolo, in the canton of Alako, settled in Fania country under the sultan of Baguirmi. The French were afraid of a Muslim reaction to aggressive recruitment methods and so left the subdivisions of Bousso and Melfi alone, but they asked Chief Taniba of the canton of Bousso to recruit all able Sara from Alako for military service. The chief did not meet his quota, having conscripted only forty young men from the five Goulaye villages. Accompanied by Corporal Bayonne and guardsman Binguinia, Taniba easily caught twenty-eight young men from the village of Kaouhabolo. When he entered Sali for more recruits, however, the villagers attacked him and his two companions. The people of Sali then freed the twenty-eight young men from Kaouhabolo, separated Binguinia from his two friends, and stripped, beat, and, castrated him. Before their arrest, these men held the chief and the two men as hostages for more than ten hours.[13] Incidents of this kind occurred in many other parts of southern Chad.

Just as conscription resulted in flight and violence, low compensation contributed to resistance. In 1918, the salary of an enlisted man was fifteen francs a year, supplemented with free food. It rose to twenty-five francs a year during World War II. The late Colonel Jean Chapelle, a former administrator in the North, an army commander, and a prolific writer on Chad (interviewed in 1974) claimed that once outside the country, Chadian troops were treated just like Frenchmen with each soldier receiving a daily ration of 510 grams of rice, 150 grams of meat, and 60 grams of oil, peanuts, tomatoes, and onions.[14] By all accounts, however, life was never rosy in the colonial army.

The two world wars indirectly underscore the contribution of Chadians, mainly the Sara, in service and lives to the expansion and maintenance of the French empire in Africa. Recruits from all French colonies engaged in combat and noncombat operations in World War I, and out of this number about 200,000 perished in the war. The number of recruits from the Senegalese troops consisted of 181,000 men from West and Equatorial Africa and Somalia (Djibouti). Out of this number, 23,000 to 25,000 gave their lives for France. In World War II, the contribution of French Equatorial Africa was equally impressive. In June 1940, the four colonies had one regiment exclusively from Chad—the four battalions of the Régiment des Tirailleurs Sénégalais du Tchad or the R.S.T.) and a few artillery and service men. It is no wonder, therefore, that resistance to recruitment was so common among the Sara and other Chadians: Engagement in war was certain, and death was probable.

For all practical purposes, the North remained semiindependent throughout the colonial period as long as the sultans and sheiks stopped their slaving activities and did not interfere with the movement of the French, did not block caravan routes, and allowed supervision of major (albeit few) colonial projects in the area. Since the North refused to cooperate with French colonization, colonial administrators focused on *le Chad-utile* (the profitable or useful Chad).

As the pacification process officially came to an end, one task proved difficult for the administration—the elimination of slavery and the slave trade in the colony. In 1909, trade-related incidents prompted the Ministry of Foreign Affairs to complain that slaving activities were still going on in Equatorial Africa. Egyptian merchants posing as businessmen continued to smuggle slaves and arms throughout the region, including Chad.[15] In 1925, this led an American Protestant missionary, identified in the archives simply as Reverend Terman, to accuse the French government of not doing enough to stop the slaving activities in the colony. Outraged, the administrator of Moyen-Chari wrote the governor, accusing the minister of "hallucinations and cowardice and of echoing Wilsonian propaganda against the French colonial empire." Although 1917 is heralded as the year the slave trade was eliminated, incidents of capture continued into the 1920s.

Forced Labor

Bringing colonial personnel to fulfill essential government responsibilities was also difficult. Thus by 1928, approximately 45 percent of the European civil service positions in Chad remained unfilled; bureaucrats stayed in Chad only an average of twenty months. Isolation was exacerbated by the distances from the ocean and Chad's landlocked location. Fort-Lamy (N'Djamena), for example, is 728 miles from the Atlantic Ocean; Moundou, 893 miles from the nearest port; Abeche, 1,754 miles from the Red Sea; and Faya-Largeau, in the Sahara Desert, 1,026 miles from the Mediterranean Sea.

Because of their personnel shortages, local administrators were forced to collaborate as much as possible with village and canton chiefs. Quite often they resorted to excessive force to instill fear and submission in the people. Chad's participation in World War II under the initiative of Governor Félix Eboué (1938–1941), who also served as governor-general of French Equatorial Africa (1941–1944), finally drew the attention of Paris, and more resources were allotted to develop the colony.[16]

The need to tap the economic resources of the colonial empire compelled the French authorities to impose three kinds of obligations on the Africans. First, administrators were entitled to call upon any African, at any time, to work on government projects and for private companies. The second type of forced labor came in the form of unpaid work by the Africans on government projects labeled as emergencies for a specified period of time—from a week to a month. The third type of "community" contribution was extracted from prisoners. The governor gave his orders to the administrators, and the latter passed them to the *chef de canton,* who transmitted them to the *chef de village.*

The *goumiers* or *miliciens*—the guardsmen—in charge of forced labor often carried out the chiefs' orders to the letter and used essentially three methods of recruitment. The first consisted of going to the villages and capturing women and children; the victims would be taken to hostage camps or *villages de liberté* located in the woods until their parents and husbands fulfilled certain work obligations. The second method, most commonly used, was a visit to a village whose young men were difficult to recruit. During the visit, chickens, goats, sheep, and other types of movable property were taken by the recruiters. The final method, widely employed by the concessionaire companies, entailed the burning of houses and crops and other property and was performed by a specially recruited force called "armed workers," or the *travailleurs armés*.[17]

In the process, women were not spared from the *système de prestations* and quite often worked alongside their husbands; they carried dirt, cut grass, cooked for the workers, transported stones, brought grain for the camps and settlements, fetched water, and provided entertainment. Working time for the nonassimilated Africans, announced in a decree as early as July 21, 1876, was twelve hours a day. When forced labor was criticized, Victor Augagneur, governor-general of French Equatorial Africa (1920–1924), justified the system this way: "Since French citizens are subject to compulsory service, and African laws acknowledge that the weaker has to obey the stronger and that force confers rights, forced labor is, therefore, justified and necessary. If we do not use force [the African] will consider us to be cowards."[18] The statistics presented in Table 2.2 support the governor-general's testimonial.

Chadian respondents and European humanitarians attest to the fact that deaths from hard, forced work, or *corveé*, ill treatment, beatings, and lack of adequate food were common. Evidence collected from former forced laborers in their sixties and seventies during the 1970s suggests a death rate of 4 percent.[19] As expected, Africans' resistance to forced labor was as frequent as their resistance to military service. At times this resistance resulted in deaths, as Denise Moran, a French eyewitness, teacher, and wife of an administrator, relates. Criticism of the practice prompted Marcel de Coppet, governor of Chad (1926–1932), to order that the number of recruits destined to work away from their home could not exceed one-twentieth of a district's population.[20]

Interestingly, the Muslim- and Arabic-speaking populations simply refused to accept military recruitment and forced labor, as they considered manual labor to be degrading and viewed the French as intruders. In precolonial times, slaves and captives did this work for them. In fact, a 1924 government circular comparing the Muslim North with the South advised the use of southerners over northerners: "The Southern populations, the Sara, are docile and passive, but socially much less advanced than the Muslim population. They are useful particularly as a reservoir of manpower."[21] It should be pointed out that forced cultivation of cotton (discussed later), introduced in the South in 1926 to 1930, was another form of forced labor.

To meet their quotas, some chiefs allocated a certain portion of the land and a number of workers for their personal cotton production. This resulted, in certain areas, in nearly 90 percent of the cotton produced belonging to the chief and his *patias* (assistants). Known as *le système des cordes*, the practice led to several murders of chiefs and collaborators in such areas as Baibokoum (1946), Bodo (1949), Moundou (1950), and Bebalem (1952).[22]

One of the most infamous forced-labor projects, involving almost exclusively the Sara, was the construction of the railroad from Pointe-Noire to Brazzaville. Construction started in 1921, was halted temporarily, but resumed in 1924.

TABLE 2.2 Number of Forced-Labor Recruits, 1923, 1930, 1932, and 1936

1923

Fort-Lamy	3,315	Massakory	1,760
Massenya	200	Bokoro	100
Melfi	100	Ft. Archambault (Sara)	2,000
Koumra (Sara)	1,500	Behagle	200
Doba (Sara)	200	Bongor	200
TOTAL	5,315	TOTAL	4,260

1930

Fort-Lamy	3,000	Bongor	200
Massakory	500	Lere	200
Melfi	200	Am-Timane	200
Massenya	250	Bousso	200
Bokoro	200		
TOTAL	4,150	TOTAL	800

1932

Fort-Lamy	3,000	Bongor	200
Massacory	500	Lere	200
Massenya	250	Am-Timan	200
Bokoro	200	Bousso	200
Melfi	200		
TOTAL	4,150	TOTAL	800

1936

Fort-Lamy	800	Koumra	2,500
Massacory	200	Bongor	200
Melfi	200	Massenya	200
TOTAL	1,200	TOTAL	2,900

SOURCES: See *Journal Officiel,* p. 1084; *Journal Officiel* 1, December 1, (1930): 1085; *Journal Officiel* 1 January (1923): 137; and *Journal Officiel,* 12–13.

Completed in 1934, the project spanned a distance of some 450 km, or 298 miles, cost 1,551,000,000 French francs ($310,200,000), and employed 120,000 Africans, 200 Europeans, and 600 Chinese. The Sara, approximately 20,000 from the Moyen-Chari Prefecture, constituted a major portion of the workforce. At least half of the workers never returned home, and an estimated 10,000 workers died in the *chantiers* (work settlements). At Mayombe, a hilly area 60 miles from Pointe-Noire, 2,600 workers died in the 1930–1932 period alone.

Conditions were so deplorable that even Europeans used to say that "while one African died for every cross-tie, one European perished for every kilometer." In France, criticism leveled at the government was such that construction was almost halted, prompting Governor-General Marius Antonetti (1924–1934) to challenge the project's critics: "Either we accept the sacrifice of six to eight thousand men or we renounce the railroad." When work was completed, "12 million cubic meters of dirt had been removed and 12 tunnels dug, one of which was 1,594 meters long beneath the Mayombe." In addition, 162 large bridges and 92 viaducts were built.[23]

Interviews with former Sara railroad workers revealed that recruits referred to Brazzaville ("Barsaouli") as a "cemetery, a place of mourning, and not of celebration." Here, the weather was either too hot or too foggy and humid, and mosquito-borne diseases infested the whole region. Stung by criticism and concerned about the reluctance of the Sara to enlist for railroad work, Governor-General Marius Antonetti appeared at Fort-Archambault for the first time by car in 1926 and ordered that workers be recruited from all villages with one-fourth allowed to bring their wives with them.

Used extensively throughout the colonies in Africa, porterage was another common form of forced labor; as a French colonialist once remarked, "Coloniser c'est transporter." Within the colonial system, any individual considered physically fit for forced labor could be recruited to transport goods, ammunition, and colonial agents. In 1925, for example, a thousand porters were recruited by Moulin, chief of the subdivision of Koumra, to carry loads destined to Brazzaville for railroad construction. Understandably, Chadians avoided porterage, and violent incidents were commonplace throughout the colonial period. For example, when Lieutenant Lavit (1920–1922) visited the Baya villages of Finade, Babaole, Goumbere, and Baibokoum in June 1920, he found that everyone had fled: "The men took refuge in the woods in order to avoid the forced work of porterage." Likewise, the Karre revolted against their administrator and escaped to the hills. Administrator Merlin wrote, "I must point out how difficult it has been . . . to recruit rowers, porters, and manual laborers since last May."[24] The price in lives due to porterage was high. According to Brazza, in French Africa at least 15 percent of the porters died from exhaustion, famine, disease, mistreatment, and physical injury caused by the heavy weights carried over long distances; some, as Auguste Chevalier notes, even became sexually impotent.

The minimum mandated load for a porter ranged from twenty-five to forty-five kilos. With such loads on their heads, porters had to travel from Loango (Congo), for instance, to Brazzaville, a distance of six hundred km, in twenty-five days to receive just twenty-five francs! The distance counted more heavily than the load. Besides low compensation, many concessionaires, instead of paying the porters in cash, kept the salary for tax purposes, so that in some instances an African could travel twenty-five km a day for nothing. To silence critics, a government decree of April 29, 1921, fixed the load allowed at twenty-five kilos per person at a salary of one franc a day for the loaded trip and half a franc for each return trip. In addition, the decree stipulated that every ten porters had to be backed up by one spare porter to relieve the sick ones and that the average walking time per day should be six hours, about twenty-five km a day.

Former Sara porters interviewed at Bedaya claimed that the hardships of the trip from Koumra to Fort-Lamy and to Am-Timan sometimes resulted in the deaths of thirty-seven percent of the porters. This trip usually took one month and twenty-five days despite efforts by overseers to make it in fewer weeks. It is interesting that according to Jacques Boisson, when explorer Casemire Maistre arrived in Moyen-Chari accompanied by 115 porters and 60 African soldiers from Brazzaville in 1897, the Sara, who received him cordially and with much curiosity, called him *bedigu-iditi,* meaning "one who forces people to carry a load on their back." Early on, therefore, the hardships of porterage had caught the attention of the Chadians.

Porterage was not only harmful to the porters and their families, it was also detrimental to the people who lived along the route of the marching caravans. Often, compelled by hunger, the porters invaded farms or villages and took whatever they could lay their hands on; the result was violence or migration. In 1910, for example, in the villages of the Imme, Mara, Bongo, Balkogne, and Yanga in Moyen-Chari, people fled to the woods as soon as they heard that the administrator was coming to recruit porters. That year, the people of Yanga killed one *tirailleur.* In 1920, accompanied by four horsemen, two guides, and a convoy of forty-five European guardsmen, administrator Sousard decided to pay a visit to his Mayo-Kebbi Circumscription in search of porters. But at Dakoutou, as he said later, even "the woods were empty."[25]

Recruitment of porters was also a perilous exercise. When Sousard approached Dakoutou, two of his guards—one who had worked with the colonial guard for seven years and the other who had served six years in the Chadian Regiment—escaped and arrived at the village earlier and tried to loot the farms (and probably abandon the convoy altogether). The administrator was shocked not only to find the whole area deserted but also to see the bodies of his two porters murdered by the populace. In 1923, when the chief of the subdivision of Pala arrived at Toubouri, where young men had attacked and wounded one African sergeant and one guard and killed one of their horses, he found a ghost town. In 1924, a European corporal by the name of Eckert was murdered near Abeche.

Whenever clandestine settlements of fugitives from porterage were discovered, the authorities allowed the local chiefs to burn them and disperse the people, forcing them to return home or settle where they could be watched, preferably along the road. In 1935, a chief of the subdivision of Kelo wrote the *chef de Département de Logone,* at Moundou, praising himself for having discovered some of these secret villages in the bush and for having burned them mercilessly. Archival sources show that this type of response to porterage was common everywhere the administration tried to enforce it. It heightened, of course, contempt for the colonial system, particularly among the Sara.

Head Taxes

Apart from their human resource needs, the French needed revenue to develop the colonies and to make each one of them self-sufficient in those sectors that did not require large amounts of capital. This need compelled the government to introduce "head taxes" in all of French Equatorial Africa in 1901. Unfortunately, in several respects, the French system contradicted Chad's southern tradition. For the first time, for example, people in the South had to contribute something regularly to a foreign authority that had established itself by force. Here, traditional taxes (if one can call them so) had been in-kind and were always proportional to one's own resources. The chief did not ask for a cow from a man who raised goats only; neither did he exact a bar of iron from a fisherman.[26] Taxation's ugliest side, however, was the collection method. Chiefs and policemen were often compelled through threats and special gifts from the petty administrators to get the amount due at whatever cost. As an incentive, they were allowed to use the *chicotte* (whip), fines, imprisonment, and the so-called *barre de justice*.

A decree of March 18, 1903—issued by Governor-General Émile Gentil (1904–1908), who reportedly killed an ex-military runaway in cold blood—prescribed that beginning January 1, 1904, one-fourth of the tax should be paid in cash and three-fourths in kind. In 1905, cash payment would increase by one-fourth, so after January 1908 all of it would be paid in cash. Regrettably, administrators often demanded taxes twice a year. In 1925, for example, Moulin, chief of the subdivision of Koumra, was unable to gather the requested amount of taxes because of an unusual number of deaths caused by smallpox. So he demanded that the living pay the taxes owed by the dead. When people began leaving the subdivision for Logone, Moulin ordered those remaining to pay for the absentees.[27]

A 1911 document explicitly stipulated that wherever there was opposition and resistance, Chadians should be taught a lesson: "Il faut donner aux rebelles les plus rudes leçons." The fugitives had to be pursued relentlessly until they paid their dues and abandoned their *chicanerie*. "Since most of our conciliatory gestures are viewed as signs of weakness," the memorandum continued, "we must wage war against them until they have submitted completely." Sometimes village chiefs, afraid of being assassinated by their own people or put in jail by the colonial authorities, paid uncollected taxes out of their own pockets. This occurred in 1924 in the cantons of Baltobo and Balkogne, "where many soldiers and government agents were murdered." Taxation had also an unfair twist to its enforcement. For example, at one point, the northerners were required to pay higher taxes than the rest of the country, probably because many owned cattle. Higher taxes in the North were no longer demanded during the 1950s, when the South was paying six times as much as the North (750 francs at Moundou and Fort-Archambault in contrast to 190 at Faya-Largeau and 130 at Abeche).[28]

Denise Moran tells unbelievable stories about the tax collection methods in Wadai and vicinity. She relates, for example, that in 1910, since tax quotas were not met in Ganatyr and Mallingue, administrators gathered their *miliciens* and sixty-four soldiers and left for Mallingue, where they fired one hundred shots, killing several people. At Arde, where Chief Abou Ouara refused to pay taxes, Sergeant T. "blew his brains out" and burned the two villages. Frightened, the Arabs immediately brought cattle and horses as tax payment; others sold their cattle and cotton cloth. In Ganatyr in 1921, a famous lieutenant known as Verver (likely a mispronunciation of "revolver") killed two village chiefs as they tendered their tax collection. Two persons who came to complain were instantly shot. Mr. Verver then ordered the men to dig a hole and throw in the cadavers.[29]

Elsewhere, the stories associated with tax collection were not different in that Chadians resisted French colonial taxation as much as possible. A good example is the story of twenty thousand Sara Dai living in Bouna, who historically fought incessantly against the slave trade and then resisted French colonial taxation. The Sara Dai not only migrated and took refuge on Dai Island and the Mandoul River in 1912 to resist colonial taxation, they completely refused to submit to the French. Encouraged by their chiefs during the 1920s and 1930s, the Sara refused to pay taxes, to provide recruits of any kind including those for World War I, to grow cotton, and to furnish food to French troops fighting the Germans in Cameroon. Resistance in the canton was also encouraged by the *chefs de terre,* who spread the belief that "the dead would resurrect to expel the French" and preached that "guns should not be feared [in Bouna country] because their bullets became water." Moreover, since 1927, Bouna resented the fact that its chief had been stripped of his power by the chief of Ngalo, and the influential men of Ngalo were marrying and abusing local women. More than anything else, however, Bouna villagers refused to pay taxes to anyone, least of all to the new chief, Batinda, who in 1928 demanded two tax payments. The assistant administrator of Moissala sent a guard named Djara to investigate the many incidents of tax evasion and insubordination among the villagers.

Between May and June 1928, news of an unfaithful Bouna woman broke out. Apparently, she had spent time with the guard and was eventually killed by her enraged fiancé. Outraged by the murder, her brothers killed one of the fiancé's sisters, prompting the authorities to send another guard to stop the feud. The guard was seized by the dead girl's family, undressed in public, murdered, and hanged from a tree. French authorities in Moissala decided then to put an end to the incidents of tax evasion and rebellion in Bouna. To accomplish the task, troops were mobilized from Fort-Lamy, Fort-Archambault, and Fort-Crampel, and the attack on Bouna was set for January 1929. French troops besieged the canton and ordered the killing of five thousand adults, the burning of the entire canton, and the slaughter of domestic animals. Only children were spared, most of whom were taken as "prisoners of war" to Fort-Archambault, their necks chained to each other. It would appear, therefore, that the causes of the war were taxation, tampering with the sanctioned traditional authority structure, and the assassination of the tax collector.[30]

Famine

A combination of environmental factors and ill-conceived colonial policies and abuses associated with military recruitment, forced labor, and porterage contributed to several famines in Chad. In Wadai, for example, two famines and epi-

demics, one occurring in 1913–1914 and the other in 1916–1918 are remembered. These famines killed over thirty thousand people. In 1924, locusts devastated Chad, destroying many farms in the cantons of Baltoubai, Alako, Moufa,
Djadja, and the area around Lake Iro. In 1930 and 1934, the entire Moyen-Chari
Prefecture experienced famine.

It is interesting that the causes of famine were usually perceived by Chadians
and many other Africans as the actions of a person—a chief or an evil man who
cast a spell over a given area. It was therefore commonplace to attribute names to
these famines, such as Mbassinda (1890s), Borman (early 1900s), Bormassi
(1910s), Kouma (1910s), Mbailao (1920s), Tabaindo (1920s), Moguinamberi
(1925), Bokibeti (1930s), and Ngodobo (1934–1935). Furthermore, the 1930 law
requiring each village to store a specified amount of grain to feed troops and
workers and to store seeds for the next planting season as prevention against
famine exacerbated the situation in some areas. The French *commandants de cercle* could not deviate from their orders. For example, in 1935, the acting governor
of Chad, Colonel Falvy, wrote, "Since I took command of Chad, I often emphasized the absolute need for our administration to force all African chiefs to establish in each village a collective or family storage of crops."[31]

Denise Moran provides a glimpse of the abuses that may have caused or contributed to famine in the area of Ganatyr, Wadai. She recounts that in order to
punish fugitive *montagnards* who took shelter in the hills, the authorities sent soldiers to their farms to harvest corn, peanuts, sesame, beans, gourds, and cotton. In
the middle of a famine, the authorities at Fort-Lamy ordered Ganatyr to furnish
two hundred tons of corn for the maintenance of troops stationed at Abeche.
Moran also asserts that in nine months, famine drastically increased the number
of thefts and murders perpetrated by bandits and gangsters roaming freely in the
countryside.

The Colonial Cotton-Based Economy

Before the arrival of the French in present Chad, trade in different kinds of commodities including slaves was flourishing within the economic free zone of western and central Sudan. Colonialism weakened the long-distance trade first by
erecting customs posts for territorial control and effective taxation and then by
introducing a new mode of transportation—human, and automotive—that replaced the camel. Trade was thenceforth diverted southward to the Atlantic
Ocean. Colonialism changed Chad's existing socioeconomic and political structures with profound impact on the economic future of the colony. By means of an
absolutist system, the *code de l'indigénat* created political and economic centralization, forced labor, and forced enterprise.[32]

Acting purely in self-interest, the French colonial administration used the state
apparatus to control domestic production, giving exclusive and monopoly powers
to French-owned firms and concessionaires over the production and distribution

of goods and services. Through taxation and forced labor, France controlled, modified, and destabilized microeconomic decisionmaking at the household level, leaving Chadians totally dependent on the whims of the colonial government. In addition to economic centralization and exploitation, the main tenets of the colonial economic legacy, the most identifiable economic impact of colonialism in Chad was the development of the cotton economy. To exclusively appropriate financial surplus from cotton produced by Chadians, the colonial administration used the strategy of forced enterprise, monopolistic concessionaires, and systematic taxation. This approach ensured dominance and guaranteed total subjugation of Chad's economy, resulting in economic dependence on France and the West as we know it today. The strategy also created interregional disparities and total neglect of the Chadian economic space.

Although some cotton production took place in the Mayo-Kebbi and elsewhere before colonialism, compulsory cotton cultivation was introduced by the French between 1926 and 1930. From that time, each tax-paying individual was forced to cultivate at least half a hectare of cotton in the West Chari region. Because the colonizer made it the supreme crop over sorghum, cotton cultivation was given the best land in spite of its restrictive growing cycle. The farmers then used a large proportion of the revenue derived from cotton to pay colonial taxes. Thus failure to cultivate cotton led to imprisonment and other severe forms of punishment.[33]

Gradually, perennial cotton production disappeared in favor of the annual cotton crop, and with the creation of COTONFRAN (Société Cotonnière Franco-Tchadienne), a French monopolistic concessionaire, efforts were made to maximize production through the use of fertilizer. In 1956, fertilizer was applied to 230,000 hectares of cotton. However, the attempt to introduce draft animals in cotton production to boost output failed. By 1952, the land area under cotton cultivation had increased from 165,000 hectares in 1950–1951 to 206. Between 1947 and 1961, there was no single year in which the cotton hectarage did not increase.

Although the land area under cotton stabilized around 230,000 hectares starting from 1955, as Table 2.3 illustrates, it reached nearly 290,000 hectares in 1960 with a total output of about 100,000 metric tons of cotton seed. Average cotton yield, however, barely exceeded 350 kilograms per hectare despite interregional yield differences. Improvement in output and yields came mainly from the increase in land areas under cotton cultivation, the introduction of new varieties by the Cotton Research Institute, *Institut Français de Recherche sur le Coton et Textiles Tropicaux* (IRCT), and the use of selected seeds and homogeneous varieties. Also, changes in the cropping calendar and official supervision contributed to increases in productivity.[34]

Christian Bouquet argues that on the one hand, by directly competing with food production, cotton helped to exacerbate hunger and famine, and because it had to be exchanged for money, the means of tax payment, it also created a more monetized economy.[35] He adds that reliance on the annual revenue from cotton sales, on the other hand, created more individualism and independence, under-

TABLE 2.3   Pre- and Postindependence Cotton Production in Chad, 1947–1988

Years	Cultivated Hectarages (thousands)	Output Including Grains (thousands of metric tons)	Yield Per Hectare (kilograms)	Yield at the Ginnery (percent)
1947–1948[a]	156	37.8	341	29.0
1948–1949	158	44.2	283	29.0
1949–1950	178	57.0	298	29.0
1950–1951	165	41.8	250	29.0
1951–1952	206	61.5	295	29.0
1952–1953	212	58.5	275	29.0
1953–1954	215	59.2	275	29.0
1954–1955	223	75.3	319	30.0
1955–1956	231	71.3	301	31.0
1956–1957	231	65.0	272	34.0
1957–1958	230	82.0	350	36.6
1958–1959	238	67.7	279	36.9
1959–1960	259	41.3	155	36.5
1960–1961	288	96.0	326	–
1979–1981[b]	160	83.0	519	–
1986	124	89.0	721	–
1987	196	113.0	575	–
1988	130	112.0	862	–

SOURCE: [a]République du Chad, *Economie et Plan de Développement,* December 1961, 5.
[b]Food and Agriculture Organization of the United Nations, *Production Yearbook 1989.*

mining social cohesion and communalism. The ultimate result was the loss of fundamental values of the traditional society.

From an economic standpoint, the effect of the cotton economy in Chad has remained negative and ruinous to the welfare of the Chadians.[36] Any improvements in income that may have occurred as a result of cotton accrued mainly to middlemen and the state (through taxation), leaving the vast majority of the producers impoverished. Furthermore, the opportunity cost of cotton monoculture was high for Chad farmers in terms of loss of production efficiency, damage to the soil, precarious economic conditions linked to cotton price instability, and the decline in food and livestock production.

The colonial authority concentrated on cotton production, ignoring basic industries. Even when it existed, the rudimentary industrial sector served uniquely as a means to maximize the exploitation of Chad's resources, especially cotton. Since cotton was the pivot of the colonial economy, other types of industrialization were negligible, and any that did arise were usually related to cotton production. These industries included a cottonseed factory and a cottonseed-oil factory at Moundou belonging to COTONFRAN. Non-cotton-based industries included the slaughterhouse of Farcha and the milk and cheese industry of Massacory, which produced only five tons of butter and five tons of cheese each year. Aside from a livestock veterinary laboratory built in Fasumrcha in 1954 and a few wells sunk by the colonial administration, other important social and economic infrastructure such as electricity and communications was ignored.

On another level, colonialism caused social disaggregation resulting in the emergence of social classes: farmers, workers, and the elite government employees. Emphasis on the French system of education contributed to a Chadian sense of cultural inferiority; it also led to a lack of entrepreneurship and an inadequate supply of skilled labor, to poverty, and to an overall low quality of life for most Chadians. Likewise, regional disparity resulted from the pursuit of one of the fundamental goals of colonialism—the promotion of the extraction of raw materials beneficial to French industries. As such, colonial economic policy and actions were more focused on the South, since it was climatically more promising for economic production than the North. Abderahman Dadi remarks that the continuation of the imposition of cotton cultivation and an educational system based on the French language created unprecedented regional, class, cultural, and economic disparities.[37]

In sum, the main goals of the colonizer in Chad were to extend the French empire, maintain law and order, and promote economic production in line with the aspirations of the colonizer.[38] The net economic effect of the Franco-Chadian encounter was, therefore, negative for the Chadians in that the French dislocated villages, instituted mandatory cotton-production quotas for farmers, and concentrated development efforts in the southern region known as *le Chad-utile*. This policy resulted in economic exploitation through the concessionaires. It created regional disparities, stagnation, and decline in food productivity; impoverishment from taxation and forced labor; and a decline in social cohesion and communalism. French colonialism was also characterized by an absence of industrial development and products for export, a lack of infrastructural development, dependence on the importation of French-made finished products, and social disaggregation.

At independence, therefore, France left the colony with an economy retarded by exploitative policies: forced production, excessive taxation, and exposure of the farmers to an international economic system in which they were not prepared to compete. Coupled with insufficient development of infrastructure, this meant overreliance on cotton and the whims of the international markets and dependence on imports for industrial and consumer goods. Thus, Bouquet argues, if colonial policy initiatives had been realistic—from the point of view of Chad— and even if they had been applied at the expense of traditional social structures, Chad would have attained independence under better conditions.[39] Unlike other French West and Equatorial African territories that were exporting wood, cocoa, and coffee to France, Chad had nothing to show but cotton.[40] Faced with colonial exploitative and oppressive policies, Chadians reacted with either violence or migration.

Migration, Violence, and Criminal Justice

The first alarming reports on the movement of *transfugés* surfaced in the 1920s. On this score, the people of Bouna, the Sara Dai, were the first to attract the attention of the administrators. Administrator La Rougery complained that the people of Bouna and Koumra were continuously leaving their villages and settling in the woods or on the islands of the Mandoul River. Why were they migrating? "They absolutely refuse to submit to forced labor, and one has the hardest time exacting taxes from them," said one administrator.

During the 1930s, the exodus of villagers to avoid taxes and forced labor had become so uncontrollable that Lieutenant Governor Marcel de Coppet (1926–1929) ordered his administrators to take the following measures: (1) Demand only the payment of obligations to the "community" from those villages located along the road, (2) desist from compelling men and women to work overtime or excessively, (3) refrain from asking villagers living along the road to contribute food for people outside their village, (4) use crop surpluses for visitors only, and (5) build worker settlements as close as possible to the villages.

Similarly, on June 3, 1935, Governor Dagain, commandant de la region du Tchad (1934–1938), ordered his administrators to scale down the displacement of individuals and enhance the chiefs' authority. All strangers in an area were to be asked to return to their original villages, but no force was to be used in the process. They were, however, to be warned of their obligation to pay taxes, to contribute their time to government projects, and to recognize *notre autorité* (our authority). Notably, 1935 was also the year the French administration stopped its antisultan policy in the North and initiated what has been called, to use a preferred French expression, *la politique de grands turbans* (the politics of big turbans) and did not resume appointing chiefs in those areas of the North.

The Sara always constituted a difficult case insofar as migration was concerned. On December 28, 1935, P. I. Marchessou, in a special memorandum (no. 1281) told authorities in Bousso and Melfi that the Sara should be returned home—"refoulés sur les pays d'origine"—because they were setting a bad precedent for the other ethnic groups. Of course, migratory movements were common in Chad, but under colonialism their magnitude, their causes, and the migrants' destinations were new. As noted earlier, migrations increased because of the introduction of taxes, forced labor, and forced grain storage, or what the administrators referred to as the *système de prestations*. The intercolony migratory movement to Nigeria, Sudan, and the Cameroons attracted more government attention than the internal movement because it meant depopulation, the loss of young men—potential manpower—and criticism from abroad. In 1925, when Commandant de Cercle Dehais asked for a second collection of taxes (*impôt supplémentaire*) in Moissala, several families left for Oubangui-Chari and other neighboring territories. In that same year (1925), the authorities asked Chief Bezo to write his brother, the Sara chief of Maiduguri in Nigeria (*Bornou anglais*), to return to him every Sara who had run away from Moyen-Chari because the flight had caused manpower shortages in the department.

One of the temptations to emigrate was that taxation was lower in the other colonies. For instance, in 1923, the *chef* of the circonscription of Mayo-Kebbi had written that whereas the Moundang in Chad paid 10 francs per year in taxes irrespective of gender, in Cameroon men paid two francs and women one franc per year. He believed that for each year his circumscription lost five hundred to a thousand individuals. In 1932, another major exodus of emigrants—"un éxode de population assez important"—headed for Cameroon and Nigeria. In the last three months of that year, 135 men, 144 women, and 71 children reportedly left for Cameroon from the village of Khozam; from Koumra some 264 individuals did the same to escape taxes. The same report adds that in 1933, there were 82,681 people in Koumra, but soon that number dropped to 80,000. At this point, the exodus was not the only cause of the decrease: a sleeping sickness epidemic in the 1930s, which forced the closing of the Kou Catholic Mission in 1932, was equally significant.

A 1938 report estimates that an average of two thousand people left the four Logone subdivisions each year for the neighboring territories. One document notes that the exodus from Moyen-Chari was higher in the rainy season because Cameroon had a greater need for manpower along its rivers, especially the Benue, where a worker could easily earn five francs a day. Elsewhere, on November 22, 1937, the chief of the Department of Salamat, alarmed by the ever-growing number of people going to the Anglo-Egyptian Sudan, sent a complaint letter to the Commander of the Region of Chad, Governor Dagain (1934–1938), noting that young men from Aboudeia and other areas crossed the subdivision of Sila and reached Mouhoud on foot. Once there, they worked for a few months to get funds for further travel. Upon achieving this goal, they paid one shilling to a local merchant, who drove them to El-Obeid, and continued to Weahad Madani after paying fewer than three shillings to a local truck driver.[41]

In response, the commander of Chad sent a circular publicizing the report and noted that from oral sources and intercepted telegrams from Sudan, young Chadians not only went to that colony but moved even farther to Ethiopia. The majority worked in the cotton plantations along the Nile. Volunteers without passports were taken by train to Kessala in Sudan, where they crossed the frontier to Sebbarot, Italian territory. Here, they were vaccinated against disease and taken to Asmara. The control post of Adre registered 685 workers from Chad to Sudan and Ethiopia in 1937. In 1939, reports of emigration from the Department of Logone were so alarming that the governor of Chad, Félix Eboué (1938–1941), sent a circular to the administrators of that department asking them to explain the migrations, which were "inquiétants pour l'avenir" (disturbing to the future). Of course, nothing could stop the migrations except perhaps self-government or the cessation of taxes. Thus, the migratory movement in Chad continued unabated until 1960.

In the process of implementing their colonial policies, the French perpetrated many massacres in Chad. One occurred in the Kokati village, prefecture of Doba, in 1919, when authorities caught an African selling beer he had brewed against government rules. Gari of Bedogo sent his guard to Kokati to arrest him. When the villagers resisted, the guard is said to have shot and killed five children. Outraged, the people of Kokati murdered the guard. In response, the administrator of Doba sent his troops to the village and seventy-five people were arrested after they were brutally beaten. Of these, sixty-five died in jail a few days later.

During the early 1900s, the chief of the village of Kon, near Fort-Archambault, refused to submit his area to French authority. To exact obedience, the army sent a Captain Marda to kill several villagers. In the village of Beti, similar retaliatory measures were taken because the people had killed three guards. The villagers of Gore also murdered a guard, and French reaction was predictable: retaliation resulting in many deaths. One episode is well remembered in Sara country. In November 1900, Mbang Ngotibai-Kouadi of Bedaya was summoned by the French who had camped at Ngondere. But the *mbang,* conscious of his authority and suspicious of their reasons, refused to go and instead sent messengers bearing gifts.

The French searched for the chief and finally ambushed him in Maingara near a river, where they killed him on March 3, 1901, took his body to the village after cutting off his head, and displayed it in the open. Fearful that the rest of the *mbang's* body might be the object of funeral ceremonies and therefore incite a rebellion, the French dumped the remains into the river; they used a similar cruel method in Balimba against chiefs Ngakoundou Guirdi, Djanta of Dobo, Dogourenoudji of Mouroungoulaye, and several chiefs in Ma and Mangara.

Another massacre, reported by General Jean Hilaire in 1930, occurred in Abeche in November 1917, after a drunken guard had killed a French marshal identified simply as Guiyades. In response, at dawn on November 15, African troops serving in the colonial forces decapitated some fifty people while they were asleep, leaving "women and children screaming in despair." The secret order also applied to Biltine, where Sheikh Abdul, his relatives and close friends, about forty in all, were arrested, taken to Abeche, and shot to death. Between 1918 and 1920, authorities in Paris suppressed any serious attempts to investigate these incidents.

Resistance to colonial rules was severely punished whenever possible with a minimum average of fifteen days in government jails. Company workers who broke the law were taken to local disciplinary jails built by the companies. As a result, in 1923, for example, the number of prisoners in Chad was so high that the governor-general of French Equatorial Africa remarked that "in 10 years, the administration of the military territory (of Chad) inflicted twenty centuries [sic] and fifteen years of detention to a population that does not exceed 1,300,000. This is certainly excessive."[42] By December 1923, there were eighty prisoners in Fort-Archambault condemned to 2,247 days of forced labor. Table 2.4 gives a breakdown of yearly prison population and amount of fines collected from 1911 to 1922. From Table 2.4 it is evident that although the prison population fluctuated

TABLE 2.4　Prison Population in Chad, 1911–1922

Year	Number of Prisoners	Fines in Francs
1911	2,912	–
1912	4,142	18,813.0
1913	6,996	50,604.0
1914	8,651	47,593.0
1915	9,402	39,919.0
1916	7,545	54,387.0
1917	9,857	63,838.0
1918	7,446	45,513.0
1919	8,452	57,120.0
1920	8,802	112,637.0
1921	5,684	52,876.0
1922	2,502	49,884.5

SOURCES: Musée du Tchad, W36, 57, 1923, 5; W32, 2-12, 1923, 1; and W32, 20, 1925, 29.

annually, it remained relatively high during the twelve-year period, reaching a high of 9,857 inmates in 1917. In 1920, a record level of 112,637 francs was collected in fines by the French colonial administration.

Although the colonial authorities considered the conduct of Africans strange and criminal, in reality, it was the abuses and ill-treatments associated with colonialism that provoked this conduct. Resistance to the French, however, resulted in harsh treatment and severe punishment. In 1924 in Mayo-Kebbi, for instance, one man was jailed for traveling one and a half days over a 20 km (13 mile) distance before bringing medication to a sick European. Other Chadians were incarcerated for refusing to transport a sick European and for abandoning mail packages on the road. In 1925, 4,114 men were imprisoned in Chad and condemned to 37,820 days of work and a combined fine of 50,718 francs. In the last three months of 1932, Fort-Lamy, the capital, had 249 prisoners with fines of 315 francs; Massacory had 805 people in jail and 680 francs in fines; and the circonscription of Bas-Chari had 919 men behind bars with fines of 635 francs. Some of the men were arrested for failing to pay taxes and for refusing to herd cattle or work on the plantations. Over 2 percent of the population of Massacory, estimated at thirty thousand, was in jail.[43] There is no doubt that it was resistance to colonial oppression that led to imprisonment and to an atmosphere of lawlessness, murder, and migration in Chad.

Post–World War II Political Reforms

Forced labor was abolished in the French colonies in 1946, and as a consequence, all Chadians were declared French citizens. Political parties were also legalized, and until 1957, as in other French colonies, Chad elected its own Territorial Assembly and selected delegates to the French National Assembly and the French

Union. The Loi Cadre (Enabling Act) of 1956 introduced universal suffrage and abolished the dual college (under which blacks and whites had voted separately).

Given the excitement brought about by the reforms, preindependence politics in Chad turned lively and relatively complex. If one follows Samuel Decalo's classification of Chad's political parties based on their objectives, among the most powerful conservative parties (briefly discussed below) stood the Union Démocratique et Socialiste de la Résistance (UDSR), founded by the European population in 1946 and affiliated with the Rassemblement du Peuple Français (RPF), a Gaullist party, in 1947.[44] The UDSR and the RPF, along with the Union Républicaine du Tchad (UTR), which had been founded in 1946 by French businessman and frequently appointed *député* Marcel Lallia, succeeded in placing several delegates in the various legislative bodies. The Action Démocratique et Sociale (ADS) and the Union Indépendante pour la Défense des Intérêts Communeaux (UIDIC) were both European-initiated and virtually throughout their existence had no African members.

The best known of the African conservative parties included the Union Démocratique du Tchad (UDT), founded in 1946 by Sahoulba Gountchome (chief of Moundang and sultan of Lere) and Arabi-el-Goni (a trained interpreter from Abeche). It became the Action Sociale Tchadienne (AST) after 1953 and catered primarily to Muslim interests. Both the UDT and the AST were, therefore, popular in Mayo-Kebbi, Batha, and Wadai. Quite often, the two parties allied themselves with those founded or led by French colonial expatriates, such as the European Union Démocratique Indépendante du Tchad (UDIT), founded in 1953 by former governor Rogué (1944–1949). The Groupement des Indépendants et Ruraux Tchadiens (GIRT), founded by Sahoulba Gountchome in 1957, did not become popular but contributed to the fall of Prime Minister Gabriel Lisette's provisional government by withdrawing support in 1959. That year, Ahmed Koulamallah (a transport merchant) founded the Union Socialiste Tchadienne (UST), which soon became defunct only to reemerge in 1959 as the Mouvement Populaire Tchadien (MPT)—a coalition of parties. The MPT formed a short-lived provisional government with Sahoulba Gountchome as premier in 1959. Then, in 1960, Koulamallah and Jean Baptiste, two archenemies, formed an uneasy, fragile coalition of the AST, the GIRT, the UDIT, and the Mouvement Socialiste Africain (MSA). They united under the banner of the Parti National Africain (PNA) to prevent the Parti Progressiste Tchadien (PTT) from rising to power.

As usual in colonial Africa, conservative parties tended to enjoy the support of the traditional authorities, particularly in the North. Indeed, some of them, in collusion with the colonial authorities, went as far as to attempt to slow down the march toward independence, particularly when they realized that the South would inexorably inherit the colonial state.[45] In fact, in 1959, in an attempt to prevent independence, Koulamallah contacted Paris to attempt to force Chad to come under the "Statut du Territorie d'Outre Mer" (overseas French territory), like Djibouti, and prevent independence.

In contrast, the progressive parties generally advocated the abolition of the traditional authorities, the end of forced cotton cultivation in the South, equal rights for blacks and whites, and the eventual replacement of Europeans by Chadians, to be followed by independence. The most important progressive party was the Parti Progressiste Tchadien (PPT), founded in 1947. It enjoyed strong support in the South, particularly among the Sara, because it opposed the forced cultivation of cotton and articulated the interests of the downtrodden southern masses. Needless to say, this party displeased the traditional authorities whose elimination it advocated. Stemming from its strength in the polls, the PPT was first to form a prototype of a locally based government in Chad—the Conseil du Gouvernement—in 1957. This occurred after it had captured fifty-seven of the eighty-five seats in the Territorial Assembly, an improvement over the 1951 campaign.

Clashing with the progressive and conservative parties were the socialist-oriented parties or "political groupings," which included the short-lived Parti Socialiste du Tchad (PST), also founded by Koulamallah in 1950, and the Parti Socialiste Indépendant du Tchad (PSIT), cofounded by Koulamallah and Adoum Aganaye. The PSIT temporarily became strong in Fort-Lamy and in the Chari-Baguirmi Prefecture. In 1956, however, it joined the PPT after the two cofounders split and Koulamallah went on to found the Parti Socialiste Koulamalliste (PSK).

Although the militant nationalist movements claimed to redress political discrimination, they had the unfortunate result of dividing the colony along ethnic, religious, and regional lines. Among them was the Union Nationale Tchadienne (UNT), founded in 1958 and made up of so-called Muslim extremists and militants led by Issa Danna, Abba Siddick (surgeon, born in the Central African Republic), and Mahamat Outman (a trader, born in Fort-Lamy). The UNT ran in the 1959 elections and won only two seats.

As if party proliferation was not enough, Ahmed Moussa (an active Muslim union leader) founded the Union Générale des Fils du Tchad (UGFT) in Cairo in 1959. This was a fundamentalist movement linked to Muslim brotherhoods that eventually joined the Front de Libération du Tchad (FLT). The FLT and its offshoot, the Mouvement National de Libération du Tchad (MNLT), fused with Ibrahim Abatcha's Front de Libération Nationale du Tchad in 1966. Samuel Decalo's typology refers to locally based groups and miniparties with limited and parochial goals, including the Union de Guera (1959), the Union de Kanem (1959), and the Union Logonaise (1959).

As the most progressive party and despite being composed primarily of the Sara, the Parti Progressiste Tchadien (PTT) enjoyed some initial support from northern sympathizers, emerging as the most powerful political force before independence. It faced several obstacles from the colonial administration, in part due to its initial affiliation with the Rassemblement Démocratique Africain (RDA), created under the initiative of the late Félix Houphouet-Boigny at Bamako in 1946, and in part because of its alliance with the French Communist party.

In January and November 1956, respectively, however, Lisette was reelected *député* to the legislature and mayor of Fort-Lamy under the PTT. Yet the unsettling reality was that Lisette was not a very likable man. Despite his French education and his marriage to a French woman, the colonial government disliked both him and his party for allegedly espousing radical ideas. How does one account for the ultimate rise of the PPT in Chad? Some scholars claim that French discriminatory practices against the North were responsible for the southern-northern political dichotomy and reinforced the southern-based PTT. The case was not that simple, however. France did not always favor the South to the neglect of the North. Its policies remained unclear and shifting throughout Chad's colonial history. It was not until the introduction of the forced cultivation of cotton and the work of missionaries in the South during the 1920s that France showed marked interest in the southern region. Until then, admiring the efficiency of the northern sultanates, the French were even appointing southerners who had converted to Islam as canton chiefs, as was the case with Bezo, made chief of Fort-Archambault, and Hassan, installed as chief at Moundou.[46]

At the root of the southern Chadians' rise to prominence in politics stands the Loi Cadre of 1956, which among other things eliminated the dual racial slates and allowed everyone who could speak and write French or Arabic to vote.[47] The law indirectly made it easier for the South, less culturally divided than the North, to wrest power from the northern politicians who had scorned Western culture and education but who, as independence approached, were moving closer to the position of the colonial administrators and the expatriates.

Southern bloc voting was further enhanced by a perception in the South that southerners, particularly the Sara, had remained the underprivileged within the colonial system. Despite differences in languages and customs, a set of similar experiences gave them a common identity, setting them apart from the northerners and the *colons*. Furthermore, as René Lemarchand notes, the French administration reinforced the polarization between North and South through the constant use of contrasting terminology: *chrétien* (Christian) versus *musulman* (Muslim); *sudiste* (southerner) versus *nordiste* (northerner); *salarié* (salaried) or *cultivateur* (field worker) versus *éleveur* (livestock breeder); *descendants d'esclaves* (descendants of slaves) versus *notables, évolu és* (cultured) and *fétichistes* (fetishists) versus *théistes* (theists); and the Communist PPT versus the "loyal" northern parties. Indeed, southern resentment had assumed such proportions that a series of violent clashes occurred throughout the colony between 1947 and 1958, especially in Fort-Lamy, between the Sara and the northerners, or *djellabah*. An alarmed Governor Rogué confided in a secret memo of May 12, 1947, to the governor-general that the Sara could be compared to "enraged sheep."

As was the case in most sub-Saharan colonies that achieved independence, the conduct of politics in Chad was also marred by conflict. Conflict that sometimes resulted in violence was often instigated by the losing candidates and used by the colonial administration to frustrate the move toward true majority rule. The most violent confrontations were in Logone during the 1952 and 1958 elections. The first incidents resulted in the so-called April 1952 Massacre of Bebalem. Allegedly, a government official, attempting to arrest a villager who had refused to pay taxes to a *chef de canton,* fired a gun into a crowd and killed a number of demonstrators. The causes for the clashes were the administration's attempt to boost the authority of the chiefs and increase cotton cultivation as well as the PPT's unwarranted support of a chief of Benoye in local elections.

Bickering and accusations continued during the 1957–1958 elections. Having engineered a temporary coalition of the MSA, the AST, and the UDIT, known as the Union Socialiste Tchadienne (UST), Koulamallah blamed Lisette's and Tombalbaye's party, the PPT, for the continuous violence between the sedentary Arabs and the nomadic Fulani in Chari-Baguirmi. Koulamallah's "dirty tricks" paid handsomely. He ended up with an unexpected victory that returned him to the Territorial Assembly in Fort-Lamy amid cheers that turned the chamber upside down. As Virginia Thompson and Richard Adloff observe, "In fact, so vociferous and rowdy did the public spectators become whenever Koulamallah rose to speak that the sessions had to be suspended several times."[48]

Beyond internal dissension, the PPT was crippled by Lisette's inability to devote his entire energies to his position as party leader because he became assistant to Félix Houphouet-Boigny, president of the RDA. Yet in spite of PPT leadership problems, the colonial administration was unable to prevent it from rising to power in postcolonial Chad. This was because the PPT had disassociated itself from the French Communist party at a time when the decline of the UDT became inevitable with the ascent of the Gaullists to power in the metropolitan areas during the late 1950s. Furthermore, the PPT was boosted by the Algerian revolution (1954–1962), forcing the French to rethink their alliance with the northern Muslims because the French saw the North African guerrilla movement as the work of Pan-Arabism (or of the *foussiers de la Ligue Arabe*).

Instead of talking of the "fetishist Southerners," as Lemarchand notes, the French now began appealing to the southern "Christians." Thus, the free-wheeling Koulamallah had to defend himself and deny publicly being a member of the Arab League or a supporter of Abdul Nasser: "I am French and I will continue to say so," he said in 1958.[49]

The first predominantly African government in Chad was formed by the PPT in alliance with the Groupement des Indépendants et Ruraux Tchadien (GIRT) in 1958, with Lisette as premier presiding over a cabinet of eight Muslims, six Christian Sara, and two Europeans. This provisional government, as it was called, lasted only from December 16, 1958, to February 10, 1959. It fell shortly after Sahoulba's GIRT defected from the coalition, forcing nine members of the cabinet to resign. On February 11, 1959, in an effort to defuse the crisis, Sahoulba was invited to form a new provisional government. Incensed, the PPT refused to collaborate with the new government and even threatened a secession of the South from Chad. Sahoulba could find no other recourse but to resign on March 12,

1959, after being premier for only twenty-nine days. This impasse enabled Koulamallah, the maverick politician disliked by the South, to pose as the power broker and the compromise candidate for the premiership, which he assumed on March 12, 1959. He selected a cabinet of four PPT, two MSA, two GIRT, two AST, and two UDT members. His fatal mistake was the deliberate exclusion of Jean Baptiste, who had joined the opposition block. Baptiste mounted increased opposition to this new government as the prevalent southern fear of a Muslim supremacy headed by Koulamallah once again paralyzed the government, forcing the premier to resign on March 24, 1959, after only twelve days in office.[50]

Lisette's political career had also come to an end. Muslims continued to label him "the foreigner," and Sara politicians such as François Tombalbaye viewed him as an obstacle to their own political aspirations. Thus Tombalbaye formed his cabinet of seven PPT, three GIRT, and three UDT members on March 24, 1959. The March 31, 1959, elections resulted in a landslide victory for the PPT, which received 68 percent of the vote and captured fifty-seven of the eighty-five seats in the Territorial Assembly. This government, the fourth of the four-month-old republic, was dissolved three months later. On June 16, 1959, it was finally replaced by a permanent government under Tombalbaye.

In retrospect, the following observations can be made regarding the nature and impact of the politics of the 1946–1959 period. First, despite the enthusiasm for political reform and the degree of political turmoil, neither the Territorial Assembly nor its government had much political power in Chad. Major decisions were still being made by the colonial executive. Second, the multiplicity of parties, with rifts aggravated by cultural and religious differences, resulted in political instability, as seen by Chad's four short-lived provisional governments. As one political scientist notes, "The functioning of the parties added to the ancient social divisions, or replaced others; likewise, the parties reinforced the ethnic and religious differences, the Sara being the PPT and the Muslims the AST (popular in Wadai, Batha, Salamat) or the MSA (strong in Baguirmi)."[51]

Conclusion

Chad's troubled past underscores the difficulties the country faced in its move toward true nationhood. With hindsight, the inevitability of disaster was clear right from the end of the nineteenth century. The whole region had for centuries remained chaotic, with states becoming easy prey for powerful nations through sanctioned and organized state and individual violence, slave raiding, looting, burning, and breaking of treaties, often done in the name of religion or ethnicity.

It must also be stated that a careful analysis of Chad's history does not support the thesis that France deliberately favored the South over the North. In fact, one could argue that the opposite was the case. Government activity was more pronounced in the South not because the French loved southerners but because of the economic resources the region was able to offer toward the success of the colonial enterprise. Understandably, this was especially true of cotton, the main commodity that spurred French interest after 1928. Before that period, the colonizer had ignored both the South and the North.

Fearful of the North, the French willfully followed differential policies that targeted the South for the recruitment of manpower for the army, forced labor, porterage, and the concessionaire companies. As a result, violence in the North subsided after 1920 and people there resumed their precolonial aristocratic and nomadic or seminomadic lifestyles; conflict escalated in the South. Here, far from Fort-Lamy, the capital, desperate administrators enforced and abused the colonial laws. The African response to taxation, manpower recruitment, cotton cultivation, and mistreatment often took the form of violence, migration, and pent-up frustration. These reactions to the inhumane and oppressive actions of the colonial administration constituted "crimes" in the eyes of the colonizer.

The only reason the South eventually had a relatively larger number of literate citizens and a more developed physical infrastructure was that the French realized they could not benefit from its resources unless they spent some energies and money there. Indeed, the result of France's discriminatory practices in favor of the North was the disintegration of southern social and political institutions while those in the North remained virtually intact. Notably, the northerners rejected Western education on the basis of religion and traditionalism. Yet perhaps the only great loss in the North was the partial weakening of the power of the sultanates and the forced abandonment of the reliance on slavery and the slave trade, which had become an important part of life.

Undoubtedly, although southerners benefited from the abolition of slavery brought about by the French presence, they saw forced labor and forced cotton cultivation as another form of slavery. Thus, when all is said and done, the achievements of the southerners occurred in spite of and not because of French preference for their ethnic groups.

Notes

1. D. Lange, "The Kingdoms and Peoples of Chad," in D. T. Niane, ed., *General History of Africa, IV* (Paris: UNESCO, 1992), 239.

2. John Collier, "Historical Setting," in Thomas Collelo, ed., *Chad: A Country Study* (Washington, D.C.: U.S. Government Printing Office, 1990), 9.

3. Ibid., 8.

4. Louis Brenner, *The Shehus of Kukawa* (Oxford: Oxford University Press, 1973), 100.

5. See Mario Azevedo, "Power and Slavery in Central Africa," *Journal of Negro History* 67 (Fall 1982): 204.

6. Jacques le Cornet, *Histoire politique du Tchad dès 1900 à 1962* (Paris: Librairie Générale de Droit et Jurisprudence, 1963), 22–23.

7. Allen Fisher and Humphrey Fisher, *Slavery and Muslim Society in Africa* (New York: Doubleday, 1972), 174, 194.

8. S. P. Reyna, *Wars Without End: The Political Economy of a Precolonial State* (Hanover: University Press of New England, 1990), 166.

9. Glauco Ciammichella, *Libyens et français au Tchad (1897–1914)* (Marseilles: Éditions du CNRS, 1987), 12.

10. Pierre Lapie, *My Travels Through Chad* (London: John Murray, 1943), 68–69; and Pierre Kalck, *Central African Republic* (New York: Praeger, 1971).

11. Virginia Thompson and Richard Adloff, *The Emerging States of French Equatorial Africa* (Stanford: Stanford University Press, 1960), 10.

12. Archives, Musée National du Tchad, N'Djamena; W90, 1–10 (1940), 1–17.

13. Musée du Tchad, N'Djamena, W90, 1–10 (1940), 4.

14. Azevedo, interview with Colonel Jean Chapelle, N'Djamena, May 15, 1974.

15. See *Gabon-Congo IV, Dossier 20,* 18 Septembre 1909 (Paris: *Société Anti-Esclavagiste de France,* 1945).

16. Brian Weinstein, *Gabon: Nation-Building on the Ogooue* (Cambridge: Cambridge University Press, 1966), 250.

17. Chambre des Députés, Session Ordinaire de 1906, *Compte rendu analytique,* 20 Janvier (Paris, 1906), 8.

18. *Journal Officiel* (November 1923), 1084; *Journal Officiel* (1 December 1930), 1085; *Journal Officiel* (1 January 1923), 137; and *Journal Officiel* (1 January 1936), 12–13.

19. Azevedo, interview with former railroad workers, Bedaya, Sarh, and Moissla, Chad (June 1974).

20. *Journal Officiel* (1 December 1930), 1085.

21. Musée du Tchad, N'Djamena, W1, 11 (1924), 12.

22. See René Lemarchand, "The Politics of Sara Ethnicity: A Note on the Origins of the Civil War in Chad," *Cahiers d'Études Africaines* 20/4 (1980): 456.

23. Michel Manot, *L'aventure de l'or et du Congo-Océan* (Paris: Librairie Sécretan, 1946), 283–284.

24. Musée du Tchad, W29, 1 (1920), 31 and W37, [n.n.] (1925), 13.

25. Musée du Tchad, W29, 1 (1920), 27–29, and W32, 7 (1920), 27. Much of the following data and information are taken from archival sources.

26. Henri Barth, *Voyages et découvertes dans l'Afrique septentrionale et centrale, I,* vol. 3 (Paris: A. Bohne, Librairie, 1861), 279.

27. Musée du Tchad, W37, 15 (1925), 6.

28. Quoted by Lemarchand, "The Politics of Sara Ethnicity," 409.

29. Denise Moran, *Tchad* (Paris: Gallimard, 1934), 84, 71–84.

30. Azevedo, interview with the Bouna village chief and his advisers, Bouna, Moissala (June 27, 1974). See also interview at Koumra (June 19, 1974); and interview at Moissala (June 26 and 28, 1974).

31. Musée du Tchad, W91, 1–10 (1935), 1.

32. Gatta Ngothé Gali, *Tchad: Guerre civile et désagrégation de l'état* (Paris: Présence Africaine, 1985), 31–37; and Harold D. Nelson et al., *Area Handbook for Chad* (Washington, D.C.: U.S. Government Printing Office, 1972), 31.

33. Christian Bouquet, *Tchad: Genèse d'un conflit* (Paris: Harmattan, 1982), 87, 94–95.

34. République du Tchad, "Économie et plan de développement," *Ministère du Plan et de la Coopération* (December 1961), 5 (annex).

35. Bouquet, *Tchad,* 109.

36. Azevedo, "Rubber, and Colonial Government in Chad (1880–1940)" (unpublished manuscript, March 28, 1983).

37. Abderahman Dadi, *Tchad: l'État retrouvé* (Paris: Harmattan, 1987), 35.

38. Gali, *"Chad: Guerre civile,"* 35.

39. Bouquet, *Tchad,* 101.

40. Michel N'Gangbet, *Peut-on encore sauver le Tchad?* (Paris: Karthala, 1984), 14–15.

41. Musée du Tchad, W53, 17 (1937), 1. Much of the following information is also taken from archival sources.

42. Musée du Tchad, W36, 57 (1923), 5.

43. Musée du Tchad, W37, [n.n.] (1925).

44. See Lemarchand, "Politics of Sara Ethnicity," 461.

45. Jean Chapelle, *Le peuple tchadien* (Paris: Harmattan, 1980), 237, 243.

46. Bernard Lanne, "Les deux guerres civiles," in *Tchad: Anthologie de la guerre civile* (N'Djamena: Yamoko Koulro-Bezo, 1981), 55.

47. Patrick Manning, *Francophone Sub-Saharan Africa, 1880–1985* (Cambridge: Cambridge University Press, 1988), 143.

48. Virginia Thompson and Richard Adloff, *Conflict in Chad* (Berkeley: Institute of International Studies, 1981), 437.

49. Quoted in Lemarchand, "Politics of Sara Ethnicity," 466.

50. For more details on the several colonial reform governments, see Samuel Decalo, *Historical Dictionary of Chad* (Metuchen, N.J.: Scarecrow Press, 1987), 253–266.

51. Cornet, *Histoire politique du Tchad,* 52.

3

POLITICAL EVOLUTION AND THE CIVIL WAR IN CHAD

At the onset of their rule, the French attempted to seriously dismantle the powerful northern sultanates, but by the mid-1930s they realized that the local political traditions were deeply *ingraine* in the social structure and that the region did not offer much hope of contributing to the colonial enterprise. Realizing that the only profitable economic activity was livestock breeding and that the inhabitants would continue to oppose their rule, the French adopted a policy of indirect rule in the North. The French consistently applied indirect rule, leaving intact an administrative arrangement they considered expedient. The sultans were therefore left alone as long as they allowed the French free access to the region, paid their taxes (however reluctantly), and maintained law and order.

In the South, notwithstanding their effort to apply an assimilationist policy that would rely primarily on European personnel, the French were forced to keep the traditional chiefs as long as they remained submissive to the colonial administrators or the *commandants de cercles*. Thus unlike in the North, where they applied indirect rule, in the South the French practiced both direct rule and indirect rule on the local level. They remained essentially satisfied provided the chiefs guaranteed manpower for military service, forced labor, government projects, assistance to concessionaires, tax collection, and cotton production. This was generally the state of affairs up to about 1958, when Chad became an autonomous republic within the French Community. The dichotomous colonial policy created resentment in the North and the South and set the stage for the political instability and conflict that characterized postcolonial rule in Chad. It is within the context of this colonial policy that we discuss the postcolonial rule, especially as it concerns Chad's political rivalries between 1960 and 1965.

The Postcolonial Era

Chad entered the era of independence on August 11, 1960, with a constitution and a government that, although heavily favoring the power of an executive president and his council of ministers, prescribed the sharing of power among three branches, namely, the executive, the judiciary, and the legislature. The nation's first president, François Tombalbaye, was also the chairman of the country's only party, the Parti Progressiste Tchadien (PPT) and the commander in chief of the armed forces. He appointed his cabinet members and the judiciary, including members of the Supreme Court. The president also named all the country's provincial governors, known as *prefets,* for the fourteen prefectures created in the 1970s. Following the coup in 1975, the army eliminated the Council of Ministers and replaced it with the Military High Council, or the Conseil Supérieur Militaire (CSM). In the same year, the military indefinitely suspended the Supreme Court in favor of a court of state security.

The country's unicameral legislature was called the National Assembly, which replaced the preindependence Territorial Assembly. Unfortunately, the National Assembly turned out to be nothing but a rubber stamp for the president's decrees and legislative whims. As the civil war intensified during the 1970s, none of the branches was actually functioning. Thus during the 1979–1982 period, by and large and as a result of Nigeria's effort, the country was ruled by the ineffective Government of National Union of Transition, or the Gouvernement d'Union Nationale de Transition (GUNT), which served as the executive (in fact, as the legislature as well) until Hissein Habre promulgated his Fundamental Law in 1982. The GUNT was to be disbanded once elections, which never materialized, were held.

Under Habre's provisional constitution, the president, to be selected by the Command Council of the Armed Forces of the North, or the Conseil de Commandement des Forces Armées du Nord (CCFAN), held unparalleled powers over the other branches of government and the armed forces. To the surprise of observers, Chad was declared a "secular, indivisible republic" with French and Arabic as the official languages. Yet the Fundamental Law did not restore the National Assembly but created a 30-member national advisory council and a series of courts based on the French model, interspersed with customary, Islamic, and military courts. Holding on to the concept of a single-party state, Habre, in 1984, established his own party, the National Union for Independence and Revolution, or the Union Nationale pour l'Indépendence et la Révolution (UNIR), with him serving as chairman. The new party was made up of a fourteen-member executive bureau and an eighteen-member central committee.

The 1982 Fundamental Law was replaced by a new constitution in July 1988 that gave even more legal power to the president, including the provision of rule by decree and initiation of constitutional amendments. Under the new constitution, elections took place in 1990 for the 123-member National Assembly, replacing the appointed National Advisory Council. Theoretically, the 1989 reforms and others to come were to lead Chad to a truly democratic system. However, the reforms were immediately shelved once Habre was overthrown by Idris Deby in late 1990. Under pressure from France and the international community, on March 1, 1991, the new regime promulgated a national charter designed to lead the country to a multiparty system, a freely elected legislature, and an independent court system. Accordingly, but after much procrastination following a national conference, the transitional Charter of April 1993 provided the election of a transitional prime minister (with Fidel Moungar as the chosen politician) and a 57-member interim legislature called the High Council of Transition, or the Conseil Supérieur de Transition (CST). The work of the CST resulted in new laws that legalized a multiparty system, restored all freedoms, and provided for a presidential term of five years and a universally elected bicameral legislature, the National Assembly and the Senate, and a constitutional court. Postponed twice, forcing the appointment of two more transition prime ministers, Kassire Koumakoye and well-respected and seasoned politician Daniel Djimasta Koibla (April 1995), the first truly democratic, internationally supervised legislative elections were scheduled for April 1996. Presidential elections were to follow immediately thereafter.

The fragmentation characteristic of pre-1960 politics were reflected vividly in the politics of the new Chad. This has led some experts to argue that preindependence Chadian political rivalries aggravated and solidified national rifts along ethnic and religious lines, thereby reducing chances for national unity or even rapprochement.[1]

During the period before independence, the Arabs of the North, who even then constituted one of the largest ethnic groups in the country and who controlled the retail businesses in the country, were unable to come together and establish a party of their own. Arab leaders had held an extraordinary gathering in N'Djamena in 1950, and political pundits expected them to form a party. Instead, they left town after agreeing only to collect funds for mutual assistance.[2]

Meanwhile, things were different in the South, where Tombalbaye was reinforcing his political position in the PPT as independence came closer. Tombalbaye's ouster of Lisette from party leadership four days before independence (a move some have called "a coup by telegram") foreshadowed the new president's politics.[3] Tombalbaye then presided over jubilant crowds on August 10, 1960, the eve of Independence Day. People crowded in front of the Palais des Gouverneurs, dancing, singing, clowning, and listening to speeches. French president Charles de Gaulle sent his congratulatory message through André Malrau, who spoke of a day of "fraternity, a new night of history." Just before midnight, in typical laconic style, Tombalbaye rose up and told the people: "Chadians, sing of joy! It is midnight. I solemnly proclaim Chad independent and sovereign."

Tombalbaye, undeniably a skillful politician backed by the educated Sara, cleverly embarked on consolidating his power, first by merging the Parti Nationaliste Africain with the PPT in March 1961 and second by purging his opponents. As early as 1962, Tombalbaye made the country a de facto one-party state and began systematically excluding his political opponents from the regime, many of whom were from the North. In March 1963, such northern politicians as the Speaker of the National Assembly, Mahamat Abdelkerim, and three cabinet ministers who opposed the move toward a single-party state were arrested and given heavy sentences.

In 1963, people in Fort-Lamy and Am-Timan began protesting to prevent the anticipated arrest of Koulamallah and Djebrine Ali Kerallah (both popular politicians during the 1950s) as well as of Tombalbaye's former ministers of finance, interior, and foreign affairs between 1961 and 1963. Bloody riots followed; five hundred people were killed. Yet Koulamallah and Kerallah were tracked down, captured at a meeting, and jailed on conspiracy charges against the government. The president declared a state of emergency. Tombalbaye completed his consolidation of power two years later. In an attempt to show his displeasure with the French who criticized his leadership and to assert his independence, Tombalbaye demanded the evacuation of French troops from the BET Prefecture.

Apart from the fact that the new republic was divided along regional and religious lines, long-standing differences were compounded by political bickering. As two renowned scholars put it, "Much of Chad's instability and violence can be attributed to its belated emergence as an organized territory and the rapidity of its political evolution, which also helps to explain . . . the subsequent trend toward a single party and one-man dictatorship."[4] Under Tombalbaye, the North now felt as the South had felt during the colonial period. Hardships also occurred in the South, but on a smaller scale because of ethnic allegiance to Tombalbaye. Few prominent southerners dared to criticize their president in public, since they benefited from his rule. For example, once they were in power, the Sara tolerated obligatory cotton cultivation in exchange for their children's ascent to leadership positions. As a northern adage appropriately cited by Robert Buijtenhuijs says, "Le mouton ne gémit pas s'il est tondu par son propre berger" (a sheep does not moan when its wool is clipped by its own shepherd). With the institutionalization of a de facto single-party state in March 1962, which gave almost unlimited powers to the president, the PPT took control of the government and slated all candidates for party and government office. Finally, on June 4, 1964, the National Assembly declared Chad a de jure single-party state.

Scholars have disparagingly referred to Tombalbaye's post-1960 military and administrative assignment of southerners to the North as an "invasion" of the region by the Sara. However, as Buijtenhuijs stresses, this relocation applied primarily to middle-level administrative positions, the police force, postal employees, and hospital and school staff and not to the *prefet* and *sousprefet* level. Unfortunately, many of the new civil servants were not adequately trained either administratively or culturally to assume sensitive positions, and some Sara saw

their prominence in government as an opportunity to redress centuries of enslavement under Islamic, Arab, and Tubu dominance. Unwise tax levies (especially on cattle, the mainstay of the North), growing abuses under the new regime,
and discrimination against the northern populations further polarized the two
regions of the country.

Despite the negative impact of Tombalbaye's authoritarian rule, it was his fiscal
policy that sparked a northern rebellion against the regime. In 1965, the government imposed a new levy on cattle and increased personal taxes (euphemistically
called by Tombalbaye a "loan to the government") to develop projects in the
country, a decree that unfortunately was not properly explained to the population. Increased tax collection led to a revolt in Mangalme, Batha Prefecture, in
which ten government officials were murdered. In retaliation, the government ordered the killing of some five hundred Mubu in July 1966, although Tombalbaye
acknowledged the death of only 217 "bandits," as he called them, and some
twenty-four government troops.

Soon, the rebellion spread to other parts of the North, where the Tubu killed
one Chadian soldier, triggering retaliation from the regime. This caused the *derdei*
(spiritual leader), along with a thousand Tubu, to flee to Libya in 1965, signaling
the coming of the civil war. Subsequently, on June 22, 1966, some twenty-four in-
tellectuals and Muslim nationalists, including Ibrahim Abatcha gathered in Sudan
and founded the Front de Libération Nationale (FROLINAT), or the National
Liberation Front. Abatcha became its secretary-general.

Unfortunately, FROLINAT, which initiated a guerrilla campaign against the
regime in the countryside, experienced internal bickering from the start, the most
acute being over the leadership of the Front. In February 1968, Abatcha was killed
by Chadian security forces and was succeeded by the controversial Dr. Abba
Siddick, a surgeon who was a former Tombalbaye supporter and cabinet minister
(1958–1959). Ethnic differences (Tubu versus Arab, for example) and quarrels between Socialists and Communists further divided the Front. Also, problems with
communication and food distribution fueled major disagreements among the
various leaders of the Front.[5]

Tombalbaye was initially unwilling to compromise with the nationalists on the
military and political front. When the Chadian army proved unable to stop the
guerrillas in the BET and Wadai Prefectures, the president recalled the French
troops in 1968 to fight the insurgents. FROLINAT did not have a commonly accepted ideological program. The Front was, however, dominated by socialist-
oriented nationalists who, as Buijtenhuijs observes, used anticolonial rhetoric
against those from N'Djamena. French intervention and FROLINAT's major split in
1969 slowed the impact of the rebellion but led eventually to a further split of
FROLINAT as follows: (1) the First Liberation Army (established in 1969) was a
splinter group that in 1976 became the Volcan Army, with Mahamat Abba operating in the Northeast (Ennedi); (2) the Second Liberation Army (the Northern
Army) operated in the Northwest (Tibesti and Borkan) under Hissein Habre and

Gukuni Wedei, the *derdei's* son, who relied on Libyan support; and (3) the Liberation Third Army (also known as the Western Army), which operated in west-central Kanem under Aboubakar Abdelrahmane, whom Nigeria supported covertly.

Although uncoordinated, the various hit-and-run factions of FROLINAT continued to launch successful attacks on government positions in their areas of operation. They caused severe casualties to the Chadian national armed forces, which Tombalbaye criticized for "un désolant spectacle d'inefficacité et de mauvais esprit" (a sad show of inefficiency and low morale). As the rebellion escalated, Tubu Nomad Guards occupied Aouzou in 1968.

Perplexed by the continuing rebellion, in 1969 the president ordered a secret internal investigation of the roots of the northern revolt, which was subsequently carried out by the French Mission de Réforme Administrative (MRA), based in Guera. In 1970, the MRA recommended restoration of the power of the local authorities, less reliance on southerners to administer the North, and the cessation of tax collection by authorities from southern N'Djamena. In the spirit of the recommendations, the number of Muslims in the Chadian army was increased to 30 percent.

On the military front, the French army had contained the northern guerrillas and raised the morale and performance of the Chadian forces. By 1972, in order to cause a further wedge within the northern population, Tombalbaye increased the proportion of Muslims in the national armed forces to 38 percent, released six hundred political prisoners, and announced an amnesty for all rebels. Likewise, to please the armed forces, he included popular General Jacques Doumro in the Political Bureau and gave him responsibility for the defense of the republic. To demonstrate further his apparent goodwill toward the North, the president went so far as to accuse his fellow Sara of hampering national unity and encouraging a military coup against his regime. He also criticized those technocrats who sought to limit development and industrialization to the country's most productive areas in the South and assailed the politicians who had opposed his plan to allow the North to keep part of the locally collected taxes.

On the international front, Tombalbaye improved Chad's relations with neighboring Sudan and Libya, both of which thereafter restrained northern guerrillas who had enjoyed sanctuary along the eastern and northern frontiers, from where they almost paralyzed Chad's countryside. As he turned his attention toward the national army and attempted to appease the North, however, trouble brewed from his very southernmost base. Tombalbaye dealt a blow to his own southern political base by ordering, on the advice of Haitian-born physician André Vixamar, the restoration of *yondo,* the traditional Sara initiation rite that in the past included circumcision and clitoridectomy; he mandated this even to older Chadians (up to the age of fifty-one) who had not yet undergone the ritual, even if they had converted to Islam. As a result, an estimated three thousand southern civil servants, two cabinet ministers, and one colonel "went through the ordeal" between April 1973 and April 1974.[6]

In addition to *yondo*, a series of ill-conceived decisions by Tombalbaye brought the government to a virtual standstill. Among the president's mistakes were his volte-face toward the Arab world, particularly Libya, to whom he seemed on the surface to have tacitly conceded the uranium-rich Aouzou Strip in 1972; the imprisonment of several army officers in 1973; poor handling of the 1973–1974 drought through his unsuccessful self-reliant Operation Agriculture; and his Africanization policy. Tombalbaye's first three mistakes are discussed in other parts of this book.

Emulating Mobutu Sese Sekou's "cultural revolution" of July 1968, the new Africanization policy, called Authenticity, forced every Chadian to drop his or her European name and adopt an African name. Only the title of *compratriote* could be used among Chadians of all ranks. In fact, Tombalbaye went so far as to hire a famous *griot* (historian-musician) from West Africa, who would introduce him on special occasions, shouting: "Ngarta connaît tout, sait tout, ne lit jamais [a remark the president did not mind], mais sait tout. Le grand N'Garta, champion des champions, seul peut-être de Gaulle le dépasse" (Ngarta knows everything, he never reads, but knows everything. The Great Ngarta, champion of champions, perhaps only De Gaulle surpasses him).[7] For himself, the president conveniently chose the name of Ngarta (Chief) Tombalbaye.

Unfortunately, Africanization or Chadianization often meant southernization, or rather Saraization, of the country. This was reinforced in September 1973 by the creation of a new political party called the Mouvement National pour la Révolution Culturelle et Sociale (MNRCS). The cultural revolution made Tombalbaye extremely unpopular among his own southern people, especially the young and the Western-educated, whom he wished to control and humiliate. Chadian and expatriate opponents of the cultural revolution, including many Protestant missionaries, were either exiled or arrested; some were beaten to death or allegedly buried alive.[8]

As the South joined the North in criticizing the regime, rumors of attempted coups spread in the capital, compelling Tombalbaye to boast that he had survived more coup attempts than any other African leader. He blamed Jacques Foccart, the secretary-general of the French presidency, for most of them. The most bizarre episode was the June 1973 "black sheep plot," allegedly engineered by Madame Kalthouma Guembang, leader of the PPT's women's wing. Reportedly, Mrs. Guembang, joined by several other prominent southerners, including General Malloum, attempted to overthrow Tombalbaye through magic in the performance of a traditional ceremony. General Malloum was therefore arrested and imprisoned along with other alleged plotters. The supposedly Christian president was so alarmed by the traditional ceremony that just before his death, he scheduled a retrial designed to impose heavier penalties on the alleged conspirators.

Unwisely, President Tombalbaye continued to belittle and purge the army. He increased the size of the National and Nomadic Guard to three battalions at the expense of the army. He also brought in foreign advisers to bolster his internal security and hired Moroccans to be his bodyguards. No wonder, therefore, that at dawn on Sunday, April 13, 1975, a palace coup carried out by junior officers of the army and units of the Gendarmerie (led by Lieutenant Ali Dimtoloum, chief of staff, and senior Sara General Milrew Odingar) assassinated the president. Malloum was sworn in as head of the Conseil Supérieur Militaire (CSM).

What factors define Tombalbaye's fall from power? Some scholars believe that the political strife under Tombalbaye had a religious basis, but that clearly is not the case. Much has been made of Tombalbaye's alleged anti-Muslim policy. Many scholars have actually accused Tombalbaye of being insensitive toward the Muslims and of advancing only the agenda of his southern base, which was mostly Christian and traditionalist. In reality, in spite of his Protestant upbringing, Tombalbaye loved neither Christians nor Muslims. Tombalbaye fought exclusively for his own power. Yet his rise to power was achieved largely through the active involvement of the Muslim constituency, as Bernard Lanne painstakingly demonstrates. The National Assembly that came out of the 1957 universal suffrage elections was 54 percent northern, and the Conseil de Gouvernement consisted of four northerners and three southerners. Furthermore, the National Assembly that put Tombalbaye in power in 1959 was predominantly Muslim, and 65 percent of Tombalbaye's (first) cabinet ministers of March 24, 1959, were Muslim.

In addition, during the 1970s, at least 30 percent of his administrative personnel was Muslim. There were also cases when northerners were appointed *prefets* in the South, although in a smaller number compared to southern *prefets* appointed to northern posts. Likewise, when a single-party state was approved on June 4, 1964, the PPT was religiously and regionally bipartisan. Fifty percent of the National Assembly was northern and 50 percent southern, and several northern Muslim politicians agreed with the changes, including Abbo Nassour, Adoum Tchere, Baba Hassane, Mahamat Abdelkerim, and Ali Kosso.

As a result of Tombalbaye's attempted conciliatory policy of 1961 to 1971, by 1971 both the PPT National Political Bureau and the government showed a ratio of 48 percent Muslim and 52 percent non-Muslim; furthermore, the ministries of foreign affairs, interior, and economy were held by northerners. Moreover, the second most important position in the country, the presidency of the National Assembly, was occupied by a northerner.[9] Tombalbaye also broke off relations with Israel, in part to appease the North.

Evidence suggests strongly that between 1960 and 1962 Tombalbaye focused more on securing his own power without regard to region, religion, or ethnicity. Thus notwithstanding his seeming change of policy in the 1970s to accommodate the North, the large number of prominent northerners and Muslims who were arrested during the 1963–1969 period indicates that, indeed, the president had developed a deliberate policy of excluding northern politicians–not because they were Muslim but because they were more vocal in opposing the regime. Michael Kelley notes, "After 1963, perceptions of ethnic, religious, and regional differences gained new meaning for mustering support and decrying opposition," and "politicians from both the government and opposition used the differences, with their historical implications, to solidify popular support behind their position."[10] It seems, therefore, that philosophically the autocratic president had little regard for religion. The president came to believe that the state should be subordinate to the party, as he made clear at a February 27, 1967, party congress meeting.[11]

The Stage for Civil War

As we noted earlier in this chapter, General Félix Malloum came to power in April 1975 following a coup d'état carried out by junior officers in which President Ngarta Tombalbaye was assassinated. Accusing Malloum of plotting to overthrow the government, Tombalbaye had jailed Malloum before his overthrow. As the new leader, Malloum was unprepared to lead the nation, although he was certainly aware of the country's problems: dissatisfaction in the North and in the South and threats to him and to the regime from the Tubu-Arab coalition and from the Sara. During the first month of his tenure, he invited several northerners to join his cabinet. He then freed more than 173 political prisoners and called publicly for national reconciliation. As a result, half his cabinet was made up of Muslims. Several prominent nationalists, including the Tubu *derdei,* Wedei Kichidemi, who returned from his Libyan exile in August 1975, praised this move. Many guerrillas, with the exception of Gukuni Wedei's and Hissein Habre's factions, stopped fighting temporarily and rallied to the new government.[12]

In late 1975, Malloum unwisely expelled the 1,500 French troops in retaliation for France's direct negotiation with the rebels for the freedom of Madame Françoise Claustre, hostage of Hissein Habre and Gukuni Wedei in Bardai since April 1974. Captain Pierre Galopin, an officer in the French forces in Chad and one of the authors of the Mission de Réforme Administrative secret report of 1969, was also captured that year by Hissein Habre and executed on April 4, 1975.

The president executed some military officers in March 1977, right at the time when Faya-Largeau was under siege from enemy troops. Rumors of impending coups circulated in the capital, illustrated by the attempt on the president's life in N'Djamena during the celebrations of the regime's first anniversary on April 15, 1976. The situation turned so precarious that President Malloum recalled the French troops. Between March and June 1978, Ounianga-Kebir and Faya-Largeau fell to the rebels even though a Libyan-sponsored cease-fire had been signed by the government and Gukuni at Sebha in February.

In a period of six months the Forces Armées Tchadiennes (FAT), the government troops, suffered as many as 2,000 deaths out of an army of 11,500 men.[13] To avoid being perceived by the South as an appeaser, Malloum increased political repression in the country and banned all political activities. To gain favor with some of the guerrillas, Malloum appointed Habre prime minister on August 29, 1978, with France apparently acting as the guarantor of the Charte Fondamentale, signed that month in Sudan under the auspices of President Gafar el-Nimeiry. The appointment turned out to be a mistake, as Habre maintained his allegiance to the Forces Armées du Nord (FAN). Whether the French actually initiated the move to have Habre brought into the government is still a matter of debate. It is generally acknowledged, however, that at an August 23, 1978, meeting in Bangui, attended by Valérie Giscard d'Estaing, Joseph Mobutu (Mobutu Sese Seko of Zaire), Jean-Bedel Bokassa (Central African Republic), and Léon Mebiane (Gabon's prime minister), Malloum was persuaded to trust Habre.[14]

The two leaders had such conflicting personal agendas that the government reached an impasse just a few weeks after Habre had taken office, as he attempted to act as president. Each was giving orders, firing the other, and arresting the other's friends, as happened at N'Djamena airport when Malloum had the passport of Hissein Alkhali (from the foreign ministry) taken as the latter prepared to attend the Non-Aligned Nations Conference in Maputo.[15] On February 12, 1979, fighting broke out in the capital between Malloum's and Habre's troops. A French-brokered cease-fire favoring Habre's and Gukuni's factions did not solve the crisis. Had the French not forced the Chadian government to stop air raids against enemy positions in February 1979, Malloum's troops would have prevailed on the ground.

Leading a well-disciplined force of some five hundred men, Habre was reportedly joined by some twelve hundred northerners who left the FAT between February 12 and 14, 1979; the combined force of his inept enemies totaled four thousand. The civil war was bloody, resulting by February 25, 1979, in the deaths of more than a thousand people and the flight of at least eighty thousand citizens, mostly Sara from N'Djamena, making the capital, for all practical purposes, a Muslim ghost town. Subsequently, Colonel Abdelkerim Kamougue, who had commanded the government troops (FAT), retreated southward and by April 1979 had become the undisputed leader of the FAT and the southern region.

After skirmishes between FAN and FAT in N'Djamena on February 12, 1979, and with French general Louis Forest's acquiescence, Gukuni's People's Armed Forces (Forces Armées Populaires—FAP) moved from BET and joined Habre's National Armed Forces (Forces Armées du Nord—FAN) against the FAT in N'Djamena on February 19, 1979. They quickly entered the capital after humiliating Malloum's Chadian national forces (FANT).[16] For all practical purposes, this incident destroyed the Chadian state. Indeed, from February 1979, Chad remained divided into virtually three countries with three capitals and one enclave: Faya-Largeau, the capital of the North, was dominated by the factions of FROLINAT discussed earlier; N'Djamena, at the center, was under Gukuni's government; Sarh, the capital of the South, gravitated toward strongman Kamougue; and Libya controlled Aouzou.

In the end, the Gouvernement d'Union Nationale de Transition (GUNT) dominated the cabinet with the inclusion of only six southerners out of thirty ministers.[17] At the same time, according to Buijtenhuijs, massacres of southerners serving in middle-level administrative positions, the police force, the post office, and the water and forest departments occurred in many parts of the North. The situation was beyond rectification. Malloum, hampered by the total collapse of the country's finances and economy, resigned and sought asylum in Nigeria following the first Kano Accord in March 1979. In May 1979, FAP–FAN forces turned south to the Mayo-Kebbi Prefecture and made Bongor, Lere, Lai, and Kelo their operation bases to cut the supply routes to Kamougue's men.

The Kano conference of March 16, 1979, attended by representatives from FAP, FAN, and the MPLT, resulted in the first GUNT with Mahatma Lol Showa as premier, southerner Negue Djogo as deputy premier, Gukuni as interior minister, and Habre as defense minister. This was, however, a short-lived Gukuni-Habre coalition. The Lagos conferences of May 27 (Lagos I) and August 14–19, 1979 (Lagos II), under the auspices of Cameroon, Nigeria, Niger, Libya, and Sudan, oversaw the signing of an agreement by eleven factions, creating the second GUNT. Gukuni eventually became its chairman and the de facto president of Chad. In the new cabinet, Habre assumed the position of minister of state for defense and Kamougue that of vice president.

Gukuni and Habre: The Battles for N'Djamena

In N'Djamena, the two Tubu leaders, Gukuni Wedei and Hissein Habre, unable to work together, clashed on the battlefield. The bloody feud between them resulted not only in high numbers of casualties and physical destruction but also provided a fertile ground for foreign intervention, particularly Libyan. Their long-standing rivalry came to the fore and led to another civil war in February through April 1980. This war continued intermittently until December 1980.

This protracted showdown between the two adversaries forced Habre to flee N'Djamena for the second time on December 15, 1980, and to reorganize his guerrillas, making Abeche his informal headquarters. Libyan forces had intervened on behalf of Gukuni to defeat the FAN. However, under pressure from the Organization of African Unity (OAU), Libya suddenly withdrew its forces from N'Djamena in November 1981, and some 3,800 inter-African troops arrived in the capital, supposedly to prevent fighting among the factions and to enforce the Lagos Accords.

Meanwhile, Habre's resolve had been strengthened by his popular appeal, by a reported $10 million assistance package from the United States through the CIA, and by considerable financial and military backing from France. He also benefited from the tribute he exacted from merchants and smugglers in the areas he controlled. Consequently, following some pitched battles outside the capital in June 1982, the former *sousprefet* was back, victorious, in N'Djamena. In August and September 1982, Habre's troops took Sarh and Moundou, both having been the sites of the murder of ten thousand Muslims (although this high number has been disputed by some), mostly by Sara commandos, in March 1979 in revenge for the massacre of Sara in N'Djamena and in the North. Gukuni regrouped his faction after fleeing the capital city through Cameroon and vowed to regain power even if it meant selling his political soul temporarily to Libya's Colonel Muammar Kadhafi. Indeed, between June and July 1983, backed by massive military and financial support from Libya, Gukuni occupied many of the northern cities, including Faya-Largeau, Habre's hometown, and Abeche, which he made the seat of his government.

Habre was never liked by the South, which saw him as an uncompromising Muslim; the North complained that it had received nothing from him while he was premier.[18] Thus the second conventional civil war commenced on March 22, 1980, when the FAP (actually under the overall command of Libyan officer Mansur abd al-Aziz); the FAT; the Front d'Action Commune Provisoire (FACP), a coalition of factions that had requested Libyan intervention; and the FAN (assisted by Egypt and Sudan in the form of military supplies) engaged in hostilities in N'Djamena, a protracted bloody affair that did not end until December 1980 and reportedly caused some five thousand deaths.

Libya's involvement soon changed the military equation, as on April 1, 1980, units of the Comité Démocratique de Révolution entered N'Djamena in Libyan uniforms. In the North, Kadhafi's troops continued to fortify their bases, issued Libyan identification cards to the population, and introduced Libyan currency. Having won the civil war, Gukuni removed Habre from his post as minister of state for defense and fired Finance Minister Mahmat Salah (one of his supporters) and former FACP minister Hadjero Sanussi on April 25, 1980. Under pressure from Libya, Gukuni also ordered French forces out of the country. Their departure, on May 4, 1980, left behind an unstable situation.[19]

Overall, the confrontation between Habre and Gukuni was deadly because both enjoyed the support and loyalty of thousands of northern Chadians. Habre's forces had always been more disciplined, however, with their elite component drawn from the Tubu of Borkou; Gukuni's Tubu guerrillas came from Tibesti, part of Ennedi, and from Salal, and they never showed the same stamina and discipline as the FAN. Under these circumstances, the situation in Chad, particularly in N'Djamena, had changed radically. Whereas the first major (conventional) civil war, February-March 1979, was a bloody engagement between North and South, of Muslim versus Christian and traditionalist, the second civil war, February-December 1980, was a confrontation between North and North and between Muslim and Muslim.[20]

Unfortunately, from the start the OAU forces sent to N'Djamena in 1981 were poorly financed and poorly trained. France and the United States promised to provide financial assistance (the latter having contributed some $12 million), but the amount provided was not enough to boost the morale or efficiency of the disorganized and untrained OAU troops. Chaos and Gukuni's indecisiveness allowed Habre to assemble an impressive force of four thousand Goranes (Arab designation of Habre's clan), who began their westward march and triumphantly entered N'Djamena on June 7, 1982, facing no opposition.

Once in control of the capital, Habre's forces marched south, and following massive resistance and carnage, they captured Sarh in August and Moundou in September 1982. This marked the earnest beginning of the rule of the North over the South, briefly started by Gukuni two years earlier; it was a reversal of the neo-colonial situation that had prevailed in the North during the 1960s. This time, the northerners came no longer as enslavers but as rulers. Habre formed a provisional council of state, promulgated a constitution on September 29, and in 1984 created a new party, the National Union for Independence and Revolution (UNIR).

To the surprise of Gukuni and his followers, many former rebels were received cordially by Habre and given prominent ministerial positions in 1985–1986. For example, Mohammat Senussi Khatir of the Comité d'Action et de Concertion (CAC) in the GUNT broke off from Acheik Ibn Oumar's Conseil Démocratique de Révolution (CDR) and was the first to sign an agreement with Chadian foreign minister Gouara Lassou in Libreville on November 11, 1985. Djibril Negue Djogo, a southern leader of the Front Démocratique Tchadien (FDT) and former GUNT chief of staff, had signed a similar agreement on December 23, 1985, and became minister of justice in Habre's cabinet.[21] Likewise, in June 1986, Abdelkerim Kamougue, the GUNT vice president, abandoned the GUNT and was looking for a way to join Habre. Colonel Alphonse Kotiga, leader of the so-called *codos rouges* (a commando group), joined Habre in February 1986, as did the GUNT representative in Brazzaville, Salmon Yatoingar, following Gukuni's refusal to meet Habre in March 1986.[22] In addition, some 3,745 *codos* of the Forces Mobiles d'Intervention (FMI) and 10,224 members of the Bureau Intérimaire de Coordination (BIC) also reportedly rallied to Habre in 1986.

The greatest setback to the GUNT, however, was the defection of Acheik Ibn Oumar, leader of the CDR, "spiritual heir to the late Ahmat Acyl," one of the original founders of FROLINAT. Oumar announced that he was leaving or suspending collaboration with the GUNT because of Gukuni's use of torture, arrest, and assassination to eliminate his opponents.[23] Gukuni also lost his number-two man, Mahamat Idris, as well as Hissein Grinki, both of whom were former leaders of the FDT. Grinki became minister of culture, youth, and sports. Ngarnayat Mbailemdana, another prominent FDT member, accepted the office of minister of finance and data processing. Gukuni's political career seemed to have ended in mid-1985. Yet the civil war would continue with Libya's heaviest involvement.

As noted earlier, Gukuni's military successes threatened N'Djamena, but he was halted temporarily by Habre's troops and by French troops who returned once again, in July 1983, to carry out Operation Manta in support of the government in power. Once the French had declared south of parallel 16 off limits to the rebels and their Libyan backers, a stalemate ensued, forcing Kadhafi and French president François Mitterrand to meet on September 7, 1984; Libya and France agreed to withdraw their troops from Chad simultaneously. By mid-November, the French had withdrawn their forces, but Colonel Kadhafi had not removed a single soldier from the North.

Gukuni and Kadhafi neither would tolerate Habre's seeming successes in the country nor were willing to abide by a unilaterally declared French *cordon sanitaire.* Thus in early February 1986, Libyan tanks and troops crossed parallel 16, or the Red Line, and occupied several northern towns in an apparent advance toward N'Djamena; a series of battles between government and rebel forces ensued.

Habre, the Desert Fox

The February 1986 southern advance of the GUNT–Islamic Legion was a military attempt to pressure Habre and to probe his capability to prevent access to N'Djamena. To the surprise of everyone, Habre's forces completely and overwhelmingly defeated the attacking forces. The easy answer to why Habre was so successful is the presence of the French military. But closer examination shows that this answer is too simplistic. For one thing, the French troops did not take the initiative; nor were they in the front line. They had not promised him complete air cover for his forces, and they discouraged him from crossing the Red Line.

For a more complex answer to why Habre was so successful, we must look not only to the low morale and inadequate training of Gukuni's men and their Libyan allies but to Habre himself and the growing military proficiency of his commanders and troops as they combined modern warfare tactics with centuries-old traditions. As noted by experts, one contributing factor to previous successes in battle by both Gukuni (1979) and Habre (1982 and 1983) was their active participation as commanders in the front lines. A commander's fighting on the front line is a very old tradition of the Tubu, whom Buijtenhuijs labels as "naturally born guerrillas."

Now, in a dramatic early 1986 extension of the 1980 civil war between Gukuni and Habre, things were different. Libya backed Gukuni 100 percent, supplying both troops and the most modern and sophisticated war materiel. As noted, Habre had the collaboration of a reluctant French military, but his Chadian forces were led by the brilliant and resourceful late Commander in Chief Hassan Djamous, assisted by Idris Deby. Habre's confident FANT troops, composed of experienced Goranes, *codos,* and Hadjerai, were determined to succeed because they smelled "Libyan blood."

Libyan contingents in Chad were equipped with some of the most modern and sophisticated weapons equipment, as became clear from the war materiel captured by the FANT in early 1987, particularly at Ouadi-Doum. But by 1987, Chadian troops—many of whom had received excellent training at Belgian-staffed military schools in Zaire—had grown in stature and self-confidence. At the same time, Libyan troops and Islamic Legionnaries, even though well equipped, suffered from a variety of adverse factors that contributed to low morale, including "officer corps surveillance" by revolutionary committees that "controlled the weapon arsenals"; lack of or delay in payment of monthly salaries to the troops in northern Chad; a high number of casualties among Libyans involved in the Chadian conflict; and frequent rumors of imminent coups in Tripoli, fueled by the defection of army officers to Egypt. Additionally, Libya suffered humiliation in April 1986 when the United States bombed Tripoli and Benghazi.

Interestingly, after the bombing of Libya by the United States, N'Djamena could not contain its joy. Chadian foreign minister Gouara Lassou commented that "Chad approves of the historical lesson inflicted on Gaddaffi by the United States."[24] At the same time, Chad's president and Radio N'Djamena were fueling the anti-Kadhafi and anti-Libyan feeling among the Chadians through broadcasts that referred to the colonel and the Libyans with such epithets as "the devil," the "wolf-Kadhafi, the Libyan slave traders, who must be ejected from the motherland's soil."

But Habre's determination, his military prowess—proven since the days of his return from the Sudanese border in 1982—and the high morale of his soldiers receive the most credit for his success against the larger and better-equipped Libyan forces. Indeed, Habre's military accomplishments have been called the result of "the most successful collaboration between a Western army and a Third World army in modern times."[25] But it also took great skill to combine and coordinate all the factional elements of that army and to maintain command and control in both the rugged mountains of Tibesti and the expansive desert plains of eastern Chad. Most Western observers agreed at the time that because of their desert fighting experience, "Habre's FANT [were] well-equipped for the semiguerrilla warfare in which they excel," and "their successes . . . [were] assisted by poor Libyan tactics, for Libyan units favored conventional Soviet-style operations in which infantry are backed up by armor, making them vulnerable to the FANT's hit-and-run tactics."[26]

The 1986–1987 northern campaigns began with the February 1986 GUNT–Islamic Legion's southern advance across the 16th parallel. By the end of 1986, the FANT began a very active guerrilla campaign against the Libyans in the Tibesti region; by early 1987 the war escalated to a more conventional encounter against Libyan forces on the eastern axis in Ennedi and Borkou. Military analysts are most interested in the rather distinctive Chadian style of operations in this campaign. The FANT had consistently decentralized battlefield decisionmaking authority down to the local operative level "within the framework of generally understood goals," as William Foltz puts it, harnessing traditional fighting methods to its overall plan. On the battlefield, Chadian behavior was described by French army captain Mun-Koefod as a "twirling combat," an adaptation of age-old desert tactics.[27] Qualified observers, such as Lieutenant General Bernard Trainor (USMC ret.), correspondent for the *New York Times*, termed Chadian tactics as "those of their desert forebears, with crew-served weapons and agile trucks replacing spears and camels."

On January 1, 1987, Habre's forces effectively used a high-speed attack to take Fada. They quickly overwhelmed the defenders, penetrating their positions and inflicting severe casualties. Libyan attempts to counterattack were frustrated by the slowness of their heavy armor, which could not cope with FANT's rapidly moving light armored cars and Toyota trucks mounting antitank weapons. Nor could the Libyans make effective use of their heavy artillery because of the close-in intermixed fighting. The ultimate price to the Libyans for this adventure in desert warfare at Fada was high: seven hundred killed in action (KIA), eighty prisoners of war (POWs), and a hundred destroyed armored vehicles out of a garrison of about a thousand. Chadian losses reportedly consisted of only twenty KIA.

When Libyan commanders at Ouadi-Doum organized a task force to recapture Fada, their men did not prove any better at coping with the Chadians in the open spaces than they had from their dug-in positions at Fada. Surprised, Kadhafi's forces bombed Arada, 120 km south of the 16th parallel. On March 19–20, government forces defeated two Libyan contingents near Bir-Kora (Yerbi-Kora), 50 km south of Ouadi-Doum, and captured Zouar in the Tibesti the following day. Two Libyan armored battalions were destroyed in these engagements. After detecting the approaching Libyan forces, the FANT set up antitank ambushes in the sand hills surrounding the desert tracks. Milan missile and rocket-launcher firing positions were deployed on the tops of these hills, and light armored cars were placed at key junctures. Once the trap was sprung, armed Toyotas joined the melee. Once again, the Libyan tanks were outmaneuvered in the sand by what Lieutenant General Trainor has labeled "the Toyota charge." About half of the sixteen hundred–man Libyan force was killed in action, allowing Habre's forces to advance toward a major prize: the capture of Ouadi-Doum on March 22. During this confrontation, a thousand Libyans reportedly died and hundreds of prisoners were captured, including the local commander, Colonel Khalifah Abdul Affar. Five days later, Faya-Largeau, Habre's hometown, which the Libyans had held since August 1983, was liberated as Kadhafi's troops pulled back to the Aouzou Strip, a move necessitated by the fall of Oaudi-Doum. The defeat of the Libyan contingent was all the more surprising because, as was clear from the war materiel captured by the FANT, Libya was equipped with the most modern and sophisticated weapons. Left behind were SU-WW bombers, L-39 light attack aircraft (Czech), Marchetti SF 260 light ground support planes (Italian), MI-25 helicopter gunships, ZS4-23-4 self-propelled antiaircraft guns, hundreds of armed combat vehicles, radar systems, T-62 and T-55 tanks, BMP armored personnel carriers, BM-21 multiple rocket launchers, and "various other types of military equipment."[28]

The victories at Fada and Ouadi-Doum dealt a severe blow to the Libyans, who lost $1 billion worth of military equipment, vehicles, aircraft, and ammunition left behind as they retreated swiftly. As Captain Mun-Koefod recounted, firing distances for FANT weapons were very short: Milan antitank missiles, 400 meters; Panhard armored cars with a 90-mm gun, 200 to 300 meters; and light antitank rocket launchers (French LRAC and U.S. M72A2 LAAW), 50 to 100 meters, and some Soviet-made RPG-7s, 20 meters, "often wounding or killing the gunner." In this close, chaotic combat, targets were in a sense engaged rapidly and instinctively.[29] Habre's potential loot was such that Colonel Kadhafi ordered his pilots to bomb the area and destroy the abandoned war materiel, some of which had already been transported to N'Djamena. The fall of the towns of Bardai (which Libyan backers lost to FANT troops and their allies in December 1986), Zouar, Ouadi-Doum, Faya-Largeau, and Fada meant a collapse of the Libyan forces in northern Chad, prompting the colonel to announce on May 11, 1987, that he had withdrawn his forces from Chad.

Thus a number of factors contributed to Habre's success in the 1986–1987 northern campaign. Chad used a combination of modern conventional warfare (in Ennedi and Gorkou, where the desert distances are long, interspersed with sand hills and small mountains) and guerrilla tactics (in the Tibesti mountains, where vehicles and heavy armor can barely move) against the rebels and their Libyan supporters, most of whom were unfamiliar with Chad. Other factors favored Habre's forces; for example, it was clear that among the Mauritanians captured in August 1987, most members of the Islamic Legion had no enthusiasm for the war because they never quite understood why they were fighting in Chad. The same might also be said of the regular Libyan troops deployed to Chad, many of whom were conscripted students and military reservists. To counter the enemy's ground forces, Libya resorted to air attacks and bombed such towns as Arada, Kouba Olanga, and Oum-Chalouba. But since they flew at high altitudes to avoid ground fire, their bombings were never effective. Pilots feared being shot down by Chadians, who were then equipped with Red-Eye and other antiaircraft missiles.[30] Trainor wrote that because of a lack of firm leadership, Libyan "officers and troops alike feared the Chadian warriors to the point of paralysis."

Internationally and domestically, things were now looking up. Although Chad's economy was still precarious, it began to improve considerably during Habre's rule. For instance, by sheer coincidence, following a four-year drought, the rains were abundant in October 1985, contributing to an impressive harvest of millet, sorghum, and cotton. In addition, problems associated with food transportation and distribution were reduced thanks to the completion of a new road and bridge in 1985, the first ever bridge over the Logone River, linking N'Djamena with Kousseri in northern Cameroon.[31] Schools doubled their enrollment, thousands of refugees returned home, and the international community began to pay more attention to Chad.[32] Unfortunately, one-third of the country's budget still had to be spent on the war effort. Thus of the total budget of $68 million for 1986, 34 percent went to defense and 18 percent went to servicing the 1986 national debt.[33] Military spending supported an army of 28,000 men (excluding the Presidential Guard) organized into four battalions in 1987, with a salary of some $70 a month per soldier.[34]

From a political point of view, the powers of the president increased in the new republic. Habre's Union Nationale pour l'Indépendance et la Révolution (UNIR), founded in 1984 to bring together all warring factions that left the GUNT, had a central committee made up of eighty members and a powerful fifteen-member political bureau chaired by the president himself. The president also created a five-member military council (cabinet) that represented the country's major ethnic groups. He divided the country into twelve military zones and subzones, leaving the North as a separate military region. As proof of his conciliatory effort, in 1984 ten of the twenty ministerial positions were occupied by southerners, including the pivotal Ministry of Foreign Affairs. Many of the new members had served in the cabinets of Tombalbaye, Malloum, and the GUNT. Of the ten secretaries of state, five were southerners.[35]

Exuding confidence wherever he traveled, Habre was willing to talk to his northern adversaries, but on his own terms. For example, he integrated the army but only at his own pace and judgment; he saw the need for legal protection of refugees and citizens but did not favor the creation of special courts, as many would have liked him to do. He was willing to sign conciliatory accords with his opponents through OAU mediation but opposed moves to have international bodies (such as members of Union Douanière et Économique d'Afrique Centrale [UDEAC]) oversee their implementation. He favored a new constitution and the holding of national elections but opposed "the idea of a transitional period during which his government would have no authority." Finally, although promising to release all political prisoners, Habre opposed the establishment of an outside organization to oversee the process.[36]

Undoubtedly, Habre demonstrated his ability to draw people to his side, to organize, and to win battles. Contrary to all other FROLINAT factions, FAN was able to recruit technocrats and urbanites to its ranks, which gave Habre an advantage over other guerrilla leaders, who depended mainly on young rural recruits. Unfortunately, the president's leadership style continued to be basically military; orders were interspersed with authoritarianism and repressive tendencies. In contrast to Gukuni, however, Habre was always a leader who commanded respect. Those who know him contrast him with his Tubu cousin: "His troops, among whom the younger are no older than fourteen years of age, and whom they call 'patron' or 'boss,' remain silent when he talks, including his lieutenants Mahamat Saleh, Mahamat Nourry, Idris Miskine, and Michel Froud"; regarding Gukuni, "almost no one stands up when he enters the room. When the *derdei's* son, a short, indecisive man of thirty-four years of age, extremely honest, courageous but capable of violent outbursts, makes a speech, no one listens."[37]

Furthermore, Habre maintained Chad as a secular state, a well-thought-out posture; he even went so far as to arrest a few fundamentalist Muslims who wished to see Chad declared an Islamic republic with Arabic as the only official language.[38] As for Gukuni, who until the early 1990s was in Algiers and not in Tripoli, his future did not look bright. Chadians still viewed him as an indecisive leader prone to compromising the integrity of the nation and its security, as he had demonstrated from 1979 through 1982. With most of his GUNT allies deserting him, many observers expected the *derdei's* son to seek the solitude of the desert. But in Chad, things are never predictable.[39]

Overall, Habre's major contributions to Chad were the restoration of the state and the integrity of the national territory compromised by Gukuni, with the exception of the Aouzou Strip; the reestablishment of at least a modicum of law and order; an end to Chad's isolation from the community of states; and the creation, at least for more than five years, of a national army that was better trained and disciplined than ever before.

Habre's Fall and the Rise of Idris Deby

What went wrong? Habre's attempt to appease most of his former enemies was perhaps one of his greatest mistakes. It is also known that the Hadjerai, some of whom had fled to Sudan or hid in the Guera Prefecture mountains under the banner of the Mouvement pour le Salut National du Tchad (MSNT) continued to wage guerrilla warfare and to protest tax policies. The greatest challenge, however, continued to be the CDR of Acheik Ibn Oumar, as well as some former members of Gukuni's GUNT, who despite promises never reconciled with Habre.[40] The eventual revelation of Habre's human rights violations, including torture of opponents, also contributed to his downfall in 1990.[41]

More important, Kadhafi continued to support rebel factions, including one created by Habre's former commander, Idris Deby, the darling of the French army who ironically had led the defeat of Libya's forces in 1987. Pressured by the West and by the South, the new president had been perhaps too hesitant in moving the country toward adopting democratic reforms through the committee he had created in July 1988. Habre also surrounded himself with many who disliked him and his leadership style, and he authorized the torture and murder of several of his opponents in Chadian prisons. Further, Samuel Decalo believes that "his unwillingness to relax N'Djamena's heavy-handed rule over the South, and to move towards national reconciliation, sealed his fate,"[42] but this is a debatable point. There is no doubt that under Habre the reconciliation process with the South had gotten underway, albeit at a slow pace.

It turned out that Habre's greatest enemy was his former friend Idris Deby, with whom he had entered N'Djamena in 1982. What is clear is that the president's former ally, fearing that Habre would arrest him for allegedly planning to overthrow the regime, fled the capital in 1989 and gathered a rebel force in the East. At the end of 1990, Deby's force entered N'Djamena unopposed and forced Habre to flee to Cameroon and then to Senegal. While the national army deserted the president in droves, the French troops (which could have easily stopped Deby) paradoxically claimed neutrality.

Another northerner had usurped power in N'Djamena. To please France, Deby promised to move rapidly toward civilian rule and multiparty democracy, although the National Sovereign Conference did not take place until January-April 1993. Within six months, twenty-six political parties were allowed to function alongside the president's party, the Mouvement Patriotique du Salut (MPS). Yet given the political fragmentation, attempted coups were rumored days after the new president had taken office, and several rebel elements (not well organized, however) continued to disturb the peace.

It is difficult to predict how long Deby, the man to whom Caesar's *veni, vidi, vici* dictum seems to have applied in N'Djamena in 1990, will remain in power. On the one hand, the international front seems to be quiet, particularly with the favorable resolution of the Aouzou Strip in 1994 and the 1996 presidential elections, with Deby as winner. The South, on the other hand, could still present problems for Deby. It was learned on April 5, 1993, for example, that his Republican Guard massacred 104 civilians in the South, an action the government had denied.[43] The incident heightened suspicions of Deby in the South. In 1994, however, Deby allowed the exhumation of Tombalbaye's remains, which had been buried secretly in the northern sands, so that they could be reburied in his native South.

As a good omen, the new leader has not shown signs of caving in to the mercurial Libyan leader despite the fact that he freed two thousand Libyan prisoners detained in Chad and criticized Habre's harboring of some six hundred U.S.-trained Libyan contras in the country. One problem that Deby finally and wisely solved in his dealings with the West was the convening of the National Sovereign Conference on January 15–April 7, 1993. To his advantage, the opposition was fragmented with some seventy parties vying to replace his MPS. Surprisingly, the National Sovereign Conference chose Sara Fidel Moungar (M.D.) as prime minister of an interim government. But still, the North controlled the Ministry of Foreign Affairs (given to Mahmat Ali Adoum, former ambassador to the United States and Brussels), the Ministry of Defense (given to Loum Hinassou Laina, former chief of staff of the army and cabinet director under Deby), and the Ministry of Planning and Cooperation (given to Mahamat Saleh Ibn Oumar, Habre's former minister). Sadly, Moungar pleased no one even after he had reduced his cabinet from thirty to seventeen members. He was replaced by Delwa Kassire Koumakoye on October 28, 1993. On April 8, 1995, Koibla became premier.

We may note before closing this chapter that in the process of rebuilding the war-torn country, Deby, unlike his predecessors, must seek the involvement of women as a priority through the strengthening of the Ministry of Social Affairs as well as through well-articulated policies to ensure their participation in every aspect of national life. Chad's record in this respect is extremely dismal. It is known, for example, that FROLINAT has no history of recruiting women to serve in the ranks of the army. The record also shows that in 1978 there were perhaps only ten women in FAN, and between 1980 and 1982 there were only fifty women in FAP. Three of them died in combat and one, commonly known as Madame Bazooka, became famous for her military prowess.[44] The same trend prevailed in both Gukuni's and Habre's regimes. In this respect, Tombalbaye's PPT and the MNRCS had a better record, as they tried seriously to recruit and involve women in every activity of the party and the nation.

Conclusion

Chad's political history from 1960 to the 1997 can be divided into two periods: one spanning from 1960 to 1979, in which the control of the country fell into the hands of southern politicians, mainly Sara; the other beginning with the ascent to power by Gukuni and the GUNT in 1979 and the subsequent control of the state by other northern politicians, Habre and Deby, who reversed the country's ethnic leadership.

Indeed, the pre-1979 Chadian regimes, although autocratic—particularly that of Tombalbaye—maintained law and order and enjoyed as much international respect as the majority of the African states of their time. In contrast, the post-1979 era has seen the disintegration of the state; the temporary loss of national territory to political factions and to Libya; the utter collapse of independence in foreign policy, particularly during the Gukuni regime; and perennial infighting among the northern leaders with religious brotherhood playing absolutely no part when personal ambitions were at stake. Although Foltz characterizes the post-1965 period as one of "uninterrupted political disorder,"[45] it would appear to someone who may have visited N'Djamena in 1974 that the characterization fits more appropriately the regimes initiated by the northern nationalists in 1979.

Looking back, we can see that conditions following the 1975 coup provide ample evidence that no one has been able to govern Chad better than Tombalbaye did and that more human rights violations have occurred during the control of the country by the northern leaders than during Tombalbaye's presidency. Indeed, no scholar has dared to rank this slain president among the most brutal autocrats in Africa—Nguema, Amin, and Bokassa, for example. Some have argued, on the contrary, that Habre's security "apparatus" tortured and killed as many as forty thousand Chadians.[46]

Should the country succeed in remaining peaceful, beyond the problem of economic reconstruction, the process toward democratization will continue to occupy center stage. The growth and strength of civil society (there are now some three hundred civil societies) and the fearlessness of the press seem to presage a boldness never before known in Chad. Yet Deby's lukewarm embrace of democratic reforms casts doubt on the future of democratic institutions in the country. As William Miles has observed, "While he [Deby] freely worked the form and rhetoric of democratization, the willingness of the MPS to surrender power was far from certain."[47] Thus as the American adage goes, the jury is still out on Chad and Deby.

Notes

1. Jacques Le Cornet, *Histoire politique du Tchad dès 1960 à 1962* (Paris: Librairie Générale de Droit et de Jurisprudence, 1963), 308.

2. Jean Chapelle, *Le peuple tchadien* (Paris: Harmattan, 1980), 240.

3. See Thompson and Adloff, *Conflict in Chad* (Berkeley: Institute of International Studies, 1981), 13, on the way foreigners were viewed politically in Chad.

4. Ibid., 11.

5. Robert Buijtenhuijs, *Le FROLINAT et les révoltes populaires du Tchad* (Paris: Mouton, 1978), 6.

6. Dennis Cordell, "The Society and Its Environment," in Thomas Collelo, ed., *Chad: A Country Study* (Washington, D.C.: U.S. Government Printing Office, 1990), 53.

7. Michel N'Gangbet, *Peut-on encore sauver le Tchad?* (Paris: Karthala, 1984), 20.

8. Ibid., 21.

9. Lanne, "Les deux guerres civiles," in *Tchad: Anthologie de la guerre civile* (N'Djamena: Yamoko Koulro-Bezo, 1981), 57.

10. Michael Kelley, *A State in Disarray: Conditions of Chad's Survival* (Boulder, Colo.: Westview Press, 1986), 11.

11. Chapelle, *Le peuple tchadien,* 262.

12. N'Gangbet, *Peut-on sauver le Tchad?* 22.

13. Buijtenhuijs, *Le FROLINAT,* 48.

14. Ibid., 115.

15. "Vers une épreuve de force," *Le Monde,* 26 January 1979, in *Tchad: Anthologie,* 7.

16. A conference of February 23–27, 1979, at Sebha, Libya, had arranged a cease-fire that did not hold. See *Africa Research Bulletin* 15 (January 1987): 8372.

17. Lanne, "Les deux guerres civiles," 59.

18. Philipe Decraene, "Le Tchad sous les armes," in *Tchad: Anthologie,* 3–5.

19. René Lemarchand, "The Road to Partition," *Current History* (March 1984): 115.

20. Lanne, "Les deux guerres civiles," 53–56.

21. George Henderson, "Redefining the Revolution," *Africa Report* (November–December 1984): 40.

22. Henderson, "Retrenchment in Tripoli," *Africa Report* (July-August 1986): 73.

23. Ibid., 74.

24. *Africa Confidential* 28, no. 8 (April 15, 1987): 4.

25. David Ottaway, "The U.S. May Send Chad Some Stingers,"*Washington Post,* September 17, 1987, A36.

26. *Africa Confidential* 28, no. 8 (April 15, 1987): 2.

27. *Africa Confidential,* 28, no. 2 (February 18, 1987): 1.

28. *Africa Research Bulletin* (April 1–2, 1986): 8433

29. William Foltz, "Chad's Third Republic," *CSIS Africa Notes,* 1–8. Foltz, Captain Mun-Koefod, and Lieutenant General Bernard Trainor are the most important sources for our analysis of Habre's victory in the North in 1986–1987. William Tom, U.S. Army, assisted the authors in editing the language in the section on Habre's military strategy.

30. Captain Mun-Koefod, "Routing the Libyans," *Marine Corps Gazette* (August 1987): 26–27.

31. *Africa Research Bulletin* (May 15, 1986): 8084.

32. *Africa News* (April 1, 1986): 7.

33. Franziska James, "On the Battlefield," *Africa Report* (July-August 1986): 83.

34. Jean R. Tartter, "National Security," in Collelo, ed., *Chad,* 183. On how Habre had secured some $25 million from the Islamic Conference Organization, see also Pearl Robinson, "Niger and Chad's Ambivalent Relations with Libya," in *African Security Issues: Sovereignty, Stability, and Solidarity,* ed. Bruce E. Arlinghaus (Boulder, Colo.: Westview Press, 1984), 171–184.

35. René Lemarchand, "Putting Things Together Again," *Africa Report* (November–December 1984): 61.

36. Paul Michaud, "Time Running Out," *New African* (May 1986): 30.

37. Koume Tale, "48 heures dans l'enfer tchadien," in *Tchad: Anthologie de la guerre civile*, 65.

38. *Africa Confidential* 27, no. 15 (16 July).

39. See *Jeune Afrique,* 1176 (20 July 1983) on Gukuni's contempt for Habre.

40. Rita Byrnes, "Politics and Government," in *Collelo,* ed., *Chad,* 153.

41. See *Africa Research Bulletin* (February 1–28, 1993): 10897.

42. Samuel Decalo, "The Process, Prospects, and Constraints of Democratization in Africa," *African Affairs* 91, no. 362 (January 1992): 20.

43. *Africa Research Bulletin* (April 1–30, 1993): 10974.

44. Buijtenhuijs, *Le FROLINAT,* 426.

45. William J. Foltz, "From Habre to Deby: The Search for Political Order" (unpublished paper presented at Boston University, October 6–7, 1994), 2.

46. William F. S. Miles, "Decolonization as Disintegration: The Disestablishment of the State in Chad" (unpublished paper presented at Boston University, October 6–7, 1994), 11.

47. Miles, "Decolonization as Disintegration," 13–14.

4

THE ECONOMY

By UN ranking in 1992, Chad is one of the poorest and least developed countries in the world, and it has a very uncertain political, economic, and social future. Although the country is vast—the fifth largest in Africa—a large proportion of its territory is desert and therefore agriculturally useless. Economic activity in Chad started as far back as the Neolithic era, when a more settled life led to the development of agriculture, livestock production, and technical specialization such as the manufacture of stone tools and the production of pottery.[1] The more sedentary agricultural life also led to a division of labor along sex lines—men hunted and fought wars; women processed grains and collected food. The introduction of the camel and the horse engendered greater and greater economic progress. This economic progress continued in Chad through the nineteenth century, when it was interrupted by European invasion and French occupation, as described in Chapter 2.

The French colonial administration introduced military-style administrative systems, a quasimilitary judiciary system, concessionaires, the cotton industry, and an economy based on taxation. Using a forced-labor system and selective development, the colonial administration exploited the southerners and created a North-South dichotomy in the colony. Presently, an estimated 80 percent of Chadians are involved in agriculture or livestock production in a smallholder, rain-fed production system in which agricultural output depends mostly on weather conditions. Although the political arena seems to hold some promise, especially after Idris Deby intensified IMF-style economic reforms in 1990, Chad's economic outlook remains gloomy. The government has consistently run deficits and maintained a negative trade balance since 1986. Seventy percent of public expenditures are externally financed, including 100 percent of the investment budget.

Despite improvements made in the postcolonial period, all socioeconomic trends are discouraging: low human resource development, stagnant per capita incomes, low levels of per capita private consumption, absence of investment, and low growth. In addition, the contribution of the productive sectors to the growth of the domestic product is deplorably low, and birth rates are high. The problems of war, famine, and drought as well as Chad's enclave location have hampered any growth possibilities. The Chadian economy depends almost entirely on cotton exports for foreign exchange. The unpredictable and uncontrollable forces of the international cotton market have resulted in sporadic and uncertain foreign exchange revenues, hindering economic development.

Resources, Infrastructure, and Industrialization

Natural Resources and Agriculture

With a land area of 125,920,000 hectares (311,022,400 acres) Chad's population density per 1,000 hectares in 1990 was forty-five; the country shares with Gabon the position of having the fifth lowest density in Africa. (Other densities per 1,000 hectares are Mauritania, 20; Namibia, 22; Botswana, 23; and Libya, 23.) Chad's low population density can be deceptive, since a substantial proportion of Chad is of no agricultural value and has a low level of capital investment and improvement. Of Chad's total land area, 67 percent is arid, 7 percent is semiarid, and only 27 percent is humid. Land with no inherent soil constraint covers 34,160,000 hectares (84,375,200 acres), of which 81 percent is arid, 1 percent semiarid, and 17 percent humid.[2] About 84 percent of the total land area is tropical, and 16 percent is subtropical (see Chapter 1).

Like many other regions located in west Sahelian Africa, massive deforestation (mainly for domestic fuel use) has reduced significantly Chad's forest resources. Average annual deforestation between 1981 and 1985 was about 80,000 hectares (197,600 acres), or 0.6 percent of the total forests. No efforts are being made to establish a reforestation program. Other ecological problems also contribute to serious soil degradation of a significant portion of land mass: Some areas suffer serious chemical deterioration of the soil as a result of nutrient loss from low-input agriculture; areas of the Sahelian zone have been overgrazed and trampled by cattle; wind erosion, especially in the Sahelian regions, contributes to soil degradation.

Chad produces minerals but to a limited extent. In 1987, mining was a mere 0.5 percent of GDP. Clay, natron, tungsten, bauxite, uranium, and gold are quarried and mined. Some petroleum prospecting has been undertaken, but only at a limited level because of the high cost of transportation and importation of capital goods. Higher oil prices during the 1970s encouraged Conoco and Shell oil companies to extract petroleum in the Sedeigi region and in 1977, north of Lake Chad. A small refinery being built near N'Djamena processes the small amounts extracted (15,000 barrels per day), which help to meet domestic demand.

Agriculture is the primary employer, the largest contributor to the GDP, and the largest foreign exchange earner in Chad. The main export crop is cotton, but groundnuts, millet, sorghum, rice, wheat, and gum arabic are also grown.

Agricultural products constitute up to 90 percent of all exports. During the period 1978 to 1980, the major agricultural exports were cotton-cake-seed ($42 million), live animals ($42 million), and meat ($2 million). The principal livestock include cattle, sheep, goats, camels, and donkeys. The primary food crops are millet, sorghum, tuber crops, groundnuts, beans, and an assortment of vegetables grown in a mixed cropping system. Wild resources exploited to supplement protein, carbohydrate, and cash needs are date palms, gum arabic, antelopes, ostriches, and other wildlife. Cattle are the main livestock exported across the border to Nigeria and Cameroon. Significant fishing is practiced in Lake Chad and the Chari and Logone Rivers.

In 1973, the average size of a farm was 2.6 hectares. Farm sizes nationwide were distributed as follows: one hectare or less, 19.7 percent; 1–5 hectares, 69.5 percent; 5–10 hectares, 10 percent; and greater than 10 hectares, 0.8 percent. Agricultural technology is low; the ratio of tractors to each 1,000 hectares is less than 1, and fertilizer is used sparingly. In 1991, the output of major agricultural products included sugarcane, 370,000 metric tons; manioc, 342,000; millet, 302,000; yams, 248,000; seed cotton, 170,000; peanuts, 115,000; and rice, 86,000. Chad also produces sweet potatoes, corn, dates, mangoes, potatoes, onions, and sesame seeds. Livestock production in 1991 included cattle, 4,400,000; chickens, 4,000,000; goats, 2,983,000; sheep, 1,983,000; and camels, 565,000.

In Chad, private pumps are used to irrigate small plots of vegetables and fruits. Most of the irrigated production systems are small-scale for high-value crops funded mostly by nongovernment organizations (NGOs) such as CARE and SECADEV. Some irrigation is practiced by relatively large commercial farms owned mainly by government officials, rich merchants, or veterans. Irrigation is very expensive; not only has the water table been dropping since the 1950s but river and lake levels have dropped in most parts of Chad since the early 1980s. Although most water is lifted directly from rivers and lakes, pumping from groundwater has become necessary in recent times. Cheap tubewells, introduced in the early 1990s by the NGOs and used in conjunction with pumps imported from Nigeria, have become popular in the Kanem area. Small-scale irrigation can succeed in Chad only if the technology is cheap, simple, and demands few resources and if the farmer has flexibility in decisionmaking and owns and manages his own farm.[3]

Human Resources and Industrialization

Chad's labor force is composed mainly of men, and unemployment and underemployment are rampant. In 1987, the economically active population included 1,859,000 people (a 35 percent labor force participation rate for the whole population). The total labor force in 1990 was 1,971,000, of which 21.1 percent (415,880) were women. This labor force consists of 83 percent agriculture, 12 percent service, and 5 percent industry.

Although the educational system beyond primary school is improving, the literacy rate is discouraging, as Chapter 5 indicates. The labor force is therefore characterized by low productivity, low wages, low skill levels, and lack of skill-improvement opportunities. The main determinants of population change also show the difficulties faced by the Chadians. As of December 31, 1984, Chad's civil services had about 22,722 officials unequally distributed among the regions. Of this number, 53.1 percent were government functionaries and 21.8 were laborers. Chari-Baguirmi had the largest number (35.1 percent), followed by Moyen-Chari (14.8 percent) and Mayo-Kebbi (10.8 percent.)

Women are grossly underrepresented in the higher cadres. In 1984, women represented only 7.6 percent of government officials in N'Djamena, that is, 605 out of a total of 7,989 government officials. There were 27 women out of 226 ministers and cabinet officials; there were no female directors general, directors, prefects, or assistant prefects. The majority of the women were ordinary public functionaries (382 out of a total of 4,440); they were also middle-to-low-level employees in health, education, and social services. Unequal access to educational opportunities ensured that there were only three female doctors out of 41. No women held doctoral degrees. Most health care providers were trainees, nurses, and midwives. Other women served as social assistants, primary school teachers, secretaries, and low-level assistants.[4]

The industrial base and level of industrialization have not changed much in postindependence Chad. Centered in N'Djamena and Moundou, industrial production occurs in state-owned enterprises (SOEs) and consists mainly of agricultural product processing and assembling consumer durables and nondurables such as radios and bicycles. Beer, sugar, cigarettes, and cotton products are also processed or manufactured. Chad's main industrial conglomerate is COTONTCHAD, the cotton-processing concern. Sugarcane is processed in Banda through the SONASUT (Société Nationale Sucrière du Tchad), and some textiles are manufactured; these industries became increasingly important in the 1980s. One of the major problems facing Chad as it enters the twenty-first century is its lack of capital investment, which has so far resulted in the low level of industrialization in the country. Associated with the low level of capital investment is an insufficient level of saving and deficient foreign investment.

Chad is one of the very few landlocked countries without railroad facilities; this makes transportation of goods to and from seaports problematic and expensive. There are only 25 km (16 miles) of transportation infrastructure per 1,000 square kilometers (386 square miles) of land area; only 1.6 kilometers (1 mile) of waterways are navigable. There has not been any significant infrastructural development since independence in 1960. In fact, the existing physical and social infrastructure suffered neglect and damage from the civil war. Only about 240 kilometers (149 miles) of paved road are in good condition, and about 3.44 km (2 miles) of improved dirt roads are seasonally accessible. In 1983, the total length of roads was 40,000 km (24,800 miles) with only one percent paved.

Banking facilities and the financial infrastructure are inadequate for business development in Chad. The three main banks in Chad (only two were functioning in 1993) are Banque de Développement du Tchad (BDT), Banque Internationale pour le Commerce et l'Industrie du Tchad (BICIT), and Banque Tchadienne de Crédit et de Dépots (BTCD). Since branch banking is only rudimentary, most parts of the country are not served at all in terms of savings mobilization and credit provision. There are three insurance agencies, a chamber of commerce, and a few development organizations. Chad is a member of the CFA (Communaute Financiere Africaine) financial system and therefore part of the Banque des États de l'Afrique Central (BEAC) as well as a member of the customs and economic union—Union Douanière et Économique d'Afrique Centrale (UDEAC).

Government resources are limited by a small tax base and inefficient collection of taxes and duties. In 1991–1992, government revenue was 34,800 million CFA francs ($300 million), and expenditure was 48,890 million CFA francs ($448 million). The major parts of total government revenue in 1990 were from goods and services taxes (33.2 percent), customs duties (28.8 percent), and income tax (28 percent). The principal government expenditures included defense spending (23.9 percent) and administration (65 percent).

Postindependence Economic Performance

The indigenous government that emerged at the end of the colonial period was very much aware of the low level of colonial economic development and the fact that Chad lagged behind other former colonies. Led by Ngarta (François) Tombalbaye, this government decided to use development planning to close the gap and to foster massive and comprehensive economic growth. Before the national development plan of 1966–1970, generally recognized as the first five-year development plan, there were two other plans. The first plan (1948–1953) was launched before independence in 1960, and 4,114 million CFA francs ($26 million) were earmarked for overall economic development expenditures.

The plan of 1966–1970 focused almost entirely on improvement of agriculture and livestock production in the hope that this would increase export-crop production, reduce the trade deficit, and create a base for sustainable economic growth. The government expected that mobilization of all natural resources of the country would improve agricultural productivity, increase crop diversification, raise livestock and fishery production, and increase sales of all products. This plan failed to achieve its objectives due to the shortage of financial resources necessary for its implementation. Essentially the independent government pursued and maintained the colonial practice of taxing export crop surpluses; its development policy was not significantly different from that of the colonial administration. Initially, rural production was allocated the lion's share of development resources (28.4 percent), followed by road infrastructure (26.7 percent). Industry was allotted 14.1 percent, education and training received 10.8 percent, and housing and urbanization received 8 percent.

When the plan was revised, of the thirteen items in the five-year plan, ten were drastically cut. Waterways suffered the greatest reduction (98.9 percent), followed by a 98.6 percent cut in allocations for railroads, 70.6 percent for radio and communications, 64 percent for airways, 56.1 percent for housing and urbanization, and 56 percent for postal services and telecommunications.

In the second ten-year plan (1971–1980) the focus shifted from human resource and infrastructural development to exportable products such as cotton, livestock, and sugar. Undoubtedly this shift in priority was made to reinforce foreign exchange earnings and to minimize dependence on foreign aid. In 1978, a year before the post-Malloum era began, the ten-year plan was replaced with a four-year plan (1978–1981) in which 226,800 million CFA francs ($1.9 billion) were allocated. This time, the plan concentrated on infrastructure, agricultural production, and petroleum exploration. The government could not implement the plan because nearly three-fourths of the allocations depended on foreign aid, which was not available in the magnitude expected.

Following the fall of Tombalbaye's government in 1975 (see Chapter 3), General Félix Malloum took over. However, despite attempts to institute political and economic reforms, international cooperation, and bilateral relations, the Malloum government failed because of incompetence in the military, internal civil strife, and external political and diplomatic misfortunes. The post-Malloum era began in 1979 after the breakup of the Malloum-Habre alliance and the subsequent accession to power by Habre and his allies. This period was characterized by an intensified dependence on foreign aid, increased budget deficits, increased military spending, and reduced infrastructural development. The period also witnessed deteriorated terms of trade, increased trade deficits, and a worsened balance of payments. Chad's economic growth and exports deteriorated as private investment plummeted. As a result of war and instability, Chad's economy suffered tremendous setbacks that caused stagnation in key sectors of the economy. In fact, most sectors of the economy and economic performance remained unchanged for more than twenty years.[5]

The Tombalbaye government (1960–1975) had a liberal approach to economic development, encouraging free enterprise and attempting to attract foreign investment by allowing profit repatriation. In contrast, under General Malloum (1975–1979), there was an increase in state interventionism and state shareholding in foreign-owned enterprises. Faced with internal strife and a political power struggle, the state lost control of the economy and was forced increasingly to depend on foreign aid. During the Gukuni Wedei era, internal strife and dependence on foreign aid continued, and the need for radical economic reforms and investment encouraged economic decentralization in favor of the North. Hissein Habre (1982–1990) attracted more aid and at the same time increased military spending in excess of economic reconstruction; his regime was faced with both internal and external threats, especially from Libya.

In 1990, after taking over power in a coup d'état, Idris Deby's administration introduced IMF reforms to stabilize and then restructure an economy in decline. Under pressure from the World Bank, IMF, and international aid donors, the government was forced to adopt measures designed to ensure fiscal discipline and drastically cut the size and growth of the civil service. Deby's administration also planned to cut the military by nearly 50 percent (from 47,000 to 25,000 men), suspend civil service recruitment, reduce indemnities paid to government officials, and reduce salaries by 10 to 20 percent (for salaries between 30,000 [$275] and 140,000 [$1,280] CFA francs). The IMF-style reform caused other problems. During the 1990s, unemployment among university graduates increased, many state-owned enterprises were bankrupt, and tariff revenues declined due to the absence of well-trained customs officials. Although civil strife and political instability mark Chadian history since independence, some Chadian observers had reason, at first, for optimism regarding Deby's activities. For instance, due to the difficult times faced by COTONTCHAD in 1984-1985, the state-owned enterprise was reformed and restructured. To cut production costs, mills were closed, cotton hectarages were reduced, and employees were laid off. During that period, the cotton sector experienced an initial boost that was soon tempered by the collapse of world cotton prices.

Did the actual adjustment policies accomplish the objectives of inflation-free balance of payments in Chad? Given Chad's deplorable economic situation in 1996, the answer is no. Chad has been historically a country of low inflation; one cannot therefore attribute the low level of inflation to structural adjustment. Furthermore, the balance of payments has not improved during the years following the introduction of adjustment. Chad has neither the institutional capacity nor the organizational coherence to implement meaningful reforms at present, and even if the institutional capacity existed, several other negative factors have hampered the successful implementation of the adjustment program. Among these factors are the lack of resources to implement the reform program, the exclusion of Chadians from the design process, the flawed sequencing introduced by the IMF and the World Bank, the simultaneous implementation of political and economic reforms, and the lack of consideration of colonial and postcolonial legacies in sequencing the adjustment process. Insofar as the reform process has led to misery and human deprivation in Chad, its negative impact cannot be ignored. Thus the reform program adopted in Chad has slowed down due to political instability, lack of administrative and institutional capacity, and IMF's introduction of a reform policy that had little consideration of the realities of Chad.

In addition to the inconsistent economic policies, other causes of serious impediment of growth in Chad are implicit and explicit producer taxation, lack of infrastructural development, lack of emphasis on human capital development, and dependence on cotton. Economic policies not only are inconsistent but have also been sporadic, thereby hampering growth prospects.

Pre- and Post-Malloum Macroeconomic Performance

Chad's overall postindependence economic performance is weak, but judging from Figure 4.1, the post-Malloum period experienced more fluctuation than the pre-Malloum period. This trend underscores the instability that marked the period between 1978 and 1984. Figure 4.1 also shows that the real GNP for 1980, the year after Hissein Habre took power from Félix Malloum, was the lowest in the twenty-year period from 1969 to 1989.

During the twenty-year period of 1970 to 1990, six years showed positive average annual growth rates, but severe declines were recorded in 1971, 1973, 1979, 1980, 1986, and 1987. At 1987 prices, real GNP grew from 210.8 billion CFA francs ($1.8 billion) in 1969 to 228.3 billion CFA francs ($1.9 billion) in 1976, declined from 1977 to 1980, and finally grew steadily thereafter. Hence for the period 1970–1990, the post-Malloum period experienced more declines in growth rates and more instability than the pre-Malloum period. Between 1970 and 1990, average annual GDP growth was low. In fact, between 1977 and 1982 the GDP declined by an annual average of 4.8 percent, recovering in 1983. From 1984 onward, Chad's economy experienced significant fluctuations of growths and recessions.

Gross domestic investment and resource balance did not make any significant contribution to the GDP growth. Comparatively, investment was higher during the pre-Malloum period than during the post-Malloum period. Since savings and investment are directly related, the evolution of gross domestic savings as a percentage of GDP was similar to that of the gross domestic investment. Until 1979, Chad had positive gross domestic savings; thereafter, it declined and has remained negative ever since. Following the general economic trend, the GNP per capita has stagnated since 1970 and does not differ significantly in the pre- and post-Malloum years. However, as Figure 4.2 shows, since the 1970s Chad's per capita GNP has never exceeded $200. Compared to sub-Saharan Africa's per capita GNP, which was over $700 from 1980 to 1982, Chad's figures showed little improvement; they remained below $200.

Overall, more growth was experienced during the post-Malloum ten-year period (1979–1989) than the ten-year pre-Malloum period (1969–1979). Nonetheless, real per capita income fell during the post-Malloum period, indicating a worsening of the welfare of Chadians. Due to the 1984 drought, livestock production fell 19 percent from an estimated 10.5 million head to 8.5 million; cotton production plunged almost 38 percent from the 1983 levels. A decline in food-crop production was critical in the Sahelian region, where it fell 76 percent. Likewise, the official estimates show that agricultural production fluctuated greatly. It grew only 5 percent in 1983, fell 23 percent in 1984, grew 51.8 percent in 1985, fell again by 3.4 percent in 1986, and fell yet again by 9.7 percent in 1987. Industry's real value added (the difference between the value of product and cost of materials) to total national output

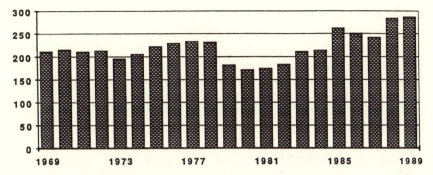

FIGURE 4.1   Real Gross National Product for Chad (billions of 1987 CFA francs), 1969–1989

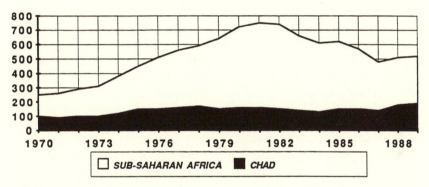

FIGURE 4.2   Gross National Product Per Capita for Chad (U.S. dollars), 1970–1989

dropped successively from 1984 to 1987. This was the case with cotton fiber, cloth, cigarettes, beer, and carbonated beverages. Oil, sugar, and soap value added declined, especially in 1985, but grew thereafter.

It is difficult to distinguish between the pre- and post-Malloum periods in Chad's economic history by merely examining historical trends because available data are often unreliable, and they show either wide fluctuations in the two periods or intermittent stagnation. Nonetheless, where the changes are progressive, historical trends have been easier to determine. For example, real GDP figures improved on the average in the post-Malloum period, but the growth rate decline was more pronounced and severe after 1989. Also, GNP per capita as a broad measure of economic development stagnated and did not vary significantly between 1970 and 1988, a period that spans the pre- and post-Malloum Chadian economy. Ten-year averages (1969–1979 and 1979–1989) of annual change in real GNP for Chad indicate that whereas the pre-Malloum period recorded a 4.7 percent growth rate, the post-Malloum period experienced a decline in growth rate of 1.5 percent. This rate of economic growth is less than the population growth. With a fair amount of certainty, one can conclude, therefore, that the welfare of Chadians worsened during the post-Malloum period.

Turnover of the main industries improved slightly (by 3.2 percent) at the end of 1990 thanks to government protection and improvement in payment of salaries. Although such industries as SONASUT (the sugar factory), Brasseries du Logone, Boissons et Glacières du Tchad (BGT), and the Manufacture des Cigarettes du Tchad (MCT) improved their performance, the textile manufacturer Société Textile du Tchad recorded a remarkable decline. Automobile sales increased; consumer nondurables fell. The production of electricity improved by 15 percent; at the same time, consumption increased 78.7 percent. The water supply also increased, and the sale of petroleum products rose 22.8 percent. Prices rose 2.4 percent in 1990 from 1989; previously, the price index in 1989 recorded a decline relative to 1988. The budget deficit for 1990 was 6.6 billion CFA francs ($6.9 million) compared to 14 billion ($14.1 million) in 1989. The reduction is attributed to a mild progression in aggregate wages and improvements in revenue collection. Revenue in the 1991 budget was estimated at 33.9 billion CFA francs ($32.5 million), and expenditure was 43.8 billion ($42.1 million) with a provisional deficit of 9.9 billion ($9.5 million) expected from external aid. Personnel remunerations, which represented 52.1 percent of the operational expenditure, increased by 18.1 percent. An investment budget of 95.5 billion CFA francs ($91.8 million) for 1991 was slightly less than the 98.8 billion ($1 billion) for 1990. Net reserves improved because of cotton; money supply decreased; and since 1988, total short-term debt decreased but not in a significant way. Government debt also fell slightly, by 3.6 percent.

Agriculture is the most important economic activity in Chad. About 400,000 families rely on cotton, the main cash crop, for their survival. Judging from official government figures shown in Table 4.1, the record production of 62,000 metric tons of cotton fiber from the 175,000 metric tons of raw cotton obtained in 1975–1976 was followed by a progressive decline lasting up to 1982 due to Chad's political turmoil. In 1983–1984, after a semblance of peace was restored, cotton production improved 57 percent. However, the drought of 1984–1985 caused a 40 percent drop in cotton output (see Table 4.1). Prices continued to decline throughout the 1980s, and although producer revenue increased from year to year to reach 12 billion CFA francs ($12 million) in 1983–1984, it still remained a small fraction of total cotton export revenues.

Government figures for food production shown in Table 4.1 indicate that after the large increases recorded for millet, sorghum, peanuts, and rice in 1980–1981, output declined progressively during the remaining four years mainly due to unfavorable climatic conditions and drought. Estimates of grain deficit are 140,000 metric tons in 1982–1983; 160,000 metric tons in 1983–1984; and at least 300,000 metric tons in 1984–1985. International agencies such as the Banque Arabe pour

TABLE 4.1   Agricultural Performance in Chad, 1974–1985

Year	Cotton Fiber (1,000 metric tons)	Average FOB Price (Kg/ CFA franc)	Export Revenues (billions of CFA francs)	Producers' Revenues (billions of CFA francs)
1974–75	52.9	220	11.6	–
1975–76	62.1	280	17.4	–
1976–77	54.0	378	20.4	–
1977–78	45.4	316	14.3	6.3
1978–79	50.1	306	15.3	6.8
1979–80	33.1	338	11.2	4.6
1980–81	31.2	400	12.5	4.3
1981–82	26.2	460	12.0	3.6
1982–83	38.1	586	22.3	7.1
1983–84	59.9	750	44.9	12.7
1984–85	35.5	724	25.7	8.7

Year	Millet and Sorghum Output (metric tons)	Peanut Output (metric tons)	Rice Output (1,000 metric tons)	Wheat Output (1,000 metric tons)
1974–75	–	–	–	–
1975–76	–	–	–	–
1976–77	–	–	–	–
1977–78	390.0	96.0	20.3	–
1978–79	272.1	93.8	20.7	–
1979–80	253.1	98.5	25.6	–
1980–81	533.3	152.1	47.0	–
1981–82	430.0	77.7	43.0	–
1982–83	459.0	75.2	29.3	–
1983–84	450.0	–	18.0	–
1984–85	350.0	–	15.0	5.3

[a]FOB = Free on board.

le Développement Économique en Afrique (BADEA), International Development Association (IDA), Fonds d'Aide et de Développement (FAD), Fund for Aid and Cooperation (FAC), USAID, OPEC, and European Development Fund (EDF) considered financing some agricultural development projects that were aimed at improving food production in the Sahelian region through land development and irrigation.

Approximately two-thirds of Chad's animal production in the form of meat and hides are exported to Nigeria. However, Nigeria's deplorable economic conditions and the depreciation of the naira caused the Nigerian market to become unattractive to exports. As a result, cattle exports have fluctuated since 1983: About 64,000 head of cattle were exported to Nigeria in 1987, 37,000 in 1986, and 170,000 in 1985. Since Chad's rain-fed pastoralism is extensive, climatic conditions play the major role in determining the level and conditions of production. This is why livestock farmers suffer tremendous losses during periods of drought. It was not until 1972 that an animal-production policy was adopted with the help of the World Bank and other external bodies. Thus the Chadian government created state-owned enterprises (SOEs) to stimulate cattle production, but their impact has been minimal in terms of restimulating production.

Drought and insufficiency of wells result in overgrazing in the Saharan and Sahelian regions and have forced the pastoralists to move southward in search of grazing zones, where they have encountered the tsetse fly and the wrath of crop producers. Over the years, livestock production and exports have provided tax revenue for the government, and they have contributed overall to economic, employment, and income improvement. Since the late 1980s, the government has taken steps to improve the animal-production subsector through institutional, structural, and sectoral reforms. However, it is too early to judge the effectiveness of these policies.

During the period 1990–1991, Banque des États de l'Afrique Central (BEAC) reports also show that cotton purchases increased nearly 48 percent, rising from 18,194 metric tons in 1989 to 26,899 metric tons in 1990. This improvement is attributed to the reform of the cotton subsector as well as favorable producer prices. Cotton-fiber exports increased 55.9 percent (from 48,329 metric tons in 1989 to 75,325 tons in 1990). The main importers of these products were Portugal, 26.5 percent; Germany, 22.3 percent; Japan, 14.4 percent; and Spain, 7.9 percent. However, the increase recorded for cotton did not occur in food production during the period 1990–1991. Grain production fell from 781,000 metric tons in 1989–1990 to 604,700 metric tons in 1990–1991. A period of inadequate rainfall is blamed for this decline, and it is estimated that the grain-supply gap widened from 80,000 to 200,000 metric tons. Oil-seed production recorded larger declines due to unfavorable weather conditions and a 63.3 percent decline in hectarages in the Sahel. In the Sudanese Zone, hectarages fell 13 percent and output fell 20 percent. At the end of 1990, meat production at the Farcha abattoir stagnated at 8,512 metric tons. Beef slaughter, which constitutes 81.6 percent of total output, increased slightly (by 1.8 percent; camel and pork production improved by 63.5 percent.

Food and agricultural production and productivity have remained stagnant over the years. Although the total agricultural production index increased from 99 in 1978–1980 to 124 in 1988–1990, the index of per capita food production stagnated within the same period, from 101 in 1978–1980 to 100 in 1988–1990. Productivity stagnated between the years 1969 and 1989. Compared to figures for all of Africa, Chad's average grain yields were low: only 645 kilograms per hectare as opposed to 1,198 kilograms per hectare for Africa in the three-year period 1988–1990.

Data compiled by Victor Lavy on food production, aid, and imports for several African countries during the 1970–1987 period show that variability of food production was relatively high for Chad in terms of deviations from the average production. Lavy's data also indicate that average emergency food aid as a ratio of total food aid was 59 percent during the period 1970–1987. Chad is likely to receive more food aid, since, as Lavy reveals, "Cross-section correlations indicate that countries with a high coefficient of variation of production receive more aid (as a percentage of total domestic production)."[6] Undoubtedly recent droughts and wars rampant during the post-Malloum years have threatened food self-sufficiency in Chad. Using World Bank data, Shamsher Singh estimates food self-sufficiency ratios in Chad to be on the average 100 in 1964–1966 compared to 90 in 1978–1980.[7]

Since the 1970s Chad has been experiencing serious financial difficulties. Whereas in the 1960s both government revenues and expenditures increased pari passu, in the 1970s defense expenditures surpassed development investment. Although there were no national budgets between 1980 and 1982, in 1983 the budget deficit was approximately 34.7 million U.S. dollars. Since 1983, deficits have increased progressively, forcing the government to rely more on foreign aid to maintain government services. According to the American embassy's 1991 "Background Notes" in 1989, recurrent expenditures rose by 30 percent, pushing the budget deficit up to 13.5 billion CFA francs ($13.6 million). Despite the economic reform program established by the Chadian administration, the budget adopted for 1991-1992 still presented a deficit of 14.09 billion CFA francs ($13.5 million). By the end of September 1991, the deficit stood at 15.3 billion CFA francs ($14.7 million) with a revenue of 17.4 billion CFA francs ($16.7 million) and an expenditure of 32.7 billion CFA francs ($31.4 million).

Cotton dominates foreign trade as the primary export; fuel, food, machinery, and equipment are the main imports. Chad imports practically all of its energy, and it benefits from cheap fuel sold illegally across the border from Nigeria. The trade shows negative net imports; just how negative the balance is depends on the cotton crop's world price. Net exports have remained consistently negative, fueled in part by high freight costs due to Chad's enclave location. Both the resource balance, in billions of 1987 CFA francs, and the balance-of-payments current account (before official transfers in millions of current U.S. dollars) have remained negative since 1980. The current account balance has actually been negative since the 1970s. Furthermore, net official transfers increased significantly between 1980 and 1989.

Of the seventeen countries that appeared in Banque des États de l'Afrique Central (BEAC) records as Chad's trading partners in 1983, ten of them had trade surpluses with Chad. In 1973, Chad recorded trade deficits with fifteen out of twenty countries with which it traded. In 1980, Chad had trade deficits with eleven out of eighteen trading partners. Figure 4.3 shows the imports, exports, and trade balance for Chad from 1960 to 1989. BEAC figures do not agree with those of the World Bank for the period 1978–1982. In spite of this discrepancy, the overall trends were the same: stagnation of imports and exports in the late 1960s and early 1970s, growth in imports and exports during 1975 and 1976, de-

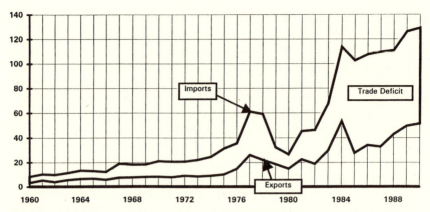

FIGURE 4.3   Chadian Imports, Exports, and Trade Deficit (billions of CFA francs), 1960–1989

cline in both imports and exports from 1977 to 1980, and an explosion in imports from 1984 onward that created record trade deficits (see Figure 4.3).

The terms of trade, which show at what prices the exported and imported goods are exchanged, declined steadily from 1971 to 1975 after some improvements in 1969 and 1970. The declining trend indicates unfavorable and deteriorating Chadian terms of trade vis-à-vis the rest of the world. Chad trades considerably more with the OECD countries than with fellow members of BEAC (Cameroon, the Central African Republic, Gabon, Congo, and Equatorial Guinea). As BEAC reports show, in 1970 over 58 percent of Chad's imports came from OECD countries, whereas only 13 percent were from BEAC countries.

In 1990, imports were worth 77.7 billion CFA francs ($80.9 million); exports were worth 51.5 billion CFA francs ($53.6 million). Of the total imports, petroleum products represented 16.8 percent; cereal products, 16.8 percent; and pharmaceutical products, 11.5 percent. Other imports included machinery and transport equipment, 7.3 percent; electrical equipment, 5.7 percent; textiles, 2.9 percent; and raw and refined sugar, 2.3 percent. The main exports were raw cotton, 91.1 percent; live cattle and frozen bovine meat, 1.8 percent; and hides and skin, 0.4 percent. Other export commodities were cattle, textiles, beer, and fish. The major export markets are France, Nigeria, and Cameroon. Goods worth an estimated $204.4 million were imported into Chad in 1990, mainly machinery and transport equipment, industrial goods, petroleum products, grains, pharmaceuticals, telecommunication equipment, and foodstuffs. The major foreign suppliers are Cameroon, Nigeria, France, the United States, and the Central African Republic (CAR).[8]

Two opposing tendencies characterized the balance of payments in 1989: a net deterioration in current account balance and an increase in foreign capital transfer. The negative current account balance shrunk progressively to a level of 5.5 billion CFA francs in 1988, but this improvement was short-lived because imports of goods and services grew to a new high. Since aid-related imports remained stable, private-sector imports were responsible for the increase. The deficit of the service account reached a record 56.5 billion CFA francs, indicating continued external support; the private transfer balance was negative, revealing a small level of foreign investment.

Chad's average official exchange rate, which is linked to the French franc, fluctuated only moderately from 1960 to 1980. Historical trends from the International Monetary Fund's database, the source of the data used in this section, show that between 1948 and 1991 the Chadian currency depreciated progressively relative to the U.S. dollar. During the ten-year period 1948-1957, the exchange rate was on the average 174.98 to one U.S. dollar. This rate changed to 209.87 in 1958 and thereafter remained constant at 246.85 during the next ten-year period, 1959–1968. Beginning in 1969, the exchange rate fluctuated more but never fell below 211 or rose above 277. However, this trend changed, Chadian currency depreciating to 328.61 in 1982, 436.96 in 1984, and 449.26 in 1985. The exchange rate jumped from 378.78 francs per SDR (special drawing rights) in 1987 to 407.68 in 1988 and fell to 364.84 in 1990. In January 1994, Chad joined the other twelve members of the franc zone in devaluing the CFA franc by 50 percent. This currency depreciation has been favorable to cattle and cotton exports, although it has generated considerable inflation. The beginning of the post-Malloum period was marked by an expansionary monetary policy. Money supply grew gradually up to the early 1980s but substantially increased to almost 70 billion CFA francs ($21 million) in 1984. Beyond this period, it has remained at high levels but below 80 billion CFA francs ($24 million). The monetary expansion of 1984 was undoubtedly inflationary, since the rate of inflation the same year reached an all-time high of 24 percent. On balance, the post-Malloum years saw more levels of monetary expansion than the preceding years. Aside from the 1984 record high inflation of 24 percent, inflation rates have been low, at less than 10 percent. For most African countries, rampant inflation is a constant burden that plagues their economies. Indeed, deflation occurred for three years following the 1984 blitz. After an inflationary 1988, disinflation occurred in 1989. Overall, the inflation rate has remained manageable in light of comparatively worse conditions in most other African countries.

Impact of War on Chad's Economy

Accurate statistics on Chad's military expenditure are hard to find. However, various estimates show that expenditure on military hardware and maintenance of personnel has been significant over the years. For instance (using UNDP and World Bank data), during the years 1984 to 1986, military expenditure represented between 34 and 38 percent of the total budget; it was $39 million (4.3 percent of GDP) in 1988. Public expenditure on the military compared with expenditure on health and education clearly underscores the disparity caused by the Chadian war. The World Bank estimates that as a percentage of GNP, Chadian military expenditure in 1986 was between 5 and 10 percent compared to 2 percent for health and education. According to the U.S. Arms Control and Disarmament Agency's *World Military Expenditures and Arms Transfers 1990* (p. 100), Chad's arms imports represented 4.6 percent of total imports in 1981; 22.1 percent in 1984; and 27.3 percent in 1978. In Chad, military personnel far outnumber teachers and physicians, according to UNDP data. The ratio of armed forces to each 1,000 people in 1987 was 3.7 (compared to 2 for sub-Saharan Africa). In 1987, there were 2.4 armed forces personnel per teacher and 170 armed forces personnel per physician. The ratio of social investment to arms import improved somewhat from 0.25:1 in 1987 to 1.7:1 in 1988–1989.

The main economic effects of Chad's war and civil strife were resource diversion (resource drain and allocative inefficiencies), degradation of the productive forces, deterioration in the balance of payments, and destabilization of the economic system and markets—labor, capital and financial, and natural resource. Military confrontation and war diverted resources away from productive investment and social spending to the nonproductive war sector and caused economic development to be abandoned. The war also caused considerable decline in investment, disappearance of industries, disruption of international trade, massive corruption, and looting of the national treasury.

Aside from instability created by war, the Chadian society faced such problems as worker absenteeism, general indifference, corruption, smuggling, prostitution, and commodity trafficking, all of which undermined authoritative structures, morality, and state finances. Roads and water-distribution systems were damaged, agriculture and agro-based industries were destroyed, and urban public-sector services were disrupted or closed down.[9] Notably, considerable damage was done to urban centers, especially N'Djamena—the theater of the second stage of the war between GUNT (Gouvernement d'Union Nationale de Transition) and FAN (Forces Armées du Nord)—and Abeche. Likewise, incessant guerrilla attacks and instability coupled with the unbearable living conditions in rural areas caused large-scale rural-urban migration. The toll on human life in terms of deaths and forced migration has been immense. In 1983, Amnesty International recorded widespread human rights violations: extrajudicial executions of civilians and unarmed former soldiers; arbitrary detentions of men, women, and children; systematic ethnic-based elimination of prominent citizens suspected of collaboration with the enemy; and disappearances. The civil wars were the main cause of Chad's humanitarian crisis; summary executions occurred during both the Habre and Deby regimes, women were forced into prostitution and political prisoners were tortured and murdered.[10] Most of the human rights violations came in the form of interethnic revenge and vendetta; for example, in the purges of January 8 and 9, 1992, at least a dozen Kanem leaders and businessmen were executed and others were imprisoned by Idris Deby's Republican Guard.[11]

A large number of Chadian refugees of that war emigrated to Cameroon and Nigeria. *Africa: South of the Sahara 1992* estimates that about 25,000 refugees fled to the Central African Republic. According to the *Economist* of December 2, 1990, the rebels who placed Idris Deby in power claim to have killed 2,000 and captured 3,000 of Habre's men during the offensive that began at the border with Sudan. Perhaps between 200,000 and 400,000 people died as a result of the Chadian wars[12] (although this large number has been disputed by some observers). Fighting in Chad reduced food production and hampered relief efforts, especially after the 1984 famine. Because some of the armed conflicts and guerrilla activity took place in the rural areas, they caused rural depopulation and emigration to urban areas as well as a breakdown in law and order.

In summary, Chad's war and military confrontations created widespread economic disruption and destabilized the infrastructure, public administration, the financial sector, and business. Industrial development and cotton production declined, especially in the early 1980s, with a general economic slowdown. The decline in industrial production resulted from the contraction of effective demand and irregular payment of public servants working in the capital. Finally, the war contributed to looting of the national treasury and the complete disappearance of the banking system by generating corruption, problems of political continuity, and power vacuums. Scarce resources were diverted away from productive investment and social spending to the nonproductive war sector. Physical infrastructure was destroyed and economic development was abandoned.

Overall (that is, on the basis of different socioeconomic performance measures), the post-Malloum period is worse than the pre-Malloum period in many respects. Chad still suffers violence and war, climatic and ecological disasters, and socioeconomic uncertainty. Although a few areas of improvement may be found, such as the growth rate of output between the periods 1969–1979 and 1979–1989 and the lowering of infant mortality, conditions remain largely deplorable. The government exhibited urban bias in its distribution of national wealth following the colonial legacy, favoring the urban class over the rural dwellers. These disparities have created regional (North-South), gender (male-female), and urban-rural wage and income gaps characterized by high-income differentials between the haves and the have-nots. Notwithstanding these economic inequalities, the devastation caused by the series of wars that occurred in Chad have more significance. Since Chad has long depended on external aid for its survival, it is therefore pertinent to examine the impact of foreign aid on the future of the country.

Foreign Assistance and Chad's Survival

Chad's dependence on foreign aid for its survival since it gained independence in 1960 is continuous and total. Indeed, without massive international assistance its economic viability and planning would be jeopardized. As shown in the second section of this chapter, Chad's dependence on France in particular began during the colonial era. This period was marked by underinvestment as well as coercive and exploitative fiscal policies of the colonial military administration that laid the foundations for much of Chad's postindependence underdevelopment and dependency.

The Republic of Chad is classified by the UN as an official borrower, since more than two-thirds of its total liabilities outstanding at the end of 1990 are owed to official creditors. Although its debt situation has not reached alarming proportions, it will not be long before Chad joins the rank of the severely indebted low-income African countries. The public and publicly guaranteed long-term debt was $33 million in 1970 but jumped to over $430 million in 1990. There were no private nonguaranteed long-term debts in 1990. Chad used only $3 million dollars of IMF credit in 1970, but in 1990 it used $31 million. The increasing importance of Chad's debt is illustrated by the World Bank's figures, which put total short-term debt at $31 million in 1990; total external debt was $492 million in the same year. From the World Bank's records, total external debt as a percentage of exports of goods and services improved from 305.9 percent in 1980 to 207.1 percent in 1990. Yet as a percentage of GNP, total external debt went from 30.2 percent in 1980 to 44.8 percent in 1990. Both the total debt service and interest payments as percentages of exports of goods and services remain low.

Through the International Development Association (IDA), the World Bank advanced twenty-four cumulative credits totaling $331.9 million as of June 1991. An $11 million project was approved in November 1990 for IDA assistance in the fiscal year 1991 for petroleum and power engineering projects. Chad also borrowed $11 million from the IDA for preparatory studies of methods to ensure the most efficient and least-cost method of implementing a proposed petroleum and power project (which would involve the construction of a petroleum pipeline, a refinery, and a power plant). The European Investment Bank (EIB) is expected, as a cofinancer, to supply the remaining $3 million for a projected total cost of $14.5 million.

Owing to its growing debt burden, Chad finds it increasingly difficult to make debt service payments and pay arrears. Chadian officials met with the Paris Club in 1989 and 1990 to discuss loan rescheduling. As a result, $92 million of principal and interest of Chad's loans were rescheduled, and $9 million of debt was canceled. This left less than $15 million of payment arrears by the end of 1990.[13] Since Chad has been adjusting its economy since 1987, it became eligible in 1989 for the World Bank's Special Program of Assistance (SPA) for debt-distressed countries in sub-Saharan Africa, which allowed access to additional concessionary nonproject funding.

Chad's dependence on bilateral and multilateral official development assistance (ODA) has accelerated over the years. ODAs are concessionary nondebt financial flows that aim to promote economic development. As shown in previous sections, the foreign savings made available to Chad through ODA flows constitute a sizable proportion of the country's GDP, the national budget, and domestic invest-

TABLE 4.2   Western Countries' Total Economic Aid Commitments to Chad (millions of U.S. dollars), 1980–1990

Years	1980	1983	1984	1985	1986	1987	1988[a]	1989[a]	1990[a]
Amounts	30	63	87	194	164	181	310	400	324

[a]Including both multilateral and bilateral commitments and excludes other official flows. Data for the earlier years and bilateral commitments of ODA and other official flows including trade credits.

SOURCE: CIA, Directorate of Intelligence, *Handbook of International Economic Statistics 1992* (Washington, D.C.: GPO, 1992), 210.

ment; in fact, all capital investment finances come in the form of financial aid from abroad. As a percent of total revenue, grants to government averaged from 7 percent in 1985 to 17 percent in 1987. Therefore, foreign aid is of great significance to Chad's economic performance. The contemporary and future impact of aid in Chad is underscored by the relationship between net ODA flows and their relative importance to the main economic and demographic indicators in Chad.

During the period 1970–1989, the CIA's *Handbook of Nations* (1992) reports that U.S. commitments to Chad totaled $198 million. The CIA handbook also shows that non-U.S. Western countries' ODA and bilateral commitments during the same period amounted to $1.5 billion, and OPEC bilateral aid between 1979 and 1989 was $28 million. Aid from Communist countries totaled $80 million from 1970 to 1989. Table 4.2 shows the evolution of total Western economic aid commitments to Chad from 1980 to 1990. Evidently, Western aid commitments continued to increase over the years; from $30 million in 1980, Western aid doubled to $63 million in 1983 and tripled to $194 million in 1985. So far the highest amount of Western aid, $400 million (including multilateral and bilateral commitments), was reached in 1989; this was more than thirteen times the level of aid ($30 million) in 1980. In 1990, per capita gross national income was $170 and per capita ODA was $55, approximately 32 percent of per capita national income. As a percentage of GNP in 1990, net disbursement of ODA from all sources was 28.6 percent. In the period 1982–1984, the figure was 15.2 percent; in 1987–1989 it rose to 24.8 percent. France is the major source of external aid to Chad.

Since the 1940s, France has been providing aid to Chad in increasing amounts, especially in the form of military assistance and financial support to prevent state bankruptcy. The main avenues for this aid include the Fonds d'Investissement pour le Développement Économique et Social des Territoires d'Outre Mer (FIDES), the program of l'Organisation Commune des Régions Sahariennes (l'OCRS), the Fond d'Aide et de Coopération (FAC—Fund for Aid and Cooperation), and the Fonds Européen de Développement (European Development Fund).

The *Bulletin de l'Afrique Noire* of May 1985 illustrates the increasing French government aid to Chad, from 8.59 billion CFA francs ($2.6 million) in 1982 to

12.27 billion CFA francs ($3.7 million) in 1983. In 1984, it was 15.39 billion CFA francs ($4.7 million); in 1985, 17.2 billion francs ($5.3 million). The main sources of French government aid are direct public aid, subsidies of the French Ministry of Cooperation, and loans from the Caisse Centrale de Coopération Économique (CCCE). In 1985, direct public aid was the largest source of French assistance to Chad. French support came in the form of technical assistance by expatriated personnel, scholarships, training, and food aid. It also came in the form of financial aid for the support of high-priority budgetary expenditures such as roads, electricity, and water supply.

France provided large amounts of weapons to Chad, helped it purchase the famous Toyotas used in the numerous battles, and also provided assistance in the form of personnel. During its numerous interventions in the Chadian conflicts, France provided military assistance to one faction after another. From 1960 to 1973, Chad received 30 percent of French military assistance to sub-Saharan Africa (except South Africa), which was the largest amount of all French military aid to that region. More than 80 million French francs were supplied to purchase five helicopters, five mobile machine-gun transports, a DC-4 aircraft, and medical equipment. From 1977 to 1980, France provided 269.3 million French francs worth of military aid to revamp the Chadian army.[14] Following an incursion from Sudan by Idris Deby's forces, France reinforced its troops from 1,200 to 1,800. There was a repeat performance in 1990, when France provided logistic and military support to Habre's forces.[15] To support Idris Deby, whose forces came under attack at the end of December 1992 and early January 1993, Paris sent military backup of 450 paratroopers to N'Djamena plus four French air force Jaguar aircrafts stationed in Dakar, Senegal, on January 1 and 2, 1993.

Unlike France, the United States concentrated mainly on military aid, as noted in Chapters 3 and 6. It is noteworthy that in 1987, the United States decided to supply seven Stinger launchers and twenty-four missiles as well as $2 million worth of military training to the Chadian government in its war against Libya.[16] Aside from military assistance, governmental organizations and NGOs such as AID, CARE, and the Peace Corps have been used for Sahel development, rural sanitation, food delivery, the strengthening of development ministries, and food-crop research. The United States also gave food aid, small-scale infrastructure assistance, financial management assistance, and institutional-strengthening support to Chad in 1990. The main organ of U.S. development assistance to Chad is USAID, which in addition to cooperating with NGOs such as CARE, AFRICARE, and VITA, works through the Peace Corps. Dependence on external aid has forced Chadian leaders to do unusual things. For instance, because of its desperate need for capital equipment and spare parts, the Deby administration recently received "humanitarian supplies"—automobiles and military hardware—from Libyan colonel Muammar Kadhafi in exchange for the release of Libyan prisoners held by Chad.

What is the impact of aid on the future of Chad? Although economists tend to agree on the use of aid as a means to alleviate economic distress, there is considerable disagreement about the advantages and disadvantages of permanent economic dependency. The main disadvantage is that a country suffers welfare losses and an erosion of its political autonomy if it permanently depends on aid from abroad. Nonetheless, most scholars tend to agree that the problem of economic assistance lies not in the assistance itself but in the rationale of the donor, the form of aid, the timing and timeliness of its delivery, and its use by the recipient state. In the case of Chad, foreign economic assistance exacerbated aid addiction and dependency. Dependence on foreign aid encouraged fiscal mismanagement and created uncertainty in planning for economic development. Chadian dependence on foreign aid has also postponed the improvement of macroeconomic management, fiscal reform, and the mobilization of domestic resources in the manner suggested by the World Bank's *World Development Report 1991*. Moreover, aid has adversely affected domestic savings and created a climate of uncertainty, since actual expenditures continually deviate from planned expenditures in the development plans presented by Chadian administrations. Technological aid has not been very successful because it is often redundant and does not necessarily fulfill the needs of the Chadians. Along with aid-induced problems and distortions, the main impact of Chad's economic dependence is its subjection to political manipulation from donors, resulting in a lack of foreign policy independence.

The historical realities and uncertainties of the twenty-first century should prompt Chad to reexamine its understanding of economic development. Gone are the days when the Chadian state monopolized development efforts and created jobs. As adjustment occurs, markets should be relied upon to dictate and rationalize demand and supply of goods. Inward-oriented strategies based on implicit and explicit discriminatory agricultural taxation to finance economic development must be replaced by outward-oriented strategies. Chad's policymakers have to understand that development is a multidimensional process involving a combination of appropriate internally derived strategies through regional cooperation and more integration into the world economy. For Chad, self-reliance and regional cooperation should mutually reinforce each other. Geopolitically, Chad faces questions of survival as it tries to cope with its multifarious troubles, unrests, insurgencies, civil conflicts, and wars. With so many troubled spots in the world, Chad in particular, and Africa in general, have lost priority in the West. Even former superpower Russia has joined the developing countries in competition for aid. Western Europe is preoccupied with the success or failure of the European Community, and individual countries are grappling with serious economic recessions. Based on these realities that underlie the new world order, the adoption of a more radical and more realistic self-reliance strategy by Chad becomes essential.

The collapse of the Soviet block, the collapse of bipolarism (replaced by multipolarism), and the emergence of three main trading blocks—North America, the European Community, and Japan—represent a different international economic order. Because of multipolarism and the need for realignment rather than non-alignment, Chad must consider changes in dialectics involving growth versus nongrowth and economic independence versus dependence in aligning itself. This is the main implication of regional cooperation for the new world order. Chad, and the bulk of Africa, are not well integrated into the global economy; unlike other regions that can align themselves with the proximate poles, Chad does not have such luxury. But is there really any hope for Chad?

Undoubtedly Chad represents an economic development challenge by virtue of the complexity of its political situation, prospects for renewed disturbances, and widespread poverty. Despite being one of the poorest countries in the world, long-term growth prospects are good provided its main development challenge—political instability resulting from several years of strife—is contained. This positive prognosis is based on recent accomplishments in growth rates, primary school enrollments, the small size of Chad's civil service, and the resilience of the Chadian people, who have endured years of deprivation caused by war. The private sector is also potentially dynamic, and Chad possesses oil reserves that could be exploited and exported. Despite improvements in fiscal management, the economic reform program yielded modest results, and the deficit is widening due to increased military spending. The improvement in the cotton sector following restructuring, together with infrastructural development and low inflation, should also yield benefits and help to set the economy in the right path.

Conclusion

The Republic of Chad has faced numerous problems since its independence from France in 1960, such as unstable economic growth trends, disparities and imbalance in the national accounts and public spending, trade deficits, and a negative balance of payments. Chad has also depended on aid and international borrowing to offset shortfalls in domestic discretionary fiscal expenditure. However, in spite of its dismal performance in social, demographic, and environmental areas, it is important to note that the foundations of these problems were laid by the exploitation, neglect, and devastation caused by colonialism. Whereas population growth rate has been sustained since independence in 1960, productivity has stagnated. Achievements in the area of human development are also mixed, and environmental degradation and constraints served as destabilizing forces on economic production.

Many analysts attribute Chad's low economic performance to the country's remoteness, inadequate infrastructure, war, climatic disasters such as drought, an ecologically fragile environment, cotton-based monoculturalism, and insufficient natural resources. However, postcolonial Chad is the product of the French colonial experience and legacy as well as of cultural, ethnic, religious, locational, and political forces. These are factors that combine to cause the instability that has prevented Chad's economic development. In summary, therefore, the primary destabilizing factors of the Chadian economy are both exogenous (colonial experience and legacy, postcolonial French engagement and external aggression by Libya and Nigeria) and endogenous (climatic and environmental factors, the Cold War, political instability and war, inadequate and incoherent government policies, dependence on foreign aid, and locational factors).

In the short run the Chadian people cannot effectively address the problem of Chad's colonial legacy or control climatic and environmental factors. Thus Chad must focus on dealing with its disastrous political instability through negotiations and on alleviating the excessive economic cost of its landlocked situation; this can be accomplished through more aggressive bilateral and multilateral arrangements with such neighbors as Nigeria and Cameroon. In this regard, it is crucial that railroads are developed to connect Chad with its access-to-the-sea neighboring countries. Chad's government must also develop policies that will not stifle economic development but rather ensure growth enhancement and structural changes. These goals can be achieved by getting rid of the sources of market and economic distortions such as commodity boards and direct government investment and control of the business sector. The Chadian government must ensure that economic aid is used not for supporting a large and inefficient bureaucratic civil service but for development of human capital and the infrastructure, thereby creating an enabling environment that is conducive to economic development.

Notes

1. Jean Chapelle, *Le peuple tchadien: Ses racines et sa vie quotidienne* (Paris: Harmattan, 1980), 18–19; and J. Courtin, "Le neolitique du Borkou," *Anthropologie* 263, cited by Chapelle, *Le peuple tchadien*, 9.

2. No inherent constraint concerns soil that is not affected by the following: steep slopes, shallow soil, poor drainage, low nutrient retention, aluminum toxicity, acid soils, phosphorous fixation, amorphous material, vertic properties, low potassium reserves, calcareous soil, soil salinity, excess sodium, acid sulfate soil, and gravel. *World Resources 1992–93: A Guide to the Global Environment, Toward Sustainable Development*, a report by World Resources Institute, in collaboration with United Nations Environmental Program and United Nations Development Program (New York: Oxford University Press, 1992), 281-282.

3. Ellen P. Brown and Robert Nooter, "Successful Small-Scale Irrigation in the Sahel," World Bank Technical Paper no. 171 (Washington, DC: World Bank), 9–10.

4. République du Tchad, Ministère Delegué à la Présidence de la République Chargé du Plan, "Fonction Publique Tchadienne au 31–12–84" (1984): 12–15.

5. Jesse Mckee, Eddie Lewis, and Robert Jenkins, "The Geo-Economics of Cameroon and Chad: The Road to Development," in Mario Azevedo, ed., *Cameroon and Chad in Historical and Contemporary Perspectives* (Lewiston: Edwin Mellen Press, 1988), 43.

6. Victor Lavy, "Alleviating Transitory Food Crises in Sub-Saharan Africa: International Altruism and Trade," *World Bank Economic Review* 6, no. 1 (January 1992): 128.

7. Shamsher Singh, "Sub-Saharan Agriculture: Synthesis and Trade Prospects," World Bank Staff Working Papers no. 608 (Washington, D.C.: World Bank, 1983).

8. Duncan Robinson, "Trading With Chad," *Journal of Commerce* 386, no. 27374 (Dec. 13, 1990): 11A. These figures should, like many others, be used with caution, since undocumented trade between Chad and its neighbors, especially Nigeria, are quite substantial and may indicate a different ranking if considered.

9. Gilbert Lam Kaboré, "Tchad: Trente mois pour oublier le passé," *Jeune Afrique* 1589 (2–18 June 1991): 33–52. See also George Joffe, "Turmoil in Chad," *Current History* 89, no. 546 (April 1990): 157.

10. Isata Nabie and John Prendergast, "The Battleground of Chad," *Africa Report* 35, no. 4 (Sept.-Oct. 1990): 62.

11. Assane Diop, "Plus ça change," *Africa Report* 37, no. 2 (March-April 1992): 25–27.

12. Jeff Ramsay, *Global Sudies: Africa* (Sluice Dock: Dushkin Publishing Group, 1991), 71–73.

13. World Bank, *Annual Report* (Washington, D.C.: World Bank, 1992), 148, 182; and World Bank, *Trends in Developing Economies 1992* (Washington, D.C.: World Bank, 1992), 104.

14. Michael P. Kelley, "Weak States and Captured Patrons: French Desire to Disengage from Chad," *Round Table* 296 (1985): 329.

15. Kaye Whiteman, "The Gallic Paradox," *Africa Report* 36 (January-February 1991): 17

16. J.J.G. Cox Mbe, "Chad: France in Africa," *Army Quarterly and Defence Journal* 118 (April 1988): 161.

5

SOCIETY
AND CULTURE

Creating a clear linguistic, ethnographic, social, and demographic picture of Chad is a major challenge. This is because for centuries, migrations from north to south, east to west, together with an influx of immigrants from Libya, Sudan, Niger, Nigeria, Cameroon, and the Central African Republic, have made Chad a melting pot in certain regions but have created a well-defined mosaic of ethnic groups and languages in others. Scholars are confused with regard to the proper classification of the country's different languages and ethnic groups, some classifying certain languages as dialects and others combining ethnic groups that perhaps should not be clustered together. To complicate matters further, some ethnic groups and other sizable human clusters perceive themselves as cohesive and culturally identifiable social units, but they have no language in common. Finally, demographic data on Chad's ethnic components, as in most of Africa, are usually not available or are often outdated and inaccurate. Census projects have been further hindered by political unrest and the uncontrolled, continual movement of people from one region to another.

Ethnicity and Demographic Patterns

Chad is the fifth largest country in Africa with a population estimated at 5,500,000 in 1995. Most anthropologists and linguists claim that some 110 distinct languages are spoken in Chad by at least 200 ethnic groups.[1] It appears that at present some 85 languages have been clearly identified, and another 25 or so are yet to be defined. If the conclusions of linguists bear any resemblance to reality, Chad defies the common assumption that for each ethnic group there is a corresponding distinct language.[2] Some linguists group Chadian languages into four groups: Sudanic, Nilotic, Arabic, and Saharan. The Sudanic group consists of Sara, Tupuri, Banana, Moundang, Baguirmi, Youlba, and Rounga. The Nilotic group encompasses languages spoken by the Arabized populations such as the Wadai, Kodoi, Malange, Madaba, Debba, Abissa, Dekker, Djema, Masalit, and Lisi as well as the Bulala, Kuka, Midogo, Abusemeu, Mubi, Karbo, Mesmedje, Kenga, Babalia, Diongor, Saba, Yalna, Tunjur, and Torom. The Arabic linguistic group includes Hassauna and Djoheina, and the Saharan group comprises the Kanembu and Turubu. In the following section, we have summarized some features of the country's major ethnic groups in order of population size. Since Chad has never had a census, the numbers are estimates based on a total population of 3,300,000 in 1964 and 5,500,000 in 1995 (for an annual growth increase factor of approximately 1.54). The main demographic characteristics of the country are presented in Chapter 1.

The Sara

Among the most populous of the Chadian societies are the Sara of southern Chad, who at present constitute about one-third of the Chadian population (1,800,000) and are found mainly in the Moyen-Chari, the Eastern Logone, the Western Logone, and the Tandjile prefectures (as well as in parts of the Central African Republic). They consist of about a dozen clans, including the Gambaye (the largest), the Mbaye, the Goulaye, the Madjingaye (known as the pure Sara), the Kaba, the Niellim, the Nar, the Dai, and the N'gana. Contrary to some accounts and following Joseph Greensberg's classification, the Sara are non-Bantu speakers. The Sara designation seems to have been imposed on these clans by the Arabs, and it originally meant Christian (from Nassara, or Nazareth), as noted by Pierre Kalck.[3] Presumably, the Sara, like many of their neighbors, are Nilotic immigrants who settled permanently in Chad during the sixteenth century. At one point, however, they may have lived north or northeast of their present habitat and moved further south later in search of a sanctuary from Muslim slave raids and conquests.[4] Described by the French as *la belle race,* or the beautiful people, the "typical" Sara tends to be dark and robust. The Sara became prey to the Muslim and Arab *razzias* (slave raids) beginning in the sixteenth century; subsequently, they became a source of labor and military recruitment during the French colonial period.

Although the agriculturalist Sara did recognize a village chief—known as *mbang* or *nge-be* or *ngeido-namg*—who wielded some power, particularly among the Madjingaye, they did not as a rule have state communities. They lived in organized villages made up of several extended-family units. The Sara who came closest to forming a state society were the Madjingaye, centered at Bedeya. Their leader determined the beginning time for the *yondo,* the initiation ceremonies followed by almost all Sara clans. A *mbang* was assisted by a council of advisers, the *mou,* which represented the people, and a number of "militarily" trained men (called *goumiers* and led by a supervisor, or *padjal*) whose function was to protect the villages.

During the 1880–1890 period, Sudanese slave dealer Rabah Fadlallah, the conqueror of eastern-central Sudan, brought many Sara clans into his domain to be used mainly as slaves. Indeed, he incorporated Sara combatants into his army and systematically began to capture the sons of prominent chiefs as hostages and bargaining chips for the region's submission to his rule. The kingdom of Baguirmi itself, harassed and weakened by Rabah, was perhaps the most infamous for its slaving activities among the Sara, raiding as far down as Fort-Archambault (Sarh), Koumra, Doba, Moissala, Mandoul, and all along the banks of the Barh Sar River. Hence the Wadaians, looking for the Sara in particular, constantly waged war against them and raided as far south as Lake Iro and all the way into Oubangui-Chari (now the Central African Republic). The Wadaians captured thousands of victims annually. Due to French action, they stopped their raids around 1900.

These slaving activities represented about a 3 to 7 percent population loss yearly among the Sara during the 1890s, when their number was estimated to be about 400,000. Even a 3 percent demographic loss, however, was enough to depopulate entire districts, since the growth rate of the population in Chad could not have exceeded 3 percent per year at the time. In captivity, selected male slaves were castrated by their captors.[5] This must have had an adverse impact on population growth among the Sara. In principle, the Sara do not seem to have been opposed to the institution of slavery as such; they too owned some slaves who fulfilled their own needs or whom they made available to the slave raiders to spare their own people. However, they opposed the violent methods used by the northern states in the procurement of slaves.

The Fulani

Another group that engaged in enslaving the Sara were the Fulani. Coming from as far west as Adamawa (in present Cameroon), the Fulani are still remembered vividly by Sara elders and other southern populations because of their slaving activities. Pierre Lapie describes one of their devastating raids on the Sara town of Koumra that took place on May 16, 1903, after they had made Bediondo their slaving headquarters. It resulted in many deaths. In the context of slavery, Sara women were particularly desirable to Wadaians as concubines; to prevent capture, Sara families commonly elongated the lips of their women to render them less attractive to the slave traffickers. Also to minimize the impact of the slave trade, Sara chiefs would at times agree on a plan (called *amana*) with the northern enslavers (whom Sara elders usually label as *guerriers*): The Sara would provide a certain number of slaves annually to the northerners, who in return would pledge to spare the villages from violent raids.[6]

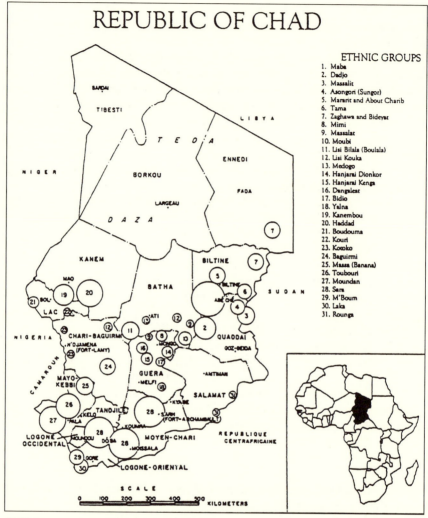

FIGURE 5.1   Major Ethnic Groups of the Republic of Chad (courtesy of Author)

The Arabs

The Arabs (at times known as Showa, Shuwa, Sua, or Aramba) never constituted more than 22 percent of the Chadian population (1,210,000) even though they had a disproportionate influence in business and Arabic is the second most widespread language in Chad. In Chad, most Chado-Arabs now live south of parallel 10 in south-central BET (in the former kingdom of Kanem-Bornu), Wadai, and Baguirmi. Most are camel herders and semisedentary; others raise cattle. Throughout the centuries, they wielded little power in the societies in which they found themselves and never succeeded in forming a state of their own. They have, however, kept their culture, religion, and language almost intact while managing to avoid isolating themselves from their neighbors. The first Arabs seem to have come to Chad in the fourteenth and fifteenth centuries from Sudan, Libya, Nigeria, and other parts of Africa.

For practical purposes, the Chado-Arabs can be divided into four major groups or clans: the Djoheina, or eastern Arabs; the Hassauna, or western Arabs (descendants of Hassan el Gharbi), found mostly in western Chad, particularly Kanem; the Awlad Sulayman (of Libyan descent), found also in Kanem (and Nigeria); and perhaps the Tunjur (of Sudanese origin), who presently are found primarily in Wadai and Kanem. As pastoralists, the Arabs travel thousands of miles every year in search of pasture and constitute almost 70 percent of the present population of the city of N'Djamena, where they dominate the business sector.

The Maba

The Maba are the third largest ethnic group in Chad (numbering about 216,800) and constituted the pillar of the former kingdom of Wadai. They were feared in the South, which they still consider to be foreign land, and claim affinity with ethnic groups in Sudan and the Maghreb. They are heavily concentrated in Abeche, Am-Dam, and parts of Biltine and lead semisedentary lives as agriculturalists, pastoralists, or stockbreeders. Interestingly, as in the past when they saw themselves as aristocrats, the Maba have continued to refuse to do manual labor and use other ethnic groups for these purposes.[7]

The Tubu

The Tubu (a word meaning "people of the Tu," or "mountain people") are the next largest group (187,341) who inhabit the BET Prefecture. According to some experts, they descend from Nilotic nomads who arrived in Chad during the seventeenth century. They played a major role in the founding of the kingdom of Kanem and embraced the Sanussiya Order during the nineteenth century. They have kinsmen in Fezzan, Libya, with whom they have maintained an extensive communication network and trade relationship for centuries.

The Tubu comprise two major clans: the Daza of Borku-Ennedi (the clan of former president Habre) and the Teda, a smaller clan of no more than 18,000 people, of which former head of state Gukuni Wedei is a member. In general, they have no strict hierarchy and are extremely dispersed, and among them individuals may virtually choose to belong to a certain clan. The Teda, who are considered to be the pure Tubu, have traditionally been the clan from which the ethnic group's spiritual leader, the *derdei,* has been selected. The Tubu are also characterized as freedom-loving, taciturn, revengeful, and almost always arms-bearing. They are mountaineers and vegetarians and enslaved others (particularly the Kamadja) to do work for them.[8] In the past, they exacted tribute from all their weak neighbors.

As seminomads who herd goats, sheep, horses, and camels, they travel constantly. Commenting on their relations with others, Virginia Thompson and

Richard Adloff label them (perhaps unfairly) as extremely clannish, representing the worst in Chad, namely, "tribalism-cum-regionalism." As pastoralists, the Tubu maintain their nomadic lifestyle for at least eight or nine months during the year, always returning to their permanent villages, where they live on dates and palm tree fruit during their short rainy season. They engage in long-distance transhumance and move their cattle to cooler areas.

The Mbum

The Mbum, or Laka, along with their kin Laka, constitute Chad's next largest ethnic group (172,480), half of whom live in the South of the country and half in the Central African Republic. They have adopted many of the rituals and the language of the Ngambaye. The Haddad (about 154,000 today), found mostly in the Kanem Prefecture, are next in size. According to Decalo, they are divided into forty clans, possess no language of their own, and in the past have adopted the languages of the people they have lived with or worked for. Indeed, in the past the neighboring ethnic groups viewed them as nothing more than slaves. They are known for their skills as tanners, shoemakers, weavers, dyers, salt miners, and ironsmiths.[9]

The Moundang

Next in size are the Moundang (sometimes erroneously classified as Sara), who have lived since the nineteenth century in southwestern Chad in the Mayo-Kebbi Prefecture (Lere Sousprefecture) and have splinter groups in Cameroon. Numbering about 138,000, they are farmers and cattle raisers and maintain a strong chief system. They have no class hierarchical structure, and those who have cattle use the Fulani as their herders. The Hadjerai ("the stone people"), about 133,900 in number, practice agriculture for their livelihood and live in the hills between Mongo and Melfi in the Guera Prefecture. Although they were settled in Chad as far back as the sixteenth century, they have never been unified, and they took refuge in the mountains against Muslim slave raiders. Consequently, they resisted conversion to Islam for a long time. The Dionkor, the Dangaleat, the Bidion, and Yalna are sometimes considered by some ethnographers as clans of the Hadjerai. Next in number are the Bulala (and their kin Kuka), about 123,200 strong, who live near Lake Filtri and Massacory, in Oum-Hadjer, which at one point controlled Kanem, Baguirmi, and Wadai. After they lost their power, they settled around Yao (Bornu).

The Toper

The Toper (Tubbier, Tupuri), perhaps 115,500 today, surround Lakes Fianga and Tiken, where they have lived since the sixteenth century. They are fishermen and are considered to be good warriors, having fought incessantly against the intruding Fulani centuries ago. The little-known Dadjo (about 100,000 in number) seem to have come from Darfur and dominated the kingdom of Wadai during the fifteenth century. They have intermarried heavily with the Maba, the Arabs, and the Hadjerai Kinga and can be found today in Chad, Dar Sila, and near Mongo, in Goz-Beida. The Kanembu (or the Beriberi), 92,000, are closely related to the Tubu Daza in language and culture and live primarily between Lake Chad and parallel 14. They consider Mao (the ancient kingdom's capital) their city, although they have become so intermixed with other ethnic groups (the Bulala, the Kotoko, the Tunjur, the Ouled Sliman, and the Haddad) that it is hard to find a true Kanembu today, except perhaps for the Magumi clan.

The Massa

The Massa, or Banana, belonging to the Nilotic group, seem to be related to the Toper. They live primarily in the Mayo-Kebbi Prefecture, especially in the Bongor Sousprefecture, where they settled during the seventeenth or eighteenth century, and perhaps are as few as 77,000. Their habitat was quite often devastated by the incursions of slave raiders from Bornu, Adamawa, and Baguirmi. Also worth mentioning are the Massalit (divided into major clans—the Massalit el Hauch and the Massalit el Batha, on the Batha River, of Wadai, who were originally from Darfur and who number fewer than 74,000 today).

The Barma

The Barma, who number about 53,900, are known as the founders of the kingdom of Baguirmi, which emerged in central Chad during the sixteenth century. They have intermingled with Sara, Kanuri, Fulani, and Massa, making it difficult to find a pure Barma nowadays. Also known as Damaky and Makwade (meaning vultures), they live along the river Chari, around Massenya (the former Baguirmi capital), in Melfi, Madiago, and north of Mandjafa. They are essentially agriculturalists and speak a language known as Tar Barma. They are known for their enslavement of the Sara and other non-Muslim southern populations. The Fulani seem to have arrived in Chad via Kanem by the end of the fifteenth century. If they live a semisedentary life—they are basically pastoralists—they can be found in the Chari-Baguirmi and Mayo-Kebbi Prefectures; they number fewer than 49,280 at present. They are aristocratic, founded several centralized kingdoms in Nigeria, Cameroon (Adamawa being a good example), and other parts of West and Central Africa and devastated Kanem during the eighteenth and nineteenth centuries. In the past, they relied heavily on slave labor. They are also known as Peul and Fellata or Bororo (when they are nomadic).

The Mubi

The Mubi (38,500 in number), live east of Abou Teflan in the Oum-Hadjer Sousprefecture and are remembered for having sparked the revolt against the government of Tombalbaye in 1965. The Zaghawa number about 30,600 at present and live in northern Chad, Biltine, eastern Chad, Wadai, and Sudan. They are closely related to the Teda, Daza, and Kanuri but sometimes have been classified as Arabs, although only a minority of them speak Arabic. The Buduma, whose largest clan are the Yedina (of the Massacory Sousprefecture), number 30,800 and are known as fishermen who use well-built canoes and as animal breeders; they have not converted to Islam or Christianity. They live primarily around Lake Chad in the Bol Sousprefecture and may have moved there during the fifteenth century.

The Bedeyat

The Bedeyat, the closest kin to the Zaghawa (fewer than 30,000 today), are found around Fada (Ennedi). They combine pastoralism with some agriculturalism. The Zaghawa practice transhumance even when they settle as agriculturalists. It is interesting how they have reversed the roles commonly assigned to men and women in most of Africa. Among them, women engage in hunting with spears and nets, food gathering, and blacksmithing; men hunt with rifles and raise live-stock.[10] The Kotoko, another small group (10,780), claim to have descended from the Sao and used to dwell in stoneless walled cities or principalities (the most re-membered being the Gulfeil in Cameroon). They can be found along the Chari and Logone Rivers and around Lake Chad, but they reside primarily in Cameroon and Nigeria, numbering altogether fewer than 45,000. They fish and own cattle. However, their cattle are tended by Arabs. In the past, they considered everyone else a potential slave. Even today, the Kotoko exact all kinds of tributes or taxes from anyone passing through "their" territory or using farming land or pasture.

The list of ethnic groups could go on, but the remaining communities in the country are small and not well known, although together they may number as many as 993,839. This section can be concluded by pointing out that the diversity of ethnic groups, languages, and social structures make Chad a complex place and, therefore, a state extremely difficult to govern.

Education

Before the introduction of colonialism in Chad, Islamic schools in the North and the East, patterned after those in North Africa, provided some education based primarily on the study of Islam and Arabic; the urban mosque was the center of learning. In Wadai, for example, from the seventeenth century to the nineteenth century, only adults and overwhelmingly males (older than nineteen years) could attend the *masjid*, or mosque school. It was not until after 1805 under Sultan Sabun that these schools were expanded.

The mosque school was led by *imams* who often taught theology at the mosque and at times recruited learned scholars—the *ulema*, also known, depending on the location, as the *faki*. These scholars taught Islam, jurisprudence, and related subjects such as interpretations of the Koran, the traditions and sayings of the Prophet, oratory, the biography of the Prophet, and Arabic grammar.[11] Children were exposed to some reading, wrote on the small portable chalkboards, and repeated over and over the words of the *suratas* in Arabic. At age nine, they would tackle the more complex *suratas* and the *isipes* and were considered experts after mastering sixty of them.

If a student wished to be a *marabout* (Muslim cleric), he would be subject to several examinations and interrogations. If he performed well, he was given the title of *goni* (master of the Koran), primarily because of his proven ability to recite the sacred scriptures by memory. Critics such as Issa Khayar and Adoum Mbaioso point out, however, that this type of education made the student passive, stifled intellectual initiative and inquisitiveness, emphasized memorization, fostered submissiveness to teachers and parents, and perpetuated the centuries-old feudal relationships that have complicated Chad's road to nationhood.

In southern Chad, informal non-Islamic traditional techniques (experience, admonition, storytelling, and observation) generally guaranteed the transmission of knowledge and values from one generation to the next. Among certain ethnic groups, as was the case among the Sara, formal initiation rites lasting from two to eight weeks were performed. Initiation assured the community that children would learn from the elders in a proper environment the social responsibilities and the values they were expected to maintain throughout their lives and transmit to their children. Such rites of passage were known among the Sara as *yondo,* or *tol ndo* (literally meaning to die socially and be reborn), and the youngsters would be bound to each other forever through special swearing rituals and a secret language.

Sex education was extremely important and remained tied to clitoridectomy and circumcision (said to have been introduced by Arab culture and Islam). This aspect of the initiation rites brought the youngsters closer to one another and made anyone else not circumcised "worthless" and "impure" in the eyes of both males and females. Indeed, even today, we are told circumcised children tend to gather and play together and examine each other, looking at and bragging about the dimensions and "superiority" of their circumcised penises. Among the Barma and Maba (who permit premarital sex), actual practice of sexual acts was expected of the girls as preparation for pleasing their future husbands.[12]

The arrival of the French did little to change the educational conditions under Islam in the North, but to a certain degree it revolutionized the South, as shown further on. It is obvious that a discussion of Western education in Africa in general, and Chad in particular, faces some major problems. As is common in Africa, Chad's statistical data on education are either incomplete or inaccurate. Furthermore, the civil war has put in doubt practically every figure on education from 1979 to 1984. Yet notwithstanding the shortcomings, trends in education in the country are discernible and some generalizations are possible.

Western education was formally introduced in the colony during the 1920s when the government built the first schools for Africans, which by 1925 received complete funding from the colonial state. Private schools, initiated by Protestant ministers and Catholic missionaries with some government support, were introduced in the South in 1921 and 1925, respectively.

During the mid-1960s, the number of schoolchildren between the ages of six and eight years rose to 17 percent (compared to 1.4 percent during the 1950–1959 period). During the colonial period, practically no girls went to school, but there have been dramatic changes ever since. In 1989, for instance, 33 percent of school-aged children attended school, 46 percent of the male and 19 percent of the female children. Chad's literacy rate for 1990 stood at 30 percent, males accounting for 42 percent and females for 18 percent of the total.[13] That year, total public and private primary school enrollment reached 57 percent among the school-age children (79 percent for boys and 35 percent for girls). For the country's secondary schools, however, the figures were less impressive; only 7 percent of the eligible students (12 percent for boys and 3 percent for girls) were enrolled.[14]

Education is compulsory for at least eight years, roughly from ages six to fourteen years. Primary (or elementary) school begins at the age of six and lasts for six years; secondary education begins at age twelve and lasts through age seventeen and is divided into the first and second cycles, lasting four and three years, respectively. The French had only a limited purpose in educating the Africans: prepare them to serve as assistants, interpreters, clerks, and teachers. In fact, French education was not only limited but discriminated against certain sectors of society. A former colonial administrator of the BET Prefecture stressed that special schools existed for the education of sons of chiefs only.[15]

Since independence, the government's effort to accelerate the rate of literacy in the country can be seen in the budget allocated for public education, which remained above 10 percent of the total budget in the 1960s. Incidentally, this amount has certainly been inadequate compared to the country's educational needs. During the 1960s and early 1970s, it averaged about 12 percent of the country's annual expenditures (14 percent in 1963, 11 percent in 1969, 9 percent in 1970). More recently, official expenditure estimates on education have remained between 7 percent and 11.9 percent ($2,297,200 in 1975 and $4,099,374 in 1983).[16] Educational expenditures amounted to 35.2 million French francs in 1977, having declined to 7.1 million French francs in 1980 and to 2.1 million French francs in 1984.

In 1921, there were only ten schools in the country, all of them primary-level institutions. By 1986, the number had risen to 1,650 and in 1989, to 1,868. The number of primary schools rose from 10 in 1921 to 154 in 1958 to 1,243 in 1975 and to 1,331 in 1987. The number of secondary schools jumped from one (in N'Djamena) in 1945 to 29 in 1965 and to 61 by 1986. Primary school teachers numbered approximately 2,136 in 1965, 2,512 in 1975, and 7,327 by 1989; in the secondary school system the number of teachers increased from 331 in 1965 to 1,422 in 1989. It is worth emphasizing that until 1942, there was no secondary school in Chad, and students had to go to Brazzaville, the capital of French Equatorial Africa, to further their studies.

In fairness to Chad, however, it must be said that relatively speaking, enrollment figures have been phenomenal. On the elementary level, the numbers stood at 55–60 in 1921, 53,479 in 1958, 178,699 in 1968, and 202,180 in 1976.[17] Secondary school enrollments went from zero in 1921 to 753 in 1958, 7,992 in 1966, 15,501 in 1976, and 58,000 in 1989. The University of Chad admitted its first students in 1971–1972; its enrollment went from 200 then to 1,046 in 1978 and 2,983 in 1989 (to be reduced to 1,643 by 1995), with a teaching staff of 25 in 1972, 141 in 1984, and 329 in 1989 (reduced again to 141 by 1995). The educational system was strengthened by an increase in the number of teacher-training institutes, from 3 in 1965 to 18 in 1988. The enrollment figures include students in private schools (mainly mission schools), the latter registering some 20,360 students in 1965. Chad has also built several vocational schools, and three of them were functioning in 1983 (at Sarh, N'Djamena, and Moundou) with a student population of 1,490. (Unfortunately, Chad has not provided the UN with any school figures for the post-1989 period.)

The Muslim North systematically refused to be "contaminated" by Western culture, and there were instances in which parents would send the children of their slaves to school rather than their own sons and daughters. Thus, for example, in 1950, there were fewer than 50 students of Muslim parents in Abeche, whereas 700 were attending the Am Sougou Koranic school (at a mosque). Consequently, it took much convincing from the leaders at Abeche to allow the French to build a secular secondary school at this Wadai capital—the Collège Franco-Arabe in 1952—as well as the École Mohamed Illech in 1968. In order to be acceptable, the schools had to adopt a curriculum that taught Arabic and the Koran.

During the mid-1960s, the North-South imbalance in the literacy rate was clear: 6.3 percent in BET, 5.3 percent in Kanem, 3.8 percent in Batha, 2.8 percent in Biltine, 3.8 percent in Wadai, and 14.6 percent in Salamat, contrasted with 22.6 percent in Chari-Baguirmi, 28.7 percent in Guera, 28.9 percent in Mayo-Kebbi, 40.5 percent in Tandjile, 55 percent in Moyen-Chari, 58.4 percent in Logone Oriental, and 61.4 percent in Logone Occidental.[18]

The Tombalbaye regime—sometimes willingly but often unwillingly—was unable to change this historical imbalance. The ability to speak French became an important vehicle to gain employment in the civil service sector and elsewhere because until the 1980s, French was the only official language in the country. Notwithstanding the problems, in the primary school, Chad has not lagged much behind other African countries on enrollment, as the progression figures among school-age children since the 1970s indicate: 35 percent in 1970, 38 percent in 1978, 50 percent in 1988, and 57 percent in 1990. Unfortunately, on the secondary level, the record is dismal: 2 percent (among potential attendees) in 1970, 3 percent in 1974, 6 percent in 1984, 6 percent in 1988, and 7 percent in 1990. The rate of females attending primary school has increased since 1970, although at a very slow pace: 17 percent (among primary-school-age children) in 1970, 18 percent in 1974, 21 percent in 1984, 29 percent in 1987, and 35 percent in 1989.[19]

As in most of Africa, population increases and shrinking resources will make the provision of education to everyone extremely difficult. Indeed, it was estimated that Chad's population would reach the 7,337,000 mark by the year 2000 and 9,491,000 around 2010, an increase of 67.2 percent between 1990 and 2010. In 1975-1976, out of the five hundred teachers employed in the *lycées* and *collèges* (high schools), three hundred were expatriates (mainly French), and 50 percent of the teachers in both categories—expatriates and nationals—had no professional training. Classrooms have always been crowded at a ratio of 90 students per teacher in many subprefectures. In the secondary schools, there have been more student candidates than the system is able to accommodate. Between 1973 and 1976, for example, there were at least 3,000 candidates but only 1,000 could be admitted. Failure and grade repetition have at times reached alarming proportions: 55,515 male repeats and 18,784 female repeats in 1976, for a total of 74,299 out of 202,180 elementary school students.[20]

Undoubtedly, Chad's performance on the elementary level has been impressive, and in that respect it has been better than the record of some other francophone African countries such as Burkina Faso, Mali, and Niger.[21] But for a poor country where the few resources available are being earmarked primarily for the maintenance of the country's independence from foreign intervention as well as to keep ambitious leaders in power, the educational challenges will remain quite significant.

Health Care

As a poor nation with a GDP slightly above $1 billion, Chad's human and environmental development are characterized by a low life expectancy, high infant mortality, low caloric intake, high incidence of diseases, low ratio of physicians to population, lack of safe drinking water, low per capita income, high levels of deforestation, and degradation of physical resources.

The profile of living conditions depicts a disheartening level of human deprivation. In 1985–1987, 2.7 million Chadians lived below the poverty line. Urban crowding has also become a major problem, as 30 percent of the population live in the city. Besides an inhospitable climate almost everywhere in the country, Chad suffers from numerous tropical diseases that continue to cause a high death toll. It is generally agreed that one of the major changes brought about by colonialism in Africa was the introduction of Western medicine. In Chad, the colonial administration took this initiative during the 1920s. Because of the few advances made by biomedicine in the treatment of most tropical diseases at the time, however, the low priority given to Africans' health care, and the new physical and social environment that transformed endemic diseases into epidemics, Chadian Africans went through a trying period of disease, death, depopulation, and migration between 1890 and 1940, as the following brief discussion illustrates.

The health areas that improved impressively between 1929 and 1946 were the numbers of nurses, consultations, and vaccinations given to the population. The increase in vaccinations corresponded to an equal increase in mobile units, especially in the fight against sleeping sickness, smallpox, and meningitis. In fact, as early as 1916, Dr. Eugène Jamot had already introduced vaccination mobile units in Equatorial Africa, including units along the Logone River in Chad. Sleeping sickness, or trypanosomiasis, is a major health problem in West and Central Africa today, affecting some thirty-two countries and exposing 45 million people annually on the continent, with 100,000 affected in Chad.[22] Epidemics of deadly sleeping sickness seem to have occurred in Chad, particularly in Moyen-Chari, the two Logones, and part of Chari-Baguirmi almost every year since 1906. Until 1916, almost all patients died because no cure or vaccination existed. Medical reports and eyewitness accounts indicate that anywhere from one-third to two-thirds of the sick succumbed to the disease.

The early work of French doctors against trypanosomiasis was so intense—and therefore so commendable—that it deserves the reader's attention. Most doctors, including M. Bouillez (working in 1914 at Fort-Archambault) and M. Kerander (working as early as 1906–1907), are of the opinion that the disease did not exist in the Moyen-Chari Prefecture prior to 1905 or that if it did, it was so confined that its effect was minimal. As described by Milleliri and Tirandibaye, the first case in the South was detected in 1914 in a woman who was found dying in the bush and was taken to Fort-Archambault. Thereafter, some 150 cases were diagnosed, prompting Dr. Eugène Jamot (the "conqueror" of sleeping sickness, as the two epidemics experts call him) to travel to Moissala from Oubangui-Chari in 1920. Relentlessly, the fight against the disease went on, achieving its major success in the period 1920–1927—the "golden age" in the fight against sleeping sickness.

In mobile clinic teams of six or ten, dedicated personnel traveled everywhere in the southern countryside, often walking thirty to forty miles a day (interrupting their rounds one or two months at a time), carrying one microscope, diagnosing the inhabitants, and distributing Atoxyl to the patients. The administration of drugs to patients had to be done carefully, and Jamot had an unhappy incident in 1923 that involved one of his assistants who overdosed patients with tryparsamide received from the Rockefeller Foundation. The mistake blinded seven hundred patients.[23]

People with confirmed cases were given zinc cards to carry around their necks for identification and further visits. A quarantine area (*camp de ségregation*) and several consultation and treatment posts were created throughout the region. In Moyen-Chari, however, cases of infection reached new heights. In Namle, Balmani, and Yngue, for example, the rate of infection stood at 35.7 percent, 43.75 percent, and 42.85 percent, respectively, in 1921.[24] In 1926, 2,901 new cases were diagnosed as positive: 1,251 men, 1,307 women, and 397 children.

Consequently, the French government put more resources into the fight, creating in 1929 the Service de Prophylaxie de la Maladie du Sommeil, based in

Brazzaville, for all French Equatorial Africa. It was directed by Dr. Muraz with Moyen-Chari receiving special attention in Sector 3 from the clinic. To its credit, Sector 3 examined a record number of people in 1930: 197,617 people diagnosed, of whom 1,991 were pronounced infected, bringing the rate of infection in the region to 3.1 percent. Several Europeans also succumbed to the disease, including missionaries. A Catholic mission located at Kou had to be abandoned in 1932 on order of the French authorities. According to Father Alcantara, the superior of the mission, Father Herriau, Father Weiss, and the Reverend Denis, a religious brother, all fell sick, and all three had to return to France. Many children and cattle died during the epidemic.

In 1944, a reorganization to upgrade the services hurt by World War II and to combat other diseases, particularly leprosy, took place with the establishment of the Services Généraux d'Hygiène et de Prophylaxie. Again, Moyen-Chari received special attention under Sector 17. As a result of these efforts, the number of newly detected cases fell to 364 in 1953, 59 in 1955, and 150 in 1967, partially because of a new drug, Arsobal, being used then. To the dismay of many researchers and epidemiologists, however, sleeping sickness still affects people in Chad today. In southern Chad, endemic foci of human trypanosomiasis caused by the *T. gambiense* and *T. rhodesiense* could still be found in the 1970s, namely in Logones Oriental and Occidental and in Moyen-Chari. As recently as 1989, for example, 2,947 agglutination card tests from preschool children and adults in Moissala confirmed nineteen cases of sleeping sickness.[25]

Meningitis epidemics competed fiercely with trypanosomiasis for victims. From 1928 to 1938 reported cases of deaths reached ten thousand. Considering that most cases were not reported and basing the estimates on the opinion of Dr. Ledentu, working in situ at the time, over twelve thousand people died in a period of ten years—about 1.2 percent of the population of Chad. In Doba alone, about 3 percent of the inhabitants were buried in 1938. Even today, Chad remains a potential breeding ground for meningitis, a disease that at times has been brought into the country by immigrants or transients such as pilgrims returning from Mecca. This happened in 1988, when a deadly epidemic of Neisseria meningococcal spread from Ethiopia to Saudi Arabia (or vice-versa) to Sudan and finally to Chad. Between February 2 and May 1, 1988, there were 4,542 cases registered in N'Djamena alone with a citywide infection rate of 0.9 percent.[26] Chad is also located in Africa's "meningitis belt," which since the 1940s has had a cyclic group A meningococcal meningitis epidemic every eight to fourteen years.

Prior to the 1970s, smallpox epidemics also decimated thousands of people, particularly children. In 1925 alone, about 3.3 percent of the prefecture of Moyen-Chari disappeared as a result of the fierceness of this disease. In some localities, the epidemic was so severe that commercial intercourse was stopped and frontiers with neighboring countries closed. Fortunately, during the 1970s, the disease was eliminated altogether, but measles has continued to afflict a high number of children—as much as 60 percent of those under age five in some villages. In 1977, at least 12,420 cases of measles with 460 accompanying deaths were recorded in the N'Djamena Central Hospital and other health facilities in the country.[27]

During the colonial period, venereal diseases seem to have been widespread in Chad, especially in the North. But in the South, the situation grew alarmingly severe according to contemporary medical reports. Recent studies (1992) by the World Health Organization in Central Africa, including Chad, have confirmed the resurgence of endemic treponematoses (which cause yaws, endemic syphilis, or *bejel,* and pinta). Malaria is the number-one ailment affecting Chadians, particularly in the southern part of the country, where it is hyperendemic. A 1970 study concluded that diarrhea and intestinal parasitic diseases are also quite frequent in Chad and remain, of course, as Buck notes, associated with poverty. His study of five villages revealed a relatively high rate of diarrhea within the twenty-four-hour period preceding his team's interviews with the villagers: 63 percent in Djimtilo, 31.1 percent in Ouli Bangala, 16.3 percent in Ouari, 8.6 percent in Boum Khebir, and 34.5 percent in Faya-Largeau.[28]

Schistosomiasis (bilharziasis) transmitted through infected water, mainly by *S. hematobium* and *S. mansoni,* ranks second in incidence after malaria in Africa and constitutes a major health problem in Chad. Buck's survey of the five villages just mentioned found that the "highest percentage of urine specimens with *ova* of *S. hematobium* was found in ten- to fourteen-year-old children" but decreased as the children matured. A 1988 study in three schools in Chad (Tikem, Youe, and Abeche) revealed serious cases of schistosomiasis among the students aged seven to fourteen years. Altogether, 50 percent of the children were infected—60 percent at Tikem and 57 percent at Youe with very few cases at Abeche.[29] Cholera epidemics have also occurred in the country, as happened in 1977 when an outbreak affected six thousand people and caused two thousand deaths.[30] To be sure, there were other diseases that afflicted Chad only occasionally but whose impact was devastating, such as the Spanish influenza epidemic of 1918–1919. Contemporary reports suggest that fifty thousand to eighty thousand people died from it by 1919 in Chad—about fifty thousand (9 percent) in Moyen-Chari alone.[31]

During the 1960s, major strides in health care were made by the Tombalbaye regime. The health budget was increased to 6.5 percent in the 1960s and to almost 7 percent (1,126,155,000 CFA francs) of the national budget by 1977. To combat the recurrent epidemics on a number of fronts, the government expanded the N'Djamena-based Service des Grandes Endémies to comprise branches in Sarh, Moundou, Bongor, Abeche, Am-Timan, and Atic, reinforced by mobile clinics. The creation of the Social Welfare Department, which improved maternity services, led to the establishment of the National Center for Nutrition in 1963. Two years later, in 1965, the Chari-Baguirmi, the Moyen-Chari, and the Logone Occidental Prefectures opened new departments of student hygiene. With assistance from the Peace Corps, the School of Government Nurses opened in N'Djamena in 1968.

Yet the health situation needed further improvement, as Chad still had in the late 1960s no more than 2 Chadian-born doctors, 4 health inspectors, 61 medical technicians, 1 licensed midwife, 94 registered nurses, 445 practical nurses, and 180 auxiliary personnel. The French did make a difference, nevertheless, through the presence of their 53 physicians (most military, though), 2 pharmacists, 5 dentists, 28 nurses, 8 midwives, 3 health inspectors, and 3 auxiliary personnel. By 1977, the situation had improved, as 100 doctors and 1,000 nurses provided services in the country and changed the ratio of doctor to population from 0.24:100,000 to 6.7:100,000.

In spite of the ravages of war, Chad had five hospitals in the 1980s (with the addition of one at the Mayo-Kebbi Prefecture), eighteen medical centers, twenty infirmaries, a hundred-twenty-seven dispensaries, and twenty social centers (one in every prefecture, except in the war-torn Borkou-Ennedi-Tibesti, plus eight leprosaria, sixteen sanitation posts, nine social centers, six major endemic disease sectors and two subsectors, and 3,500 beds attended by ninety-four physicians.[32] These services were reinforced by the existence of five private hospitals, three private medical centers, seven maternities, and thirty-nine dispensaries, owned for the most part by religious organizations. Altogether, seventy-five private facilities provided a total hospital capacity of 4,200 beds in the entire country.[33]

As a result of improvements in health care and the temporary cessation of hostilities during the 1980s, Chad's infant mortality rate fell from 180 to 200 per thousand live births in 1974 to 144 per thousand, and the doctor-to-population ratio improved to 1 per 41,900 in 1988. Life expectancy at birth was 29 years for men and 35 for women in 1964 (37 in the North, 29 in the South, and 33 in urban areas). By 1983, however, the rate had risen to 39.8 and 42.8 for males and females, respectively; this figure has jumped to 43.9 years for males and 47.1 for females during the 1990s.[34]

Unfortunately, typhoid, tuberculosis, pneumonia, whooping cough, measles, poliomyelitis, malaria, and tetanus continue to be the major child-killer diseases, most of which can either be prevented through immunization or treated effectively with modern medicine. Regrettably, immunization of children in Chad has received low priority, as illustrated by the country's polio immunization effort. On this score, Chad has the lowest immunization figure, 1.1 percent, in Africa. Lack of adequate immunization efforts accounted for Chad's continuing high infant mortality rate of 124.6 per thousand live births in 1992.[35]

In 1987, given the precarious condition of its health care facilities, Chad also had one of the highest mortality rates on the globe—about 23 deaths per thousand per year compared with 10 worldwide. The overall effect of morbidity has, of course, many other unpleasant effects. Ironically, diseases in Chad have not prevented a relatively high rate of births. High birth rates have led to an increasingly younger population in the country—about 44 percent are under fifteen years old with only 2 percent being over sixty-four years in 1987. Unfortunately, a survey conducted for USAID in 1985 found that Chad has neither instituted a primary health care program nor sustained family and maternal planning programs.[36] Chad also ranked among the lowest in health services accessibility. Only 31 percent of Chadians have had access to sanitary water, 14.5 percent to adequate sanitary facilities, and 30 percent to health care services between 1987 and 1990.

Finally, malnutrition is still a major problem in Chad, often aggravated by recurrent droughts, as happened in the periods 1969–1974 and 1984–1985. In 1985, a team of government personnel in Chad, USAID, Doctors Without Frontiers, and other international organizations conducted a survey of seven settlements of people displaced by the drought and found the health conditions appalling: Levels of acute undernutrition ranged from 8 percent to 67 percent among children between the ages of one and five.[37]

On a brighter note, it would appear that Chad is one country in Africa where the AIDS epidemic has not yet taken much hold. The government reports that there were only two cases detected in 1982, seven in 1988, ten in 1989, and fourteen in 1990. It is doubtful, however, that these figures approximate the reality, particularly when one considers the number of refugees returning from neighboring countries. In fact, studies done on four Chadian cities as recently as 1989 reveal that the infections are much higher than reported and show "a preponderance of heterosexual transmissions" of the virus.

Recent studies have also stressed the progressive advance of endemic trachomatose (onchocerciasis), which has now reached parallel 12 and has spread throughout the country. It seems that no discernible progress has been made since the 1970s toward reducing the incidents of blindness in the country. In 1972, studies confirmed that about 4 percent of the people were blind; 54 percent of blindness was due to cataracts, 14 percent to glaucoma, and 9 percent to corneal obtuseness. These figures hold today. More frightening is the fact that in settlements created by the drought in 1985, about 60 percent of the children under five had conjunctivitis.[38]

In conclusion, the health care crisis facing Chad is one not simply of a commitment to the eradication of disease but also of insufficient resources made even more scarce since the late 1960s by the civil conflict. Regrettably, France, the major contributor to Chad's health budget, downsized its assistance after 1977 from 13.1 million French francs that year to 9.5 million in 1980, 9.3 million in 1981, and 4.0 million in 1984.[39] This trend continued during the 1990s. The future is, therefore, bleak, and Chad can hardly reach the goal that many developing countries have set for themselves for the year 2000, namely, providing health care for all citizens.

Religion

As is true almost everywhere in Africa, there are three major religions in Chad today: Christianity, Islam, and traditionalism. Although the regional distribution of these three religions is not disputed, the number of adherents to each faith is a matter of debate. In 1962, it was estimated that about 1,483,000 (55 percent) of Chadians were Muslims, 958,200 (35 percent) traditionalists, and 257,654 (9.5 percent) Christians.[40] These figures had changed drastically by 1966, when the percentages were 41 percent Muslim, 30 percent traditionalist, and 29 percent Christian. The latest estimate (1992), whose accuracy is still doubtful, places the number of Muslims at 44 percent, Christians at 33 percent, and traditionalists at 23 percent.[41]

The problem of classification is complicated by the fact that many who profess Islam or Christianity are in fact traditionalists who selectively embrace elements of both religions while still worshipping in the ways of their ancestors. Christianity was appealing because it was the religion of the seemingly all-powerful colonizer. It opened doors to employment and empowerment, and it guaranteed access to other modern necessities. Islam, in contrast, was attractive mainly because of its disassociation from and resistance to colonialism (especially in northern Chad), its reputed association with literacy, and its international standing as an important link to the cosmopolitan Middle Eastern world of trade and religion, highlighted by the hajj to Mecca. Yet Christianity was a close ally of Western education, and conversion remained one of the goals of the colonial state.

Christianity encountered three major obstacles in Chad. First, there was a wave of anticlericalism in France during the 1880s, precisely the time when colonization was being introduced in Central Africa. Second, French colonials, in their attempt to appease the North, discouraged the opening of any missions in that part of the colony. Third, missions in Chad remained, until the 1930s, subordinate to those in Oubangui-Chari, as this is where the missionaries had first established their headquarters. Not until March 22, 1946, were religious jurisdictions approved by the Vatican to work in Chad.

The activity of Protestants, mostly American missionaries—Baptists and Evangelicals—which began in 1920, preceded the work of the Catholic Church in Chad with the opening of several missions, health care centers, and schools at Lere, Sarh, Doba (1925), and N'Djamena (1926). Because they did not confine their work to proselytizing, the Protestant schools enrolled some 1,380 students during the mid-1960s. As Cordell notes, however, rather than allowing a local Christian tradition to develop, "the missionaries tended to preach a fundamentalist doctrine native to parts of the United States, speaking against dancing, all alcohol, and many of the local customs, which they considered 'superstitious.'"[42] They fiercely resisted the reintroduction of the *yondo* in the period 1973–1975, which led to the expulsion of several of them by the regime of Tombalbaye, himself educated in a Protestant school. The overall number of converts to Christianity in Chad has not been impressive, however. During the early 1990s, the number of Chadian Protestants was estimated at less than 150,000.

Catholic work was first introduced in Chad by the Fathers of the Holy Ghost from Oubangui-Chari, who founded a mission with a school and a hospital at Kou, near Moundou. Due to recurrent sleeping sickness epidemics that decimated hundreds of those living in the area, both were hurriedly abandoned in 1932 and moved to Doba. Priests from Oubangui-Chari also founded Kelo Mission in 1935; the Capuchin missionaries, coming from Cameroon, established themselves at Sarh in 1939 after inheriting the Doba Mission from the priests of the Holy Ghost. Thus, the number of missions grew to 10 in 1950, 30 in 1960, and 69 by 1970; the number of Catholics rose from fewer than 1,000 in 1940 to 10,000 in 1950, 54,000 in 1960, 160,000 by 1970,[43] and some 200,000 in 1994. The cathedral at N'Djamena, rebuilt from the ravages of the war during the 1980s, remains a symbol of Catholicism in the country. (Incidentally, Colonel Jean Chapelle notes that when Kadhafi visited Chad in 1974, he remarked that the Cathedral would make "a beautiful mosque.")

Catholicism in Chad has experienced other problems. First, during the colonial period, a major stumbling block against its advance was the slow pace of Africanization of the liturgy and the teaching of the Bible in a nonvernacular language. Second was the fact that the Chadian church suffered from a perennial problem in Africa, namely, the tendency not to prepare a black clergy to assume church responsibilities. This problem was magnified following independence and the departure of several missionaries during the 1970s. The church's association with colonialism also mitigated against it, and its constant attacks on the cultural practices of the Africans, such as polygamy, became an obstacle to many Africans who otherwise would have embraced the new faith. For a long time, the most successful of the Catholic dioceses in Chad remained that of Moundou, which had 154 priests (mostly white) in 1974.[44]

Islam expanded over northern, eastern, and central Chad below parallel 13, which divides Islam from Christianity and traditionalism and the pastoral from the farming lifestyles. This expansion was gradual and relatively peaceful, without requiring major jihads, and it affected primarily towns and cities rather than the rural areas in the North and the center of what is now Chad. Experts claim that conversion was facilitated by the natural and constant advance of Islamic and Middle Eastern civilization and commercial contacts between North Africa and Central Africa even where the camel was unable to travel, to use Mazrui's analogy.

J. Spencer Trimingham cites three major factors that facilitated the introduction of the faith into Chad prior to colonization: lack of natural geographical barriers between the North and the East; the fact that the Lake Chad region became a melting pot of "cultural currents"; and the impact of the nomadic Zaghawa on Kanem.[45] In many areas, as shown in Chapter 2, the expansion of Islam was influenced by the conversion of the leaders, who made it a state religion. Once the leader had been converted, the subjects usually followed suit even if there was little understanding of the new religion. The greatest force behind the expansion of Islam, however, was the work of brotherhoods (*tariqa*). The Tijaniya, as Decalo notes, was the most important brotherhood in Muslim Chad, partly because the French encouraged its growth given "its emphasis on submission to temporal authority." Today, one finds some followers of other brotherhoods including the

Sanussiya (Sunni Sufi) the Qadiriya, the Mirghaniya, and the Tarbiya (banned by Tombalbaye in 1962).

It is ironic that the Europeans helped to spread the very religion they feared. Both the British and the French viewed Muslims as culturally and educationally superior to traditionalist Africans and favored them in supervisory roles. In the southern part of Chad, the French had started a process of appointing chiefs who had converted to Islam. As many scholars of Islam in Africa have observed, with the opening of new cities, new markets, and the improvement of communications, the colonialists unwittingly "broke down the traditional structures of society, introduced new educational and social ideas, opened markets, attracted migrants to growing cities, and indirectly promoted Islam as a form of authority and as an expression of cohesion among displaced peoples."[46]

Regrettably, Islam has neither generated a coherent political agenda nor prevented infighting among the coreligionists in the North itself. From this perspective, therefore, it is inaccurate to view the civil conflict as stemming primarily from religious differences, although the role of religion cannot be ignored. The very splits within FROLINAT and the fratricidal hostilities among Habre, Gukuni, and Deby underscore the fact that Islam has played a secondary role in the civil conflict in Chad. No one has expressed this reality better than John Obert Voll:

> Primarily, FROLINAT was more of a liberation group composed of Muslims than an Islamic movement. Its programs were not distinctively Islamic in character and were aimed at giving the Muslim sections of the population appropriate influence in the government and its policymaking process. That distinction means that the Chadian civil war was a sectional struggle for power with overtones of personal religious identity rather than a religious holy war.[47]

Presently, there is some fear that Islam in Chad might acquire the fundamentalist characteristics it has recently taken on among certain followers in Egypt, Algeria, Sudan, and Libya. The threat in Chad seems to come mainly from the Sudanese border. However, it is the opinion of many observers that fundamentalism is not a threat to the stability of the Chadian state at present.

Conclusion

Chad's divergent lifestyles—which pit the nomad and livestock breeder against the sedentary agriculturalist and fisherman, the entrepreneur Arab against the leisure-loving Kotoko—have fostered and nurtured distinct identities that decades of colonialism and independence have been unable to reconcile. The traditional social and regional structures are likewise difficult to overcome and have, for centuries, pitted the aristocratic North against the quasi-egalitarian South. Religion, especially Islam, more than anywhere else in Africa except perhaps in Sudan, has remained more of a divisive than a uniting force between North and South. Northerners, still living in feudal societies and by and large refusing manual labor, enslaved the South. Unfortunately, this enslavement was carried out in the name of religion—for the Sharia allowed slavery over the *kirdi* of the *dar-es-bila,* or the "pagans," in the land of the slaves—and carved a regional and religious wedge.

The colonial interlude, even if it had been an earnest effort to amalgamate the various peoples and regions, was bound to fail, since it was carried out by a foreign occupier who had little in common with the region's traditional societies and cultures. To be sure, the problems facing Chad today in education, health, and religious differences are, in one way or the other, experienced by many other countries in Africa. Yet in Chad, the differences have been so magnified by the centuries-old regional, ethnic, and religious violence and social ostracism that it is hard to find a parallel case on the continent. The recent political reversal in the country, in which the North dominates the South, renders the situation even more volatile than it was during the 1970s and 1980s. This is because the North is more divided within itself than the South, less educationally equipped to hold the reins of power, and less willing to use peaceful means to bring about change, as the civil conflict of the past quarter-century has clearly demonstrated.

In this chaotic situation, a glimmer of hope lies in the fact that both the North and the South have vowed to attempt to preserve Chad as one political entity, indivisible in its national territory. This commitment may counteract any tendencies by ambitious self-serving leaders to pursue blatant regional, ethnic, and religious policies. As the national crisis continues to unfold, however, it is doubtful that the present leadership can solve the national social problems entirely. Indeed, the advances in education and health, characteristic of the Tombalbaye regime during the 1960s, have been reversed.

Notes

1. Jean *Chapelle, Le peuple tchadien* (Paris: Harmattan, 1980), 40; *World Almanac* (New York: Press Publication Company, 1993), 741; and Donald G. Morrison, Robert Cameron Mitchell, and John Naber Paden, *Understanding Black Africa: Data and Analysis of Social Change and Nation-Building* (New York: Paragon House and Irvington, 1989), 412.

2. See one of the most extensive studies of Chadian languages in Barbara Grimes, ed., *Ethnologue,* vol. 1 (Austin Tex.: Summer Language Institute, 1992), 215–229.

3. Anthony Arkell, *A History of the Sudan from the Earliest Times to 1821* (London: Athlone Press, 1961), 194; and Richard Grey, "Christian Traces and a Franciscan Mission in Central Sudan, 1700–1711," *Journal of African History* 8, no. 3 (1967): 383–393.

4. Dennis Cordell, *Dar al Kuti and the Last Years of the Transaharan Slave Trade* (Madison: University of Wisconsin Press, 1985), 25.

5. George Schweinfurth, *The Heart of Africa* (London: Sampson Low, Marston and Searle, 1873), 413.

6. Mario Azevedo, "Power and Slavery in Central Africa," *Journal of Negro History* 67, no. 3 (Fall 1982): 206–297.

7. Samuel Decalo, *Historical Dictionary of Chad* (Metuchen, N.J.: Scarecrow Press, 1987), 181.

8. Christian Bouquet, *Tchad: Genèse d'un conflit* (Paris: Harmattan, 1982), 45–46; and Jean Cabot et Christian Bouquet, *Le Tchad* (Paris: Presses Universitaires de France, 1973), 31–37.

9. Decalo, *Historical Dictionary,* 144.

10. Marie-Joseph Tubiana and Joseph Tubiana, *The Zaghawa from an Ecological Perspective* (Rotterdam: A. A. Balkema, 1977), 31.

11. Issa H. Khayar, *Les refus de l'école: Contribution à l'étude des problèmes de l'éducation chez les musulmans du Ouaddai (Tchad)* (Paris: Librairie d'Amérique et d'Ouest, 1976), 56. Many of the following remarks on Islamic schools are derived from this unique source.

12. Adoum Mbaiosso, *L'éducation au Tchad: Bilan, problèmes et perspectives* (Paris: Karthala, 1990), 73, 74, 78, 89–90. Much of the information on traditional education is taken from this source.

13. Europa Publishers, *Africa: South of the Sahara* (London: Europa, 1993), 268.

14. Ibid.

15. Chapelle, *Le peuple tchadien,* 231.

16. *Statistical Yearbook 1988–1989* (New York: UN Department of Economics and Social Development Statistical Office, 1980), 127; and Cordell, "Society and Environment," in Collelo, ed., *Chad: A Country Study* (Washington, DC: U.S. Government Printing Office, 1990), 78.

17. Figures on education are scattered throughout different sources. For more details, consult Mbaiosso, *L'éducation au Tchad;* Khayar, *Le refus del'école;* Chapelle, *Le peuple tchadien;* Nelson et al., *Area Handbook for Chad* (Washington, D.C.: GPO, 1972); Azevedo, *Cameroon and Chad* (Lewiston, N.Y.: Edwin Mellen Press, 1988); *UN Yearbook;* Europa Publishers, *Africa: South of the Sahara;* and *World Encyclopedia.*

18. Henri Bassis, *Des mîtres pour une autre école: Former ou transformer* (Brussels: Casterman, 1978), 69.

19. Bouquet, *Tchad,* 178–179.

20. Ibid., 2.

21. Adama Ouane and Yvette Amon-Tanoh, "Literacy in French-Speaking Africa," *African Studies Review* 33, no. 3 (December 1990): 27.

22. J. M. Milleliri and H. N. Tirandibaye, "Historique de la trypanosomiase humaine africaine dans le Moyen-Chari (Tchad)," *Médicine Tropicale* 49, no. 4 (October-December 1989): 381.

23. For details, see John McKelvey, *Man Against Tsetse: Struggle for Africa* (Ithaca: Cornell University Press, 1952), 130–131. A historical account of epidemics in Chad is provided by Mario Azevedo, "Epidemic Disease Among the Sara of Southern Chad," 118–152, in *Disease in African History,* ed. Gerald Hartwig (Durhan, NC: Duke University Press, 1978).

24. Milleliri and Tirandibaye, "Historique," 383.

25. A. Stanghellini, P. Catan, N. Tirandibaye, P. Emery, J. M. Milleliri, and G. Cordoliani, "Epidemiological Aspects of Human African Trypanosomiasis in South Chad," *Médicine Tropicale* 49, no. 4 (October-December 1989): 395–400; J. M. Milleliri, H. N. Tirandibaye, and B. Nana-Madjoum, "The Focus of Human African Trypanosomiasis in Moissala (Chad): Prospective Study of Sixteen Villages Using the Direct Card Agglutination Test (Testtryp CATT) and the Ion Exchange Mini-Column (MAECT)," *Médicine Tropicale* 49, no. 3 (July-September 1989): 253–258.

26. See Patrick Moore, John Hierholzer, Walis DeWitt, Koulienga Gouant, Dezoumbe Djore, Theo Lippeveld, Brian Plikayis, and Claire V. Broome, "Respiratory Viruses and Mycloplasma as Cofactors for Epidemic Group A Meningococcal Meningitis," *Journal of the American Medical Association* 264, no. 10 (September 12, 1990): 1271.

27. World Health Organization, *Evaluation of Health and the Social Situation in the Republic of Chad* (Brazzaville: WHO, 1982), 32, 82.

28. A. Mathews and G. M. Antal, "The Endemic Treponematoses: Not Yet Eradicated," *World Health Statistics* 45, no. 2–3 (1992): 228–237. Sara elders honestly held the belief that venereal diseases were introduced in Chad by French males who had contracted the diseases from French women who had intercourse with dogs.

29. P. L. Gigase, E. Mangelschots, R. Bockaert, Ph.

Autier, and L. Kestens, "Indicateurs simples de la prévalence et de l'intensité de la bilharziose urinaire au Tchad," *Annales de la Société Belge de Médicine Tropicale* 68, no. 2 (1988): 123–132.

30. WHO, *Evaluation of Health,* 32, 82.

31. See Charles M. Good, "Salt, Trade, and Disease: Aspects of Development in Africa's Northern Lakes Region," *Intercontinental Journal of African Historical Studies* 5 (August 1972): 572, on how intercommunication during the colonial period spread epidemics.

32. Cordell, "Society and Environment," 83; WHO, *Evaluation of Health,* 8; and *World Almanac* (New York: Pharos Books, 1993), 741.

33. Cordell, "Society and Environment," 84.

34. *International Marketing Data and Statistics,* 196.

35. See WHO, *Evaluation of Health,* 33–34.

36. *International Marketing,* 482.

37. MNWR, "Leads from MNWR," *Journal of the American Medical Association* 254, no. 20 (November 22–29, 1985): 2878, 2880.

38. P. Resnikoff and Yankalbe Matchock-Mahound, "Effect d'une conjonture difficile—premières mésures," *Révue Internationale du Trachome et de Pathologie* 63, no. 1–2 (1980): 133–143.

39. Michael Kelly, *A State in Disarray: Conditions for Chad's Survival* (Boulder, Colo.: Westview Press, 1986), 94.

40. Chapelle, *Le peuple tchadien,* 148–149.

41. *The World Factbook,* 68.

42. Ibid.

43. Chapelle, *Le peuple tchadien,* 161.

44. Cordell, "Society and Environment," 76.

45. John J. Spencer Trimingham, *A History of Islam in West Africa* (Oxford: Oxford University Press, 1970), 104–105.

46. Ira Lapidus, *A History of Islamic Societies* (Cambridge: Cambridge University Press, 1988), 824.

47. John Obert Voll, *Islam, Continuity and Change in the Modern World* (Boulder, Colo.: Westview Press, 1988), 261.

6

INTERNATIONAL RELATIONS

Africa's foreign policy has often been characterized as ad hoc because it was bound intricately to the personality of the presidency.[1] Since then, however, significant changes have taken place across the continent, and this is no longer true for most of the African states. Many of the regions that gained independence in the 1960s have matured and prospered; others have not fared so well. African states have been accepted since the mid-1970s as full members of the UN, where they wield considerable power. As political conditions became more settled after the 1960s, state administrators saw the wisdom of regional and international cooperation. Over time, each nation's international behavior has been influenced by its national maturity and the length of tenure of its executive. As discussed in this chapter, regional geopolitical realities and considerations have transcended individual leaders and nations. A country's foreign policy can no longer be changed suddenly or radically.

Chad and Its Neighbors:
Cameroon, Nigeria, Libya, and Sudan

Chad has had the misfortune of being surrounded by relatively powerful but often unstable and unpredictable neighbors. To the north Libya has, since the late 1960s, attempted to pursue a policy of territorial expansionism disguised in Pan-Arabic and Pan-Islamic brotherhood. Cameroon, to the south, the least unstable of all neighbors, experienced a bloody attempted military coup in 1984 and has recently been plagued by a violent rift between anglophones and francophones. In Cameroon also, an uneasy relationship exists between the Muslim North and the rest of the country, and the evolution toward democratization has not been smooth. Since the mid-1980s, Sudan, to the east, has been subjected to a series of fanatic fundamentalist autocrats who have plundered the country's resources and forced the enactment of Islamic laws simply to humiliate and subdue the Christian-traditionalist South, which has been engaged in a liberation war since the 1980s. To the southwest, Nigeria, lately a pariah state in the international arena, has experienced several quasi-religious and ethnic civil wars; its military has followed a policy of intimidation of some of its neighbors, including Cameroon and Chad.

In this section, we concentrate on Chad's neighbors that have played a significant role in its international relations and deliberately pay less attention to Niger and the Central African Republic, which have not been prominent in the conflict. The most significant determinants of Chado-Cameroonian relations are (1) the 800-kilometer (656-mile) border shared by the two countries, (2) a relatively similar colonial legacy (although Cameroon's triple colonial heritage is more complex), (3) formal and informal economic links, and (4) similar ethnic and religious problems in an important geographical region. Cameroon's foreign policy toward Chad can be traced to its first president, Ahmadou Ahidjo, and his perception of Cameroon's role in the international arena between 1960 and 1982. Ahidjo viewed African state boundaries as permanent features that guaranteed national and international peace and secured continental unity.

Consequently, for Ahidjo and for Paul Biya, his successor, northern Chad in its totality,[2] including the Aouzou Strip, was and should continue to be an integral part of the Republic of Chad. It is understandable, therefore, that when the Chadian clashes of the 1970s (see Chapter 3) intensified, Cameroon was one of the first African states to question Libya's support of FROLINAT. In addition, as a member of the OAU Conciliation Committee on the Chadian conflict since 1977, Cameroon was instrumental in establishing negotiations that led to the brief cease-fire between Félix Malloum's government and the National Liberation Front, or FROLINAT, in 1978. In a sense, throughout the 1970s and 1980s, Cameroon remained the conscience of Central Africa whenever France attempted to support moves that might result in the division of Chad along ethnic or geographical lines.

On June 15, 1979, following intensive fighting in N'Djamena among the factions of Habre, Gukuni, and Malloum, French Director at the Foreign Ministry M. Guy Georgy flew to Yaounde to suggest that talks among the factions be held there.[3] However, suspecting that the envoy might encourage secession or the formation of a federal state in Chad, Ahidjo refused to host such a conference. Although some political analysts have indicted Cameroon's policy as lacking a clear ideology and as reactive and conservative rather than proactive and progressive,[4] most others characterize it as pragmatic and constructive. Observers have pointed out that although Cameroon "had the greatest interest in a peaceful settlement of Chad's civil war" among the six states that participated in the Kano I and II and Lagos I and II Accords in 1979, its low-key approach to foreign policy forced it to be "the least censorious of Chad's transitional government, and the most disinterested."[5]

Cameroon's carefully crafted policy toward Chad has been dictated by its fear that given the political similarities between northern Chad and northern Cameroon, the conflict could spill across the border.[6] In fact, immediately after Cameroon achieved independence, religious and cultural differences surfaced. In 1961, northerners, who felt alienated, voted in a UN-sponsored plebiscite for union with Nigeria. This adverse tide was stemmed by the presence of Ahidjo, a northern Fulani Muslim, who instituted a type of "affirmative action" to gradually bring his discontented kin into Cameroon.[7] Outright northern revolt by the Presidential Republican Guard occurred only when southerner and Catholic Paul Biya assumed power following an early election victory in April 1984.

Throughout the Chadian conflict, Cameroon absolutely refused to allow any faction to use its territory as a springboard from which to destabilize whatever regime was then in power in N'Djamena. When Habre was defeated in 1979–1980 but refused to sign the Lomé cease-fire agreement of November 22, 1980, he "disarmed and interned the FAN." Ahidjo granted Habre a private audience but told him in no ambiguous terms that asylum was out of the question. Yet Cameroon has provided assistance and asylum to displaced Chadians since the beginning of Chad's civil conflict. Experts estimate that through May 26, 1980, some 200,000 Chadians had left N'Djamena and vicinity to seek refuge in Kousseri. This created real danger for Cameroon because Kousseri is less than a mile from N'Djamena, which was then a true battleground.

As fighting in Chad escalated in the 1970s and 1980s, factions multiplied and the OAU seemed impotent to resolve the conflict. Cameroon was one of the few states that advocated intervention by the UN.[8] In a 1983 interview, Biya made it clear that Cameroon's refusal to attend the OAU Tripoli Summit in 1982 was in response to Kadhafi's behavior toward Chad and his resort to military means. At that time, Biya recognized only Habre as the legitimate head of state in Chad.[9] It would be naive, of course, not to recognize that Cameroon's policy toward Chad is motivated also by economic self-interest. In 1959, the four French equatorial colonies (Gabon, Chad, Congo, and CAR, joined by Cameroon) were organized by France into a customs union known as Union Douanière et Économique de l'Afrique Centrale (UDEAC), from which Cameroon has benefited more than any other member. This prompted Tombalbaye to convince CAR president Jean-Bedel Bokassa to withdraw from the Union in 1968 and to join him in forming the Union des États de l'Afrique Centrale (UEAC). Tombalbaye is said to have been so elated with his coup de grâce against Ahidjo that he called his UEAC "an association born almost of divine thought." Overall, however, Cameroonian diplomacy toward Chad has been cautious and reserved, favoring no Chadian faction.[10]

For several reasons Nigeria has played a pivotal role in Chad's internal and international conflicts. Certain regions of the two countries share the same ethnic groups and the same religion, Islam, through which fundamentalists could play a major role in shaping this region's politics. Likewise, along with Cameroon and Niger, Chad and Nigeria share the resources of Lake Chad. Foremost, economic ties have been a major determinant in the bilateral relations of Nigeria and Chad. In fact, Nigeria has recently surpassed France as Chad's major provider of oil, industrial products, meat, and fish.

During the mid-1960s, relations between the two neighbors were cordial, and Tombalbaye, departing from French foreign policy, supported Nigerian general Yakubu Gowon's federal government and not General Emeka Ojukwu's secessionist effort during the 1967–1970 Biafran War. Accused of supporting factions in Chad, Nigeria's government has denied providing aid to the Forces Armées de l'Ouest (FAO) or FROLINAT's Third Army, which was led by Aboubakar Abdelrahmane. He allegedly received considerable military and financial support in Kanem and in Maiduguri beginning in 1977. Beyond the dispute, Nigeria acquired leverage with both the movement and with France when it put pressure on the FAO rebels to release two young European hostages it had abducted in the Lake Chad area on January 18, 1978, for whose freedom it was demanding a 500 million CFA ransom. Unfortunately, as one of the six permanent members (along with Cameroon, Senegal, Mozambique, Algeria, and Gabon) of the OAU ad hoc Conciliation Committee on Chad, established on July 2–5, 1977, Nigeria often used the committee's forums to advance its own policies on Chad.

Most memorable are the accords of Kano I and II (March 10–16, 1979, and April 7, 1979) and Lagos I and II (May 26–27, 1979, and August 14–21, 1979), which brought together Chad's several political and military factions for the establishment of a provisionary government. Kano I, attended by Malloum, Habre, and Gukuni, led to Chad's first Government of National Union in Transition (GUNT) under an unknown politician, Mahamat Lol Showa (April 29–August 29, 1979). Besides creating the GUNT, the Kano Accords mandated a cease-fire to be supervised by Nigerian troops and a 100 km demilitarized zone around N'Djamena. Lagos II (signed by eleven factions) created a second GUNT in August 1979, which led to the appointment of Gukuni Wedei as chairman and later as de facto president of Chad in November 1979. At both the Kano and the Lagos deliberations, Nigeria's diplomacy was heavy-handed, in part to placate Libya. For example, at Kano, when Gukuni and Habre refused to include in the upcoming government Libyan-sponsored candidates, Nigerian authorities held the two Chadian leaders under house arrest. It was then widely known that President Shehu Shagari of Nigeria preferred Gukuni over Habre.[11]

The March-April 1979 Kano Accords became void almost immediately because of factional disagreements, and Nigeria closed its border with Chad. Michael Kelley observes that this neighbor of Chad then went from a "moderate stance to outright arm-twisting" and that "by attempting to dictate a solution for Chad at Kano II, and Lagos I, Olusegun Obasanjo (the Nigerian military leader) lost legitimacy in the eyes of the main Chadian protagonists."[12] Apparently incensed by the fact that Habre was visibly contemptuous of General Shehu Yar' Adua, the leader of the Nigerian delegation, Nigeria changed its stance and insisted on the inclusion of Libyan protégés in the GUNT.

Following the signing of the Kano I Accord, Malloum resigned as president of Chad and sought asylum in Nigeria. Some speculate that he was simply tired of politics and others, that he was forced out by pressures from leaders of the neighboring countries, particularly Nigeria; still others claim that too much criticism and military and psychological pressures from Habre and Kamougue in particular left him no choice but to "abdicate." In any case, most Chadians distrusted Nigeria. Popular hostility toward Nigeria heightened when a contingent of Nigerian cease-fire supervisors who arrived in N'Djamena in March 1979 was said to have been so undisciplined that it behaved as an occupation force. News of the previous house arrest of the two Chadian leaders by the Nigerian authorities in Kano created such a potential for threat to the supervising contingent from Habre's and Gukuni Wedei's troops that the Nigerians were forced to leave Chad on June 4, 1979; ironically, they were protected by the French expeditionary force under General Louis Forest.[13]

One of Nigeria's most decisive measures regarding the Chadian conflict was its strong stand against Kadhafi on January 6, 1981, following announcement of a merger between Libya and Chad. As a show of force to warn Gukuni, Nigeria dispatched its fourth infantry division to Bornu, on the Chadian border. This show of force was made despite a placating visit to Lagos by the GUNT leader, who declared that the merger was not real but (using Kadhafi's words) a "union of the two peoples" and that "the integrity, unity, and sovereignty of Chad" would be safeguarded. Yet President Shagari declared that an attack on Chad would constitute an attack on Nigeria.

At the end of January 1981, Nigeria closed the Libyan embassy and called for sanctions against Libya and the withdrawal of its troops from Chadian soil. No wonder, then, that Nigeria joined the OAU peacekeeping force, which was under the command of its own General Geoffrey Ejiga, in November 1981. In spite of Nigeria's apparent good intentions, Chad was never comfortable with its neighbor's solutions; if they were not followed, there was an implicit threat to Chad's oil supply and the potential for military intervention.

Stemming from cultural and geographic affinity, the people who now constitute northern Chad have for centuries maintained close ties with the Libyans. At the turn of the twentieth century, for example, the Sanussiya Brotherhood carved a significant sphere of influence in northern Chad. Libya's claim to Chadian territory goes back only to January 4, 1935, when a secret Laval-Mussolini agreement extended Chad's border south to "a line just north of Agoza, near the Sudan border, Tekro, Yebbi Bou, and Bardai, and westward to Toummo in Niger."[14] This would have included Chad's Aouzou Strip, a piece of land 100 km long and 60 kilometers wide (some say about 96,200 square kilometers, or 114,000 square miles, in surface area.) The annexation, which was never recognized internationally, went against the 1955 border agreement between France and Italy, which upheld the 1899 boundaries. The matter gets more complicated, however: The French Senate unanimously approved the secret treaty, and the Chamber of Deputies did the same by a vote of 555 to 9; but the French president never signed it.[15] The present borders were sanctioned by the OAU in 1964.

Until 1969, Chad's northern neighbor served only as an informal training ground for the northern nationalists and was a haven for Chadian political refugees; it was not a platform from which rebels could mount attacks on Tombalbaye's regime. In the aftermath of an attempted coup in N'Djamena in August 1971, however, the late President Tombalbaye accused Colonel Kadhafi of complicity, and on September 8 he protested Libya's assistance to the rebels and its protection of the *derdei*. Tombalbaye announced then that he would openly provide refuge to anti-Kadhafi Libyans while immediately severing diplomatic relations with Libya. This move forced the colonel to reciprocate by recognizing FROLINAT as the sole representative of the Chadian people. To buttress his stand, Kadhafi offered Abba Siddick a guerrilla base in Tripoli. Thereafter, Kadhafi gave full support to the northern rebels, supplying them with arms, vehicles, and advisers with the explicit intent of toppling the regime in N'Djamena, all the while calling Tombalbaye an "Israeli agent."[16] Yet when Tombalbaye broke diplomatic relations with Israel in 1972, Libya and Chad resumed their diplomatic ties and signed a pact of friendship under Niger's auspices.

In reward, Libya promised Chad an aid package of $920 million, a promise that was hardly carried out, although Kadhafi provided a loan of 23,000 million CFA for several industrial projects and established a Chado-Arab bank in N'Djamena. Unfortunately for Chad, Kadhafi had already reinforced his troops around the Aouzou Strip, which he had occupied in 1972, and later fortified it with ground-to-air missiles. Some observers think that the annexation occurred with Tombalbaye's consent; many others disagree, and the Chadian president himself denied the allegation at a party congress in April 1974.

Indeed, Bernard Lanne argues that if a secret treaty had been signed, the Libyans would have produced the document at the OAU 1977 meeting in Libreville, where they were condemned for the annexation. Lanne concludes emphatically: "In our opinion, there has never been a treaty of cession, neither secret nor public."[17] The most plausible explanation seems to be that Tombalbaye and his regime could do nothing to stop Kadhafi from occupying the strip. The annexation contributed indirectly to the civil war in Chad because it created a major rift between Habre and Gukuni. Gukuni and Habre, leaders of the Second, or the Northern, Army of FROLINAT (operating in Tibesti and Borkou), wrestled with the issue. Whereas Habre urged nationalists to challenge Libya's occupation of any parcel of Chadian territory, Gukuni thought they should leave the issue alone and concentrate on one enemy at that time: Tombalbaye.

In fairness to Gukuni, it appears that he never approved the annexation of Aouzou. Even when he was receiving Libyan assistance, Gukuni told the press:

"We have not changed our position regarding the occupation of Aouzou. In fact, we have denounced it repeatedly. If today we cede some territory to Libya, tomorrow maybe we will give some to Sudan, and then what will be left of Chad?"[18] Malloum criticized Kadhafi's "conqueror's appetite" and protested his assistance to Gukuni Wedei's forces. Shortly thereafter, on February 23, 1978, and March 24, 1978, Malloum suffered severe humiliation when he was forced to fly to Sebha to negotiate a cease-fire agreement arranged mainly by Kadhafi and his protégés, marking the first time since the rebellion began in 1966 that the government met officially with representatives of FROLINAT.

What were Libya's intentions? Colonel Kadhafi revealed his true objectives for Chad when he forced Gukuni's representatives in Tripoli to sign a treaty of friendship and cooperation on June 15, 1980. The treaty allowed the immediate airlifting of two hundred Libyan soldiers (four thousand, according to some sources) who were flown to N'Djamena through Maiduguri airport December 8–14, 1980, to fight Habre. Eventually, Libya assembled a force of a thousand Islamic Legionnaires, five or six armored companies of between fifty and sixty Soviet-supplied T-54 and T-55 tanks, and six hundred Libyans, some "carrying multiple rocket launchers and eighty-one mortars." They were reinforced by Gukuni's FAP and Kamougue's FAT *codos* and by several East German and Soviet advisers. Dougia, a base the French had evacuated some forty miles from N'Djamena, was occupied by Libyan "guest" forces.

The real political bombshell was yet to come. On January 6, 1981, following Gukuni Wedei's state visit to Tripoli, Chad and Libya announced a merger. Reaction from African capitals, particularly Lagos, was swift and negative; the two signatories were forced to declare that their agreement was nothing more than an initial move toward a future merger. It was just "a partnership," in the words of Gukuni, who added that the Libyans were simply "invited guests." Intimidation and promises of financial and military assistance seem to have played a major role in the affair. Kadhafi pledged so much financial aid to Gukuni at the time, mainly in civil service salaries (about $3 million for six months with as much as 2 million CFA more to come in 1982), that some analysts have characterized the assistance as the Marshall Plan for Chad.[19] Chad's delegation, however, composed of Mahamat Abba (interior minister, member of the FLP-FACP), Lossinian Naimbaye (minister of agriculture, member of FAT), and Tchari Assounon (education minister, FAO member) and excluding Foreign Minister Acyl of the CDR-FACP, "refused to cooperate with the Libyans, and even Abba disassociated himself from Acyl."[20] At home, Christians and Muslims alike were shocked, and people in N'Djamena demonstrated against the merger on January 12, 1981. A Libyan merchant is reported to have exclaimed: "Even the dogs in Chad oppose the unification." The Sara threatened to secede, and Kamougue, their leader, called it an "impossible marriage." Abroad, Oumar Bongo called the merger "imperialism," and Sékou Touré and Ahmadou Ahidjo (both Muslims) in a joint declaration characterized it as Libyan "expansionism."

Paradoxically, even prior to October, GUNT forces had been fighting Libyans in the eastern Sahel to safeguard the national territory; Gukuni was asking the French to leave Chadian soil. Libya's seeming noninterference in N'Djamena at the time prompted French foreign minister Claude Cheysson to praise Kadhafi as a moderate leader with whom the French "intended to gradually resume normal relations."[21] Libya withdrew its forces from N'Djamena at the end of 1981. Most observers were surprised at Kadhafi's withdrawal even though, on February 8, 1981, he and his right-hand man, General Abdessalam Jalloud, had announced that at the request of the GUNT or Gukuni, Libya would withdraw its troops anytime. Why did he withdraw his troops from Chad? The reasons were many. First, the OAU and all neighboring states had openly denounced the merger, and the French stood firmer this time. Second, the FAN was causing serious reverses to Libyan forces supporting Gukuni in Salamat, Ennedi, Biltine, and Wadai and had lost between a thousand and perhaps fifteen hundred men since the beginning of the civil war in Chad. Furthermore, the Libyan economy was hurting because of the oil crisis. Finally, Kadhafi wanted to become OAU chairman in 1982.

Hostilities between Chad and Libya resumed, of course, after Habre evicted Gukuni from N'Djamena on June 7, 1982. After the French, as agreed, withdrew all their troops from Salal, Moussoro, Arada, Biltine, Abeche, Ati, and N'Djamena in November 1984, the Libyans secretly began fortifying their positions. The Chadian bloody drama makes it obvious that Colonel Kadhafi was not simply interested in gaining recognition of his claim of the Aouzou Strip. As for France, Chad is strategically located in the heart of Africa and would facilitate, in the words of Neuberger, "any Saharan unification under Libyan hegemony," whereas the Aouzou Strip's uranium might help develop what has been called the "Islamic bomb."[22] Strategic and political insecurity seems also to have been at the root of the hold on and obsession for Aouzou.

Experts point out that Colonel Kadhafi has not forgotten that in 1970, two of his major critics, Omar Shalhi and Prince Abdallah al-abid al Senussi, launched a destabilizing attack on Sebha (now known as the Black Prince conspiracy) that involved some two hundred retired security officers loyal to the former regime. Observers also suspect that the Israeli Mossad, which was then training Chad's "crack security unit–the Compagnies Tchadiennes de Sécurité (CTS)"—was involved in the affair.[23] Kadhafi's constant accusations of Tombalbaye and later of Habre being "tools" of Israeli imperialism have their origin partly in this episode.

Regarding the aborted 1981 merger, those who know Kadhafi point out that he has never given up the principles and ideals he outlined in his *Green Book* and his *Third Universal Theory*. Kadhafi is a strong follower of Rousseau's theory of democracy and a believer of some of Marx's theories; he is convinced that he is the heir to Gamal Abdel Nasser and must unify the Arabs, and he advocates eventual elimination of the state in favor of what has been called a "peopledom," similar to his concept of Jamahiryya. He hopes to develop a brand of socialism based on Islam that will do away with profit and money altogether. His unsuccessful attempts at unity with Syria, Egypt, Morocco, Tunisia, and Chad (which he has characterized as an Arab country) come from his inner conviction that all Arabs are bound to some day become one nation. David Blundy and Andrew Lycett write that Kadhafi "believed he could use Libya's traditional ties in Chad to strike a blow against Western neocolonialism and establish the first link in what he hoped would be a Libyan dominated Islamic empire in Africa."[24] On closer analysis, Kadhafi's activities in Chad reveal that the colonel is flexible only to a point. In the pursuit of his goals he has often played his cards well, siding with one protagonist against another or abandoning both in favor of a third.

On the Gukuni-Habre rift and Kadhafi's role, René Lemarchand characterizes the changing alliances as a phenomenon that evokes the historical legacy of the Tubu and the Arabs, among whom "oppositions and alliances are thus constantly recalculated, commitments reconsidered, alternative combinations explored." For these groups, adds Lemarchand, the procurement of external support is a sine qua non of political survival "in which Libya, during the 1970s and 1980s, played a determining role: by constantly playing one group against another, it decisively contributed to intensifying factional rivalries."[25] Thus Kadhafi's assistance to Kamougue, a Christian, in May 1979 against his own Muslim Chadian former protégés proves that religion is a means toward Kadhafi's ultimate aim and not an end in itself. On some occasions, he has used religion directly as a weapon against his enemies.

On January 12, 1987, for example, he appealed to religious hatred when he said that Libya had to fight Habre because he "has gone over to the ranks of Christians, the crusaders, the ranks of the enemies of Islam, and he must be fought against."[26] One might say that Kadhafi is always consistent in his goals and appears inconsistent only regarding the means he uses and the strategies he adopts. On the military level, one might ask why the colonel dared to attack beyond parallel 16 in early February 1986. Several factors seem to have intervened in his decision to deploy southward some of the reportedly seven to twelve thousand Libyan troops and Legionnaires stationed in northern Chad. First, this contingent reportedly was fortified by "three battalions at Chicha, 80 km south of the main base at Faya-Largeau, backed by sixty aircraft, three hundred armored cars, and a number of Mi-8 and Mi-24 helicopter gunships" at the 4,200-meter Ouadi-Doum airstrip, protected by a battery of surface-to-air missiles.[27] Second, French elections and French inactivity since the aborted simultaneous withdrawal of troops from Chad in September 1984 no doubt played a major role in the colonel's gamble to cross the Red Line. The result of the test seems to have been unexpected: Habre was able, without French intervention at first, to stop the Islamic Legionnaires and the GUNT forces. Third, Libya mistakenly counted on usual French indecisiveness. Fourth, the attacks may also have been a desperate move on the part of Kadhafi and Gukuni given the mass defections of prominent leaders and soldiers from the GUNT that had demoralized the rebel side. As *Africa Confidential* revealed then, in late 1986 the only northern friend that Kadhafi had left was Rakhis Manani, GUNT defense minister and Acheik's former number-two man.

On the one hand, Kadhafi's attitude must also be seen within the context of the denial by the African heads of state of his chairmanship of the OAU in 1982–1983; on the other, one cannot underestimate Libya's problems with the rebels. Aside from the nonexistence of a trustworthy leader within the GUNT, the disintegration of the northern rebels was real. In fact, on August 27–28 and November 14, 1986, Libya's and Gukuni's forces clashed around Fada, where Libya lost one aircraft, three T-54 tanks, and twenty of its troops. It was reported at the time of the November battle that in late October, Gukuni had been wounded in Tripoli in a crossfire between Libyans and his supporters; in late November 1986 he was reportedly detained indefinitely in Tripoli for announcing that he was ready to negotiate unconditionally with Habre. As Gukuni's chief-of-staff, Kailan Ahmet, announced in Paris, many followers of Gukuni were arrested all over Libya and detained at Mordoum. By late 1986, Libyan forces above parallel 16 numbered perhaps up to 16,000 men. In the East, they were based principally at Fada and Faya-Largeau with their main logistic base at Ouadi-Doum; in the West, they were based on the Tibesti Mountains with garrisons at Zouar, Bardai, and Aouzou village and had their main support at Aouzou base. It is estimated that Habre had 14,000 troops available for operations north of parallel 16, based mainly at Ito, Kalait, and Kouba Olanga. As discussed in Chapter 3, Libyan troops were finally forced out of Chad in 1987, except for Aouzou, from which Libya finally withdrew by May 1994.

Apart from the actions of the West in the post–Cold War era, economic conditions will, as they did during the 1980s, partly determine Kadhafi's behavior during the 1990s and beyond. In fact, unpopular measures of austerity were enacted in the desert country during the 1980s. Oil revenues, estimated at $10 billion in 1984, fell to $8 billion in 1985 and were expected to be as low as $5 billion in subsequent years. During 1986, imports fell to $4.77 billion, 6.3 percent less than in 1985,[28] but the standing 68,000-man army forced Libya to spend a "staggering $4.2 billion to maintain it in 1983." In addition, in 1986 Libya's arms imports amounted to 25.7 percent of total imports at a cost of $1.9 billion, much of it to sustain the war in Chad. Such expenditures cannot go on unabated.

Interestingly, when Habre was overthrown in 1990, Libya was the first country to recognize the new Chadian government, immediately sending into Chad crates marked "food and medical supplies." To cement the relationship, one of Deby's first official visits abroad was an encounter with Kadhafi in Tripoli on February 8, 1991, where the latter reaffirmed the two countries' "special" relations based on their historical links.

Sudan has also been an important power player in the Chadian conflict. Prior to 1969, this neighbor of Chad provided financial assistance, military training grounds, and refuge to FROLINAT insurgents, partly because of religious and ethnic affinity. Sudan had to craft a cautious policy because Chad was home to a large number of Sudanese, whom the government of N'Djamena always threatened to expel if its eastern neighbor continued to undermine the Chadian state.

In the aftermath of the 1965 Mangalme revolt, the year 1966 saw perhaps the worst relations between the two neighbors, which were actually at the brink of war. Chad closed its borders and Tombalbaye issued an ultimatum to Khartoum to stop supporting and providing refuge to the rebels. Fortunately for both, the FROLINAT rebels had abused their welcome in Sudan, particularly in Darfur, their best sanctuary, by harassing people, pillaging crop fields for their own maintenance, and exacting tribute from merchant caravans. The rebels also became involved in deadly factional skirmishes, forcing the government of Sudan to expel them. Through the mediation of Niger's President Hamani Diori, the dispute was eventually diffused, and borders were reopened on September 30, 1967.

Even so, the tension between the two neighbors did not subside completely until the military coup of 1969, which turned Sudan into one of the most ardent defenders of Chadian integrity; Sudan's President Nimeiry grew alarmed over Kadhafi's apparent expansionism in Central Africa. Accordingly, Sudan became one of the sponsors of the Kano and Lagos Accords in 1979 and formed an undeclared anti-Libyan coalition with Egypt. An Egypto-Sudanese delegation led by Egyptian vice president Hosni Mubarak had visited N'Djamena in 1977 and openly pledged its financial, logistic, and military support to the Malloum regime. In August 1978, the Sudanese president hosted a reconciliation meeting between Malloum and Habre that resulted in the signing of the Charte Fondamentale of August 25, 1978.

Nimeiry's overthrow in April 1985 resulted in a new military regime that reversed Sudan's policies and brought Libya and Sudan closer. In fact, the West believes that the overthrow of the Habre regime in December 1990 was made possible through the assistance of both Libya and Sudan, a charge that Deby denies. Curiously, however, as soon as Deby took office, he closed the N'Djamena offices of the Sudan People's Liberation Movement, which has been fighting against Khartoum, and Sudan pledged to allow Chad access to the Red Sea. It can be said with certainty that in spite of its direct and indirect involvement in Chadian affairs over the years, the eastern neighbor has never been anyone's proxy and has had no territorial ambitions on Chad. Its policy toward Chad has been motivated primarily by its own internal dynamics.

The OAU and Other African States

The attitude of the countries sharing borders with Chad had a major impact on the position of the Organization of African Unity (OAU); an overwhelming majority of member states upheld at all cost the maintenance of Chad's territorial integrity (even though a few may have opposed some of the nationalists who vied for the country's leadership). In 1977, Malloum threatened to take the issue of Libya's annexation of Chadian territory and its interference in Chad's internal affairs to the United Nations, by-passing the OAU and thus exposing its inactivity. Malloum's string of complaints prompted the UN to establish the permanent

Conciliation Committee—made up of Algeria, Cameroon, Gabon, Mozambique, Nigeria, Niger, and Senegal—which met for the first time in August 1977. Malloum was still not satisfied; on February 8, 1978, his government complained formally to the UN against Libya's assistance to rebels and its occupation of Aouzou.[29] The UN Security Council met on February 17 but took no action because France pressured the Chadian head of state to withdraw his complaint. These diplomatic moves were followed by a National Reconciliation Conference under Libyan auspices on February 21, 1978, allegedly with French blessings; the UN had decided that the issue of Chad fell within the purview of the OAU.

On January 1981, OAU members became alarmed, and understandably so, when Chad and Libya announced a merger. An extraordinary meeting of the OAU Commission on Chad met in Lomé and condemned the proposed merger, and member states agreed to send an Inter-African Force (IAF) to Chad to replace the Libyan troops in N'Djamena. Thereafter, the OAU's major concern was to find a way to get Libya out of Chad, and the OAU's firmness may have had an impact, since Colonel Kadhafi unexpectedly (for most observers) withdrew his forces from N'Djamena in November 1981. Libya's withdrawal paved the way for an OAU force of some two thousand Nigerian, one thousand Zairean, and eight hundred Senegalese troops (the numbers vary according to sources) to enter the capital as peacekeepers. In Tripoli in 1981, OAU differences over Chad burst into the open when Habre's delegation, opposed by Libya, was not allowed to sit. The question now was, Should Habre be recognized as Chad's legitimate head of state after he had overthrown the GUNT? Apparently, France had much to do with the OAU's eventual acceptance of Habre as Chad's de facto head of state; at a francophone summit in October 1982, President Mitterrand introduced Habre as the president of the Republic of Chad. Subsequently (at the urging of France) the International Conference on Assistance to Chad held in Geneva in November 1982 recognized Habre as Chad's head of state.[30] Thus by the time the OAU held its summit in June 1983, Habre had won the support of almost every member state, and his delegation was finally allowed to participate in the deliberations. What about the role of the remaining individual states in Africa?

Zaire ranks among the strongest supporters of Chad's effort to maintain its sovereignty and territorial integrity. Mobutu and Tombalbaye had maintained excellent relations during the 1960s and 1970s, forging a similar "cultural revolution," as noted in Chapter 5. Mobutu, in an effort to assert his own power in Central Africa, resented Libya's and Nigeria's heavy involvement in Chad. It was no wonder, therefore, that in 1981 Mobutu's troops were part of the OAU Inter-African Force sent to keep peace in Chad. And once Habre had assumed power in June 1982, Zaire deployed some 1,800 to 2,000 paratroopers to guard the city of N'Djamena alongside the French troops from July to October 1983. Many observers believe that the United States had pressured Mobutu to send his troops to boost Habre's chances of withstanding Kadhafi's threat. Whether or not that was the case, it is acknowledged that by his use of Belgian military officers in Zaire,

Mobutu provided, second only to France, the most important and most modern military training to Chadian forces under President Habre.

Egypt has been a strong supporter of the regime in N'Djamena throughout the civil war and the period preceding it. Both the late Anwar Sadat and his successor, Hosni Mubarak, disliked Libya's expansionist foreign policy, which, had it been successful, was bound to have repercussions in Egypt and the region. To frustrate Libya's destabilizing impact in the region, Egypt has consistently provided significant military assistance to N'Djamena, particularly to Habre, even when he was training his Goranes before overthrowing Gukuni's regime in 1982. Working in tandem with the United States and Sudan during the 1980s, Egypt's policy toward Chad was based on two major factors: the perception of Libya's threat to all regimes in the region and the attitude of the Chadian heads of state toward Colonel Kadhafi.

Niger and Senegal have behaved as the active peacemakers in the conflict. Niger, particularly under the late Presidents Hamani Diori and Seyni Kountche, had some success in mediating on several issues related to Chad. Senegal, in contrast, participated in the 3,800-man Inter-African Force (IAF) sent to Chad in November 1981. Gabon has likewise been a supporter of the N'Djamena regime despite diplomatic differences and quarrels stemming primarily from issues of trade and leadership styles. President Oumar Bongo of Gabon served as intermediary between France and Chad during the Claustre affair of 1974–1977 and between Libya and Chad during the 1980s. His position has been clear on the Chadian issue: Preserve Chad's territorial integrity and sovereignty. He has insisted that the leaders of Chad and Colonel Kadhafi meet face-to-face to resolve their differences. To show support for the restoration of Chad's integrity, Bongo provided the first "budgetary aid to Chad" in 1980.[31]

The Central African Republic (CAR) shares not only borders with Chad but also some of the same ethnic groups, including the Sara. The issue of Colonel Kadhafi has been a major determinant of CAR's foreign policy toward Chad. President David Dacko severed diplomatic relations with Libya and the Soviet Union in 1981 because the CAR government accused Kadhafi of inciting the Central Africans against his regime. President André Kolingba managed to develop a closer relationship with Colonel Kadhafi after September 11, 1981, when the CAR received some 500 million French francs (FF) from Libya for mineral exploration. Thomas O'Toole writes that "as long as French military intervention in Chad is a major part of that nation's foreign policy, the potential for Libyan intervention in the affairs of the CAR remains real."[32] The permanent presence of French troops in Bangui, however, makes it unlikely that the CAR regime could seriously follow an anti-Chad policy in favor of Libya.

During their lifetime, Côte d'Ivoire's Félix Houphouet-Boigny and Chad's François (Ngarta) Tombalbaye were never close friends. Tombalbaye often complained to the French that they were listening too much to Houphouet-Boigny (and Senghor of Senegal), whose advice resulted in France's unwise policies in

Africa.[33] However, Houphouet-Boigny's influence played a major role in France's eventual assistance to Habre in 1983. When the 1984 troop withdrawal agreement was announced by France and Libya, Houphouet-Boigny was one of the few leaders, along with Mobutu and Habre, who convinced Mitterrand that he had "been had" by the colonel.

Togo essentially followed the position of most francophone African states toward the Chado-Libyan relations (as did most other African states with the exception of Mengistu Haile Mariam's Ethiopia, which praised the Chado-Libyan merger as conforming to OAU's unity goals). Togo's President Gnassingbe Eyadema supported the Nigerian initiatives and successfully brought together Habre and Gukuni to accept a cease-fire in April 1979 (which lasted only three days). It seems clear, therefore, that virtually every African state opposed Kadhafi's involvement in the affairs of Chad.

Chad and the World: France, the United States, and Others

French military intervention in Chad has been a constant reality since the former colony achieved independence in 1960. Underscoring the reliance of the former colony on French intervention, the French army remained in the BET Prefecture until January 1965, since peace was so precarious in the region. Tombalbaye and his successors continued to solicit the aid of the French troops to defend their regimes in the North. Accordingly, French troops returned formally to Chad in 1978–1980, 1983–1984, and 1986–1987 (although they have maintained some presence there through the mid-1990s).

During the 1967–1971 period, while Georges Pompidou was president of France, the French engaged their troops (some 300 soldiers, increasing to 2,500 by the end of 1968) under General Cortadellas in actual combat against the rebels. Under President Valérie Giscard d'Estaing French policy focused on preventing Libya from controlling the GUNT leaders, protecting N'Djamena, and ensuring that FROLINAT's leaders, particularly those of the Deuxième Armée would lead the country. This French posture became clear during the 1979 civil war in N'Djamena, when General Forest claimed neutrality. The powerful Imam Moussa of N'Djamena, whose sympathies eventually shifted to Habre, called both the French ambassador and General Forest and threatened to bring every dead body to the French embassy if the French did not prevent government aircraft from flying over the city and bombing enemy positions. The French general ordered the supposedly Chadian-commissioned pilots to discontinue the flights and raids; if they did not, he told them, he would block the airport with parked vehicles.[34]

It has also been reported that during the civil war of February 1979, Habre telephoned the same general and threatened to execute the remaining 500 (out of 3,500) French expatriates if he did not order a halt to the government's air bombings. French behavior during this civil war, which some experts have labeled "active neutrality," was criticized by several Chadian leaders. In general, French leaders have claimed that they have intervened in Chad only when called upon by legitimate leaders and only to the extent that their intervention would reassure Chad's survival as a state. However, it stands clear that France has never been willing to prevent Libyan influence. This was evident with the 1980 Opération Tacaud under General Tonquedec, which left for Bouar, Central African Republic, in May 1980. Opération Tacaud was not designed to engage in combat or to assume an offensive role but to defend government positions and to train young Chadians militarily. At the Champs Elysées on September 17, 1981, Gukuni formally requested French assistance, but the French president kept repeating that he would like to leave the problem of Chad to the OAU while at the same time warning that he would not tolerate Libya's lopsided intervention in Chadian affairs.

Almost two years later, the government in N'Djamena had changed. As a direct result, Colonel Kadhafi stepped up his assistance to Gukuni, the former leader of the GUNT. It was at this point (in 1983) that the French put Operation Manta (Stingray) in motion, deploying 3,500 French Legionnaires and forcing the invading forces to retreat to parallel 16. Spartacus (pseudonym of a French colonel) mocked the operation (which cost $500,000 a day, 560 million FF for fiscal year 1983, and 3 million for 1984) as one that was comparatively inferior to the forces that retook Kolwezi in Zaire in 1977 and to Operation Barracuda, which ousted Bokassa in CAR. The 3,500-man force had no heavy armament and disposed of only a few dozen wheeled AMX 10 RC cars, fewer than fifteen combat aircraft, thirty helicopters, and fewer than ten transport airplanes.[35]

In September 1984 in an attempt to prevent open hostilities between Libya and France, Kadhafi and Mitterrand agreed to withdraw their troops simultaneously from Chad. The withdrawal agreement, opposed by Habre, was hailed left and right by the OAU, the UN, and the French as a masterstroke of statesmanship. Habre, who had not been consulted prior to the agreement, and the American administration continued to remind the French (as early as November 14, 1984) that the Libyans would not withdraw. Mitterrand refused to accept the obvious, that he had been duped, and Foreign Minister Claude Cheysson claimed on October 12 that France actually had aerial photos showing the withdrawal of Libyan troops. General Janou Lacaze, chief-of-staff of the French armed forces, visited N'Djamena on October 12–14 and assured Habre that there was no reason to distrust Kadhafi's motives. Finally, frustrated and humiliated, Mitterrand asked Libya to withdraw its troops up to the last soldier: "L'évacuation [he said] doit être totale jusqu'au dernier soldat libyen ou français."[36] An interesting verbatim recounting of the meetings of Mitterrand and Habre in Paris and Bujumbura with Mobutu, Houphouet-Boigny, and Oumar Bongo in October 1984 and with other francophone presidents on December 11, 1984, provides a dramatic glimpse of the disagreement among the francophone leaders.

At the Paris meeting, Mitterrand was so irritated with Habre's objections that he told him: "Un jour, vous les [libyens] avez appélés à venir au Tchad, pas moi"

(You, and not I, invited the Libyans to come to Chad). Habre retorted: "Ce n'est pas moi qui les ai appélés; à cet moment-là, j'étais dans le maquis." (I was not the one who invited them; at that time, I was in the resistance.) Mitterrand snapped back: "Non. Pas dans le maquis. Vous étiez en Libye." (You were not in the bush [fighting]. You were in Libya.) Habre found no words to refute Mitterrand.[37] At Bujumbura, Habre and his francophone colleagues expressed their utter disapproval of Mitterrand's agreement with Kadhafi, prompting the French president to tell them that only he could judge what constituted a threat to the interests of "black Africa" and France. Mitterrand went on to challenge them: "If you wish me to go to the north [of Chad], Africa must ask me. You should go first. No? No volunteers?"[38] On February 13, 1986, three days after Kadhafi's Islamic Legionnaires had crossed the Red Line, or parallel 16, Quai d'Orsey warned Libya that France would be obliged "to intervene." The next day, Defense Minister Paul Quiles made a short visit to N'Djamena and concluded that the GUNT was in disarray but that an air attack by Libya could pose a serious threat to N'Djamena. Thus on February 12, Mitterrand's special adviser on African affairs made a "lightening visit," to use a reporter's expression, to N'Djamena. He assured Habre that France would respond appropriately to Kadhafi's threats and that military assistance would be forthcoming. Speculation ended on February 16, 1986, when Mitterrand ordered an air attack from Bangui airbase on the Ouadi-Doum runway, 90 miles northeast of Faya-Largeau, which Libya claimed to have built to transport food only and not armaments.[39]

At 7:02 the following morning, a Libyan Tupolev-22 flew undetected all the way from Faya-Largeau to N'Djamena airport and dropped three bombs, one hitting the runway and the other two falling on the ground as puzzled French officers looked on. The new operation, labeled Epervier (Sparrowhawk), was essentially an air mission supported by some 750 "crack troops" and 24 armored cars. A respected Air Force officer, Colonel Hector Pissochet, commanded the operation and oversaw four Puma assault helicopters, five Jaguar strike aircraft, and six Mirage F-1 interceptors at N'Djamena airport while 1,500 French troops remained on alert in Bangui. It appears the French were forced to act because of criticism of the 1983 Operation Manta, France's largest military intervention in Africa since the Algerian war,[40] and reinforced constant pressure from the United States. To Chad's detriment, the Claustre affair had made Habre a scorned leader among right-wingers because they held him responsible for the 1975 murder of Captain Pierre Galopin. In contrast, the business community and financiers in France viewed Habre as the only leader capable of restoring Chad's economic stability.[41] Why, then, has France intermittently intervened in Chadian affairs, particularly in the civil war, in 1978–1980, 1983–1984, and 1986–1987, and during the 1990s? Most experts agree that Africa's fifth largest country, located in the very heart of the continent, is strategically important for France. France also maintains its presence in Central Africa to counteract the influence of Libya and Nigeria and, prior to the fall of the Soviet Union, to prevent the advance of communism.

For Giscard d'Estaing and his advisers, Chad constituted a port of call for the French air force, linking it with its bases in Dakar and Diégo-Suarez.[42]

Notwithstanding Chad's meager agricultural resources (except for cotton), the country's potential abundance of vital mineral resources such as oil, uranium, and phosphates compels France to not abandon its former colony. Equally important is France's honor; every request by a Chadian government for intervention has been in accordance with the military pact approved by the French National Assembly on November 9, 1977. Even so, the French have played a double game—they dealt with Libya economically while attempting to oust it from Chad, as demonstrated by the aborted Elf-Aquitaine Society's oil deal in 1981.

A most troubling aspect of French policies toward Chad is the on-again, off-again advocacy of a federal government structure for the former colony rather than the present unitary system. Valérie Giscard d'Estaing, as early as 1978, was a major advocate of a federal government for Chad, which no Chadian leader had ever seriously contemplated.[43] Indeed, observers believed that a federal structure would make the North gravitate toward Libya and the South toward sub-Saharan Africa, thus sowing seeds of secessionism. France's mixed signals on Kadhafi, especially during the civil war, have also been detrimental to Chad. Pronouncements from Paris on the Aouzou Strip provide a good example. While on the one hand Foreign Minister Claude Cheysson declared on August 24, 1983, that the strip was part of Chad, Mitterrand, on the other hand, agreed with his predecessors that the issue was one of contention and debate between Libya and Chad.[44]

Colonel Idris Deby's ouster of Habre raises serious questions about France's involvement in the matter, for France immediately pledged to protect Deby's new regime in N'Djamena—which perhaps provides the most plausible explanation of Habre's sudden removal from power. Deby is a known francophile and was invited by the French to receive training at the École de Guerre while he was still in Habre's government in 1985. Defensive, Deby has denied having been "recruited" by the French. Paris circles see Deby as "less dogmatic and one who can at the same time stand against Kadhafi and Muslim fundamentalists."[45] Thus the French have continued to protect him and are assisting him in increasing the efficiency of the 40,000-man army (mostly of Zaghawa, Hadjerai, and Bideyat) by purging it and reducing it to about 25,000.

How can U.S. policy toward Chad be characterized? From 1962 to early 1982, it focused primarily on humanitarian assistance, which amounted to some $65 million in grants for the period. In 1982, only about 6.6 percent of all international assistance to Chad came from the United States; for the 1981–1982 period, the former French colony received $10 million in military aid from Washington, "mainly from Sudanese-Egyptian stocks (later replenished)."[46] Between 1984 and 1987, the United States provided $70 million in humanitarian assistance, but substantial change to include military assistance could be seen in the aid package. For example, of the $10 million requested for Chad by the administration, $5 million was earmarked as a response to "Libyan expansionism," a similar amount having been made available to Chad the previous year. The Reagan administration's perspective came from a renewal in Cold War policies and from a search for spheres of influence. With the Soviets then making inroads into Ethiopia, Angola, Mozambique, Guinea-Bissau, and Congo, the Reagan administration stepped up pressure on those governments that were either collaborating directly with the Soviet Union or behaving as proxies of that superpower. Libya was seen as a Soviet puppet, a destabilizer, a terrorist state intent on spreading its ideology in North and Central Africa, particularly in Chad. When the Chad-Libya merger was announced, the State Department and the White House mounted intense overt and covert pressure on France to act on behalf of its former colony against "Libyan aggression." Thus following consultation with Sudan and Egypt, the United States offered the French its assistance in air surveillance over Chad and Central Africa, using its sophisticated AWACS planes "to stave off and pre-empt" Libya's advances in northern Chad.

France's ambiguous response led the United States to assume a more active role by directly helping certain protagonists in the conflict. In the eyes of the Reagan administration, the candidate most likely to bring stability to Chad and oppose Libya effectively was Hissein Habre. Accordingly, the United States channeled to him some $10 million (some say $12 million) in military aid in 1982 alone as he prepared his assault on N'Djamena. Paradoxically, the U.S. position regarding Habre, particularly in 1981, went counter to OAU's policy of supporting Gukuni's GUNT and the establishment of an OAU force for Chad. The United States had pledged and delivered a $12 million package to assist the Inter-African Force. Although Paris attempted to reject Washington's dictates, American pressure was certainly partly responsible for the return of the French troops to Chad in August 1983. As Rita M. Byrnes notes, "For a time in the early 1980s, the United States' commitment to military support for Habre was more enthusiastic than that of France, which hoped to preserve its relationship with Libya."[47] In order to cement his friendship with Washington, Habre visited the White House in 1986, and the Reagan administration pledged to provide him with most of the weapons needed that France would not make available, including red-eyed antiaircraft. The April 1986 bombing of Benghazi and Tripoli by the United States must also be seen both as a move to punish Libya for allegedly masterminding the killing of an American serviceman in former West Germany and as an attempt to weaken Kadhafi's position in Chad.

It was little known prior to the overthrow of Habre that the United States had been allowed to train some six or seven hundred anti-Libyan contras on Chadian soil. At the request of Libya, Deby asked the United States in 1990 to get the commandos out of Chad. Understandably, Deby's victory was a setback for the United States, but it elated Colonel Kadhafi, who on December 13, 1990, warned African governments that if they followed U.S. policies, he would encourage rebel movements to overthrow their regimes. As Africa News observed in 1991, "Now, the staunchly pro-Western Habre has been replaced by someone with at least modest ties to Tripoli and neither Washington nor Paris seems very upset."[48] Under the Clinton administration, Chad remained one of the most favored sub-Saharan African countries, receiving U.S. aid along with Ethiopia, Cameroon, Ghana, Kenya, Madagascar, Malawi, Mozambique, Uganda, and Zaire.[49]

Elsewhere in Africa and on the globe, the Arab and Muslim states by and large have stayed away from the Chadian conflict, although Algeria supported Kadhafi's annexation of the Aouzou Strip and provided asylum and training camps for the anti-Habre regime. This explains why Algiers has always been Gukuni's last refuge whenever he felt rejected or persecuted by Tripoli. In Africa, practically every Muslim and Arab state theoretically opposed all foreign intervention in Chad, including that of France, partly because of the precedent that a partition of the country could create and partly because of their disagreement with Colonel Kadhafi's policies on the continent and around the world.

Conclusion

To the critics who maintain that France has no obligation to assist Chad, one must retort that inasmuch as bilateral military assistance treaties remain ratified, France has the responsibility to assist. Our contention in this analysis is simple: Once France pledges assistance to the regime in power and actually lands and deploys its troops on Chadian soil, it is only reasonable to expect that it will defend the regime.

Understandably, the U.S. role in Chad has been limited over the years, as France is expected to play the major role in its former colony. It is disconcerting, however, that the Reagan administration viewed Chad not as an end in itself, a country that desperately needed assistance, but as a means or a pawn in a global strategy to stop the advance of communism in the world or the expansionist policies of Colonel Kadhafi in Africa. In the same vein, the OAU and individual African states, particularly Cameroon, Gabon, Niger, Sudan, Egypt, Senegal, Zaire, and even Nigeria are to be commended in general for their attitude toward Chad during the unfolding of its civil conflict—an attitude aimed at safeguarding the sovereignty and the territorial integrity of the embattled country.

Regrettably, their responses have not constituted a meaningful, concerted, and collective effort designed to assist in solving a crisis throughout the thirty-year-long conflict in Chad. There are three major reasons for this lack of forceful action: actual fear of Colonel Kadhafi, a false reliance on France's ability and assumed willingness to rescue Chad, and internal paralysis brought on by domestic political and economic crises.

For its part, Libya has certainly learned an unexpected sobering lesson from its involvement in Chad. Notwithstanding its apparent defeat, the military and political problems for Chad will remain for as long as its northern neighbor seems to follow an erratic, and perhaps unpredictable, foreign policy in the region. Unfortunately, challenging Libya's air capability will continue to be a major obstacle for any Chadian leader if the conflict between the two neighbors ever escalates to the pre-1990s level.

Clearly, Chadian leaders have demonstrated that with a modicum of French air support, they can stop Libya's aggression. Observers have likewise asked how long Kadhafi might survive as Libya's undisputed leader. Oye Ogunbadejo points out that in view of the attempts on Kadhafi's life and the widening dissatisfaction among the educated, the business community, Muslim fundamentalists, and the army, "a change in Tripoli may not be as forlorn as it appears."[50] Unfortunately, political pundits have been so wrong in the past that it is futile to await a coup in Libya. In fact, George Henderson stresses that notwithstanding Kadhafi's accusation that Major Abdessalam Jalloud lost the war in Chad and "embroiled the army in Chad's internal affairs," the colonel "still has his all-important Qadhadhfa tribal support base spread throughout the armed forces and security services."[51]

Notes

1. I. William Zartman, *International Relations in the New Africa* (Englewood Cliffs, N.J.: Prentice-Hall, 1986), 65.

2. Doudou Thiam, *The Foreign Policy of African States,* (New York: Praeger, 1964), 77–78.

3. Jean Claude Gautron, "La force de maintien de la paix au Tchad: Éloge ou réquiem," in *Année Africaine* (Paris: Editions Pedone, 1983), 178.

4. Willard Johnson, "The Cameroon Federation Laboratory for PanAfricanism," in Martin Kilson, ed., *New States in the Modern World* (Cambridge, Mass.: Harvard University Press, 1975), 89–118; and Ndive Kofele-Kale, "Cameroon and Its Foreign Policy," *African Affairs* 319 (April 1981): 198.

5. Virginia Thompson and Richard Adloff, *Conflict in Chad* (Berkeley: Institute of International Studies, 1981), 111.

6. B. W. Hooder and D. R. Harris, *Africa in Transition* (London: Methuchen, 1967), 289.

7. See Ahidjo's speech of February 5, 1965, quoted in Johnson, "The Cameroon Federation," 345.

8. Collin Legum, *Africa Contemporary Record* (New York: Africana, 1981–1982), B25.

9. *Le Message du Renouveau* (Yaounde: SOPECAM, 1984), 304.

10. *Africa Research Bulletin* (1–30 November 1980): 5861.

11. However, Mahmat Shawa Lol became the compromise candidate for Nigeria. See Rita M. Byrnes, "Government and Politics," in Thomas Collelo, ed., *Chad: A Country Study* (Washington, D.C.: U.S. Government Printing Office, 1990), 162.

12. Michael Kelley, *A State in Disarray: Conditions of Chad's Survival* (Boulder, Colo.: Westview Press, 1986), p. 72.

13. Robert Buijtenhuijs, *Le Frolinat et les guerres civiles du Tchad (1977–1984)* (Paris: Karthala, 1987), 145.

14. Kelley, *A State in Disarray,* 38.

15. René Lemarchand, "The Case of Chad," in René Lemarchand, ed., *The Green and The Black* (Bloomington: Indiana University Press, 1988), 108.

16. John Wright, *Libya: A Modern History* (Baltimore: Johns Hopkins University Press, 1982), 168.

17. Bernard Lanne, *Tchad-Libye: Querelles des frontières* (Paris: Karthala, 1982), 230.

18. *Africa Report* 23, no. 5 (September-October 1978), quoted by Benyamin Neuberger, *Involvement, Invasion and Withdrawal: Qadhdhafi's Libya and Chad* (Tel Aviv: Tel Aviv University, 1982), 40.

19. P. Branche, "Tchad: Le bourbier," *Le Figaro* (18–19 February 1982).

20. Neuberger, *Involvement, Invasion and Withdrawal,* 51.

21. Andrew Lycett, "Hot Sands," *New African* (April 1986): 22–23.

22. Neuberger, *Involvement, Invasion and Withdrawal,* 60, 68.

23. Lemarchand, "The Case of Chad," 110.

24. David Blundy and Andrew Lycett, *Qaddafi and the Libyan Revolution* (Boston: Little, Brown, 1987), 186.

25. Lemarchand, "The Case of Chad," 112.

26. Keith Somerville, *Foreign Military Intervention in Africa* (New York: St. Martin's Press, 1990), 76.

27. George Henderson, "Retrenchment in Libya," *Africa Report* (July-August 1986): 73.

28. *Africa Confidential* 27, no. 16 (July 1986): 6.

29. Thompson and Adloff, *Conflict in Chad,* 102.

30. Kelley, *A State in Disarray,* 48.

31. Thompson and Adloff, *Conflict in Chad,* p. 106.

32. Thomas O'Toole, *The CAR: The Continent's Hidden Heart* (Boulder, Colo.: Westview Press, 1980), 137.

33. R. L. Trouze, *370 jours d'un ambassadeur au Tchad* (Paris: Éditions France, Empire, 1989), 131, 137–138.

34. Jean Gorini and Jean Claude Criton, "Les oracles et le 2e bureau étaient avec Hisseine Habre," in *Tchad: Anthologie de la guerre civile* (N'Djamena: Yamoko Koulro-Bezo, 1981), 14–15; and Buijtenhuijs, *Le Frolinat,* 116–119.

35. Colonel Spartacus (pseud.), *Operation Manta: Tchad 1983–1984* (Paris: Plon, 1985), 228. See also how George Moose, "French Military Policy," 72–79, in *Arms in Africa,* ed. William J. Foltz and Henry S. Bienen (New Haven: Yale University Press, 1985), argues on the ineffectiveness of the French presence in Chad.

36. Mitterrand hoped that Kadhafi, then enjoying his diplomatic coup de grâce, would abide by the accord.

37. *Jeune Afrique* 1689 (20 August–26 May 1993): 17–18.

38. Ibid.

39. Andrew Lycett, "Hot Sands," *New African* (April 1986): 22–23.

40. René Lemarchand, "A Sketch of Hisseine Habre," *Africa Report* (November-December 1984), 65.

41. *Africa Confidential* 27 (15 July 1986): 5; and Jean Tartter, "National Security," in Collelo, ed., *Chad,* 197–200.

42. Kelley, *A State in Disarray,* 91.

43. "Special: Tchad," in *Tchad: Anthologie de la guerre civile,* 20.

44. *Le Monde,* 26 August 1983.

45. *Africa Confidential* 13, no. 12 (19 June 1992).

46. Tartter, "National Security," 200.

47. Rita M. Byrnes, "Government and Politics," in Collelo, ed., *Chad,* 166.

48. *Africa News* (1991): 15.

49. *The Backgrounder* (Washington, D.C.: Heritage Foundation, 1993), 7.

50. Oye Ogunbadejo, "Qaddafi and Africa's International Relations," *Journal of Modern African Studies* 24 (March 1986): 68.

51. George Henderson, "Quaddafi's Waterloo," *Africa Report* (September-October 1987): 25–27.

7

CHAD:

FACING THE FUTURE

The political conflict in Chad vividly illustrates the outcome of imposed colonial rule in Africa, with the Chadian state representing the worst of the French colonial legacy in Africa. Nevertheless, the precolonial period was actually more unstable because of the coexistence of disparate and almost incompatible societies. Chadian societies not only were separated by a geographic divergence that made some regions economically poor and others rich but were also divided by religion, social traditions, and colonial policies that made unification and reconciliation difficult at any point in history.

Over a thousand years of slavery and slave trading had transformed the region into a zone of mutual distrust and social exploitation; war, raiding, looting, social casting, and conquest caused perpetual instability and prevented development of Chad's frontier. When the French appeared in Central Africa, Chadian society had experienced more periods of hostility than of peaceful coexistence. Since the "frontier zone," to use Dennis Cordell's expression, was burning with hatred and raging from constant warfare, the French presence did nothing but exacerbate those differences by playing—through haphazard, discriminatory, and regionally based policies—the role of divider and conqueror. For the most part, French rule in the North remained indirect; the South experienced direct French rule with a modicum of assimilation that introduced the *indigénat* system at its worst. It made one ethnic group, the Sara, virtually the sole source of recruitment for forced military service and government projects, labor for French monopolistic concessionaires, and porterage. Government-forced labor was dramatically highlighted during the construction of the Congo-Brazzaville railroad in 1924–1934, when out of 200,000 workers, about one-half died in the *chantiers* from harsh working conditions, disease, and mistreatment.

Over time, the reforms made by France following World War II might have provided an opportunity for the Chadians to work out their differences by denouncing what was wrong with the colonial system and devising ingenious ways to work together once they realized they would have no choice on the matter of nationhood. Unfortunately, the colonial state continued to foster divisiveness so that it could remain in power. The period designed to implement reforms was too short; the French were unable to stop colonial Africa's rapidly rising tide toward independence. It is doubtful, however, that the French would have created a better society even had they realized that independence was inevitable and the time to accomplish it brief. At the eleventh hour, they were forced to abandon their allies in the North and create conditions for the South to ascend to power in a nascent country that most observers knew would be desperately divided along religious, ethnic, and regional lines.

To be sure, Tombalbaye's unwise policies aggravated the social and political tensions that exploded in 1965. Not only did he continue to build on the country's differences but he undermined even his own position in the South, particularly through his policies on cotton cultivation and the restoration of the *yondo*. Yet it is difficult to prove that a northern leader such as Koulamallah, Acyl, or Abatcha would have done better than Tombalbaye in bringing the factions together in a country that had been so maladministered as a colony. In neighboring Cameroon, Ahidjo, a Muslim, was able to steer the new country to nationhood not only because he was a better leader than Tombalbaye but also because northern Cameroon had not been as neglected in terms of infrastructure development as northern Chad. Unlike Tombalbaye, Ahidjo instituted a type of affirmative action without polarizing the country. Had the differences in Cameroon been as sharp as in Chad, however, it is doubtful that Ahidjo would have been as successful as he was.

From hindsight, one can see that political conflict and perhaps civil war were inevitable regardless of the leadership in 1960. It seems unlikely, however, that such conflict or civil war would have taken thirty years to resolve had Libya and France not interfered in Chad's internal affairs. Libya's involvement and French limited military assistance created a series of stalemates that made it impossible for either side, North or South, to win the political and military contest. Their presence set the stage for a protracted war.

The northern nationalists' major aim was merely to wrest power from the southerners. Their personal and ethnic differences (more so than religious idiosyncrasies) prevented the northerners from developing a vision of what the new Chad should look like. Indeed, FROLINAT not only was unable to unify its own leadership in the North but did not develop and articulate a clear program for the reconstruction of the country. In the post-Malloum era, power was not redistributed equitably, and foreign policy was dictated not by Chadians but by the

French, the Libyans, or the Nigerians (Tombalbaye had a better foreign policy record than any of his successors).

If it were possible to assign degrees of responsibility for Chad's current conflict, the archaic states of Kanem-Bornu, Wadai, and Baguirmi would bear the greatest burden. Their slaving activities and the stigmatization of people different from them religiously and politically have left a legacy of bitterness that will be difficult to erase (a situation much like that in the United States). The second greatest degree of responsibility would belong to the French, who at no point in the colony's history attempted to unite the people. France equally bears the responsibility for Chad's deplorable condition because it practiced differential treatment of its Chadian colonial subjects and would not release its stronghold on Chad's destiny following independence. Indeed, if anything good came out of French colonialism, it was perhaps the elimination of slavery and the slave trade from Chadian soil.

Libya would take third place in guilt because had it not been for its active but ill-fated interventionism after the 1970s, FROLINAT would never have had such strength and impact on the physical and moral destruction of Chad and the Chadian state. Without Libya, there would have been no fratricidal wars of the magnitude the world witnessed in the North, particularly between the Arabs and the Tubu. The Sara, and more specifically their leaders—Tombalbaye and Malloum—would come next for their lack of vision and for failing in an opportunity offered them to begin healing and minimizing the centuries-old conflict between North and South. In the fifth place in the hierarchy of culpability would rank the northern leaders themselves, who, although of unquestionable nationalism and intent on preserving a united Chad, let themselves be dictated by outside forces. Just like the Sara preceding them, they put personal interests above those of the nation.

At this juncture, the survival of Chad depends on several factors, particularly the nature of its internal leadership, the role of France, and the conduct of Libya. Unfortunately, no matter who might rise as a leader in a country that is compromisingly dependent on foreign assistance, he will run the risk of being toppled by the French either through inaction and sabotage (as were Malloum and Gukuni) or through their active involvement (as seems to have been the case when Deby was victorious over Habre). The unpredictable behavior of Colonel Kadhafi also makes the situation problematic as long as the French, who have always posed as the guarantors of Chad's territorial integrity, do not back their word with action.

On the positive side, no political leader, including Kamougue and Habre, ever advocated the dismemberment of the country into two states. Against such a barometer, Chadian leaders acted not as warlords but as nationalists who lost track of their responsibility to the state and the nation. A federal structure was an option only France and Libya were willing to entertain during the 1980s as the best solution to the seemingly endless conflict. At least this fact leaves hope for the future of Chad as a nation. Indeed, few Chadian leaders, from Arab Abba Siddick to Tubu Gukuni to Sara Malloum, have endorsed any form of federalism. On the prospect of secessionism, one thing appears clear at the moment: Whereas the South can survive as a nation without the North, the same cannot be said of the North. The North has a very poor infrastructure. It lacks schools, hospitals, roads, and trained cadres and is unable to muster adequate resources to sustain an independent state. By the same token, however, given the militarization of the North and its proven effectiveness and resolve on the battlefield, the South could not sustain a successful secessionist movement if it required military confrontation.

Under the circumstances, national reconciliation, a balanced allocation of resources to develop the entire country, an independent foreign policy (to the extent that such is possible), an educational system that stresses Chadian identity, and constitutionally sanctioned democratic reforms that allocate power evenly among the fourteen prefectures may allow this war-torn Central African enclave to finally make itself a true nation. One can therefore argue that although the state has been chaotic and in disarray and sometimes has disappeared altogether in Chad, the concept of the Chadian nation never died.

It is equally remarkable that no matter how much dislike and contempt they might have for one another, Chadian leaders—Malloum, Gukuni, Habre, Kamougue, and Deby—have not attempted to assassinate each other, and they have ended up talking to each other. Even Gukuni returned to Chad to participate in the 1993 National Sovereign Conference on democracy. Significantly, at the end of the historic event, he burned, in a public ceremony with Deby at his side, a cache of weapons, thus symbolizing the end of the war and his wish to see all Chadians reconciled. From his exile in Nigeria, Malloum sent a high-level delegation to N'Djamena for the conference.

One of the consequences of the civil war and the involvement of foreign powers has been the proliferation of arms and the militarization of the country, more so than in Somalia, Liberia, Angola, and Mozambique. Here, the war was fought openly with the most modern conventional weapons found in Western Europe, the former Soviet Union, and the United States. In addition, the number of Chadians who have served in the national army, in FAP, in FAN, in FAO, and in other rival armed camps surpasses 200,000. Moreover, as the French undertake the task of training and downsizing Deby's army to encompass about 25,000 and to make it effective, more guns are made available across the landscape, making it difficult for the government to control violence and lawlessness, particularly in the North. In 1993, for example, some 3,000 Zaghawa were discharged from the national army but were allowed to carry their guns with them. A militarized Chad could pose a problem not only for its neighbors, should the wrong man occupy the presidential palace, but also for the Chadians themselves, as has happened in Somalia.

By the same token, making the Chadian army effective in the region is neither an impossible task nor an unwise dream. Habre demonstrated this in his defiance against Libyan troops that were, during the various military engagements, larger in size and superior in modern military weaponry. Given the ever-lurking threat from the North and the erratic policies of its western neighbor, Nigeria (as proven by the Nigerian-Cameroon conflict in 1994 and previously), it is certainly imperative that Chad create such an army to safeguard its territorial integrity.

Unfortunately, Chad's economic conditions make it an easy prey of foreign and neocolonial forces. As a geographic enclave, the country suffers several economic disadvantages in addition to its aridity and environmental fragility: the blatant colonial neglect of human and physical capital investment, postindependence economic problems linked to postcolonial French engagement, and external aggression from Libya (and, to a certain degree, Nigeria). Other factors have worsened the state of the country's already naturally weak economy: climatic and environmental degradation, the Cold War, political instability and civil war, inadequate and incoherent government policies, and dependence on foreign aid.

In a sense, Chad is poor because of the poor policies of its unstable leadership. It has unstable leadership due to past sociopolitical realities, French colonial and neocolonial policies, and personal ambitions and inexperience. Should the Chadians then rest on this realization and blame the past and the French for their problems? The answer is, Of course not. Although Chad's leaders should remain cognizant of exploitation and colonial devastation as well as of contemporary unequal partnerships, they cannot afford to dwell on excuses or to play the blame game. The government must focus on removing major constraints to economic growth by targeting and improving the level of savings, foreign exchange earnings, agricultural productivity, and human capital development. To improve the rate of development that approaches Chad's potential rate, a stable Chadian government must pursue appropriate macroeconomic and trade policies and show a strong commitment to developmental goals and the capacity for efficient public management.

Arguably, economic reform and structural adjustment have not been very successful in Chad due in part to the civil conflict and in part to the problems inherent in IMF orthodoxy and the inability of the international financial agencies to enforce conditionality. But more important was the paradoxical expectation of the international financial agencies that the Chadian government would willingly reduce its role in the economy through privatization and trade liberalization. The Chadian state was neither stable nor organizationally coherent enough to implement a successful reform program. At best, IMF's efforts punished the poor and created distributive conflicts resulting from the unequal sharing of adjustment-induced pain and gain.

Notwithstanding the failure of structural adjustment, Chad's policymakers need a better understanding of organizational changes in each sector or market and the sequencing of such changes. They need to modify the technique of resource allocation and policy planning at the macrolevel to reflect the resource constraints, needs, and realities of Chadian society. While focusing on making macroeconomic management more efficient, they must pay attention to the issues of income distribution, technical change, and the international aspects of development and their effects on policy. In post–civil war Chad, there is a need to completely reexamine the country's congenital dependence on foreign aid and aspire to a more self-reliant and sustainable economy.

As Chad makes the foray into the twenty-first century, its economic future looks uncertain but not hopeless. Much of the outcome will depend not just on the wisdom and the actions of the military or the former guerrillas and civilian leaders but, foremost, on the will and determination of the Chadians themselves to restore the economy, rebuild the ravaged cities, democratize and stabilize the political process, and set in motion a bureaucracy that is competent and dedicated. The task is quite challenging but not impossible.

Expanded Chronology

3000	Sao civilization
A.D. 800	Founding of Kanem
900	Sao civilization in Lake Chad region
1384	Sefuwa Magumi dynasty of Kanem Kingdom ousted to Bornu
1480s	The capital Birni Ngazargamu is founded
1512	Massenya founded as capital of Baguirmi
1611	Maba kingdom of Wadai founded under Abd-el-Kerim
1808	Birni Ngazargamu ravaged by the Fulani jihad
1814	The capital is shifted to Kukawa
1840–1842	Awlad Sulayman migrations ravage Lake Chad and Kanem regions
1846	Umar al-Kanemi deposes the Sefuwa dynasty in Bornu
1850	Abeche replaces Wara as capital of Wadai
April 1851	Heinrich Barth reaches Kukawa
1869–1874	Explorations of Gustav Nachtigal in Libya, Chad, Niger, and Sudan
1892	Massenya razed and Baguirmi conquered by Rabah
1893	Kukawa pillaged by Rabah
1896	Sanussiya headquarters moved to Kufra and in 1899 to Gouro, BET
October 1897	Franco-Baguirmi treaty of protection signed by Gentil and Gaurang
June 14, 1898– March 21, 1899	Anglo-French conventions recognizing French rights in Kanem, Baguirmi, and Tibesti
November 1899	Protectorate Treaty signed with Kanem
April 22, 1900	Battle of Kousseri
September 5 & 8, 1900	Creation of the Territoire Militaire des Pays et Protectorat du Tchad

---

Part of this chronology (up to 1984) was reprinted with permission of Scarecrow Press from Samuel Decalo, *Historical Dictionary of Chad* (Metuchen, N.J.: Scarecrow Press, 1987), pp. xiv–xxii. We changed some of the spellings to suit our style (e.g., Gaurang rather than Gouarang, Wadai rather than Ouaddai), provided further entries, and carried the chronology from 1984 to 1997.

January 1901	Rabah's son defeated; end of Rabahist challenge to French expansion in the region
November 1901	Three Franco-Senoussi battles for Bir Alali
December 1902	Franco-Senoussi skirmishes go on until 1920
1905–1909	Franco-German colonial boundaries fixed
April 20, 1907	Battle of Ain Galakka
1908–1909	Turkish outposts reestablished in Tibesti with Teda cooperation
June 13, 1909	Abeche occupied by France and Sultan Acyl elevated to the throne
1909–1912	Abeche occupied and Wadai pacified after a general revolt
January 15, 1910	AEF set up
November 4, 1911	Franco-German Treaty on mutual exchange of territory affects Chad's boundaries
June 5, 1912	Sultan Acyl deposed in Abeche; no new sultans appointed until 1934.
November 27, 1913	Borkou pacified by Col. Largeau; Ain Galakka retaken by France; Turkey withdraws from Tibesti
1913, 1916–1918	Major famines and epidemics in Wadai decimate 60 percent of the population
1914–1916	Conquest of Cameroon
1915–1918	Teda revolt (under Turkish flag) against France; temporary French withdrawal from Tibesti (1917)
April 12, 1916	Chad detached from Oubangui-Chari
November 1917	Kub Kub massacres in Abeche
1920	First civilian administrator of Chad appointed
1920	The *derdei* of the Tubu submits to French rule and pacification of BET is completed
November 11, 1929	Tibesti detached from the AOF Federation (Niger) and linked to Chad and the AEF Federation
January 1930	The "new" Awlad Sulayman emigrant wave arrives in Chad from Libya
August 16, 1940	Under Governor Felix Eboue Chad becomes the first territory to declare for the Gaullist Free French cause; Eboue subsequently promoted to head the AEF
1947	Gabriel Lisette founds the Parti Progressiste Tchadien
1952	Bebalem riots and further unrest in Sara regions
March 1957	Major PPT electoral victory
May 15, 1957	Council of Government formed by Gabriel Lisette
November 28, 1958	Proclamation of the Republic of Chad
June 16, 1959	Period of political instability and of provisional governments (including those of Sahoulba and Koulamallah) end with the rise of the Tombalbaye government

January 30, 1960	All remaining Muslim opposition parties join to form the PNA
August 7, 1960	Gabriel Lisette purged while on a visit to Israel and barred from reentering Chad; later all Europeans barred from Chadian politics
August 11, 1960	Proclamation of Independence
April 1960	"Unity Congress" of Abeche in which a single party—the UPT—is formed
1961	Tombalbaye's Parti Progressiste Tchadien (PPT) merges with the main opposition party, Parti National Africain (PNA).
1962	New constitution is promulgated. All political parties except the PPT are banned. Front de Libération Nationale du Chad is founded
January 20, 1962	One party-system established as all parties except the PPT are banned
April 14, 1962	Presidential system established in Chad
1963	Five prominent northern politicians are arrested. National emergency is declared in the wake of bloody riots in which 500 are killed
March 26, 1963	National Assembly dissolved and major purge of political opponents commences
September 1963	Major riots in Fort-Lamy subsequent to the arrest of the top northern leadership of the country, including Koulamallah
June 4, 1964	One-party system officially legitimated via a constitutional amendment
January 23, 1965	French military forces formally evacuate BET garrisons fully five years after Chad's independence
September 2, 1965	Bardai incidents
October 1965	The bloody Mangalme tax riots erupt, marking the onset of the civil rebellion in Chad
November 19, 1965	Major anti-Tombalbaye plot uncovered, leading to the arrest of three ministers and the VP of the National Assembly
January 1, 1966	UDEAC formed with Chad a member
June 23, 1966	Official founding date of FROLINAT
1968	Tombalbaye invokes Franco-Chadian agreement of 1960 for military assistance against the rebels.
April 2, 1968	With Chad's adherence, UDEAC is formed
April 28, 1968	Chad withdraws from UDEAC
May 1968	Secret "Galopin Report" on Chadian mal-administration of BET
July 29, 1968	Constituent Congress of the PPT Youth wing, the JEPPT; formal beginning of the Cultural Revolution

August 28, 1968	Tombalbaye calls on French troops to assist in quelling Tubu rebellion in the north
1969	Tombalbaye is reelected president
April 1969	The French Mission de Réforme Administrative is dispatched to Chad to overhaul the local administration
September 26, 1969	Increase in chiefly powers, reinstallment of sultans decreed as part of the MRA recommendations for the restoration of order in the country
June 18, 1970	Major amnesty of political prisoners
1971	Tombalbaye regime breaks diplomatic relations with Libya; Kadhafi recognizes FROLINAT
April 19–22, 1971	Major amnesty of political prisoners
August 27, 1971	Guerrilla attempted coup in N'Djamena
Nov. 29–30, 1971	Student strikes in Chad
June 5, 1972	Guerrilla attempted coup in N'Djamena
December 1972	Chad-Libya rapprochement leading to Chad's break with Israel
1973	Libya occupies Aouzou Strip in northern Chad
June 1973	"Black sheep" plot revealed, leading to the arrest of Felix Malloum, Kalthouma Guembang, and others
Aug. 27–30, 1973	PPT Congress of N'Djamena, dissolution of the PPT, and replacement by the MNRCS
April 21, 1974	Françoise Claustre captured in BET by Habre-Gukuni troops
August 27, 1974	Operation Agriculture launched by Tombalbaye
March 23, 1975	Arrests of senior military officers connected with an anti-Tombalbaye plot
April 4, 1975	Execution of Captain Galopin by FROLINAT
April 13, 1975	Coup d'état in which Tombalbaye is killed: Malloum becomes head of state
May 13, 1975	Formation of an 18-man provisional government
August 15, 1975	Return from Libyan self-exile of the *derdei*; rapid decline of antigovernment hostilities in the North and East
1976	New defense treaty is concluded with France; Habre's FAN troops first clash with Libyan forces in the Aouzou Strip at Oumchi
February 18, 1976	Hissein Habre's attack on Faya-Largeau
April 15, 1976	Grenade attack in N'Djamena on Malloum and other officials celebrating the first anniversary of the 1975 coup
October 18, 1976	Habre ousted from FAN by Gukuni
1977	Attempted coup against the government is reported crushed

January 29, 1977	Françoise Claustre released by Gukuni in Tripoli, Libya
March 31, 1977	Attempted coup in which Lt. Col. Ali Dabio died defending the presidential palace
1978	Chad breaks diplomatic relations with Libya after accusing its northern neighbor of occupying a 78,000 sq. km. (30,000 sq. m.) territory in the Tibesti region believed to hold uranium deposits
1978	Kadhafi steps up aid to Chadian rebels, who inflict serious casualties on government troops
January 22, 1978	Malloum-Habre negotiations in Khartoum
Feb. 23–27, 1978	Cease-fire talks under Libyan aegis lead to Sabha Agreement; despite the agreement, Gukuni continues his incursions into the central government
August 25, 1978	Malloum-Habre Accord announced
August 29, 1978	Habre assumes the premiership under Malloum's presidency as a new constitutional charter is announced
February 12, 1979	Malloum-Habre tug-of-war leads to Habre's attempted coup in N'Djamena; Chadian army routed, leading to eventual entry in N'Djamena of Gukuni forces
March 6, 1979	Anti-Muslim pogroms erupt in the South following earlier mass exodus of Sara from the capital
March 16, 1979	First round of Kano peace talks
March 23, 1979	Provisional State Council set up in N'Djamena
April 29, 1979	GUNT administration under Lol Chowa with Gukuni and Habre in key posts
August 1979	Eleven Chadian factions join to form the GUNT; Gukuni becomes de facto president
November 10, 1979	New GUNT government, including representatives of existing 11 factions, following Douguia talks
1980	Fighting resumes and over 1,000 are dead as violence escalates; Congo withdraws its troops; peace talks in Togo between rival factions fail to resolve crisis. Fighting breaks out between FAN on one hand and other FROLINAT rebel groups, including FAT, FAC, and FAP, on the other.
January 18, 1980	Congolese peacekeeping contingents arrive in N'Djamena
March 1980	FAN and FAP forces battle in N'Djamena with 5,000 killed
March 21, 1980	Civil war erupts in N'Djamena after a Gukuni-Habre falling-out; N'Djamena becomes a ghost city as 100,000 inhabitants flee to Cameroon
April 1980	Habre forced to leave N'Djamena and moves to northeastern Chad; Kamougue embraces the Gukuni regime

June 15, 1980	Chad-Libya defense agreement is signed
December 15, 1980	Aided by Libyan forces, Gukuni routes Habre from N'Djamena
December 1980	Libyan forces are deployed to N'Djamena
1981	Libyan troops occupy the capital
January 6, 1981	Chad-Libya merger announced; the ill-defined proposal triggers CIA support for Habre, who is regrouping in the East
October 29, 1981	Gukuni is pressured to request withdrawal of Libyan troops in exchange for protection from OAU forces
November 1981	Libyan troops withdraw from N'Djamena at Gukuni's request
November 19, 1981	Abeche falls to Habre units following the withdrawal of Libyan troops
Nov. 15–27, 1981	Zaire-Senegal units of the OAU force arrive but refuse to stem Habre's assaults
December 1981	A 3,800-man Inter-African OAU Force with troops from Nigeria, Senegal, and Zaire arrives in the capital
January 7, 1982	Faya-Largeau falls to Habre's troops
February 1982	Mangalme and Oum Hadjer fall to Habre's units
May 8, 1982	Declaration of N'Djamena; new provisional government set up
June 1982	Habre successfully concludes his march on N'Djamena; Gukuni flees, and OAU troops do not interfere
June 7, 1982	N'Djamena falls to Habre; Gukuni flees to BET
July 19, 1982	Acyl dies in an accident
August 7, 1982	Sarh falls to dissident FAT troops allied to Habre
September 4, 1982	Moundou falls to dissident FAT troops aided by FAN units; Kamougue flees to BET via Cameroon
September 29, 1982	New Acte Fondamental proclaimed
October 21, 1982	Habre sworn in as president of Chad
October 28, 1982	Gukuni announces the creation in Bardai of the Government of National Salvation, pledged to the ouster of Habre
January 7, 1983	Unified Forces Armées Nationales Tchadiennes set up
April 18, 1983	Chado-Nigerian troop clashes along the border
May 1983	Gukuni's counteroffensive, supported by Libya, commences in BET
June 23, 1983	Faya-Largeau falls to Gukuni Wedei
June-July 1983	Libyan and Gukuni rebel troops advance southward, capturing Faya-Largeau and Abeche; France launches Operation Manta, deploying 3,000 troops to Chad; invading forces retreat to parallel 16

July 1983	Mobutu of Zaire sends 2,000 troops to help protect N'Djamena
July 10, 1983	Abeche falls to Gukuni but is later retaken by FAN troops personally led by Habre
July 1983	U.S.-French airlift of materiel to N'Djamena
August 3, 1983	France, nudged by the United States, commences Operation Manta, creating a Red Line limiting Goukouni's advance southward
September 1983	FAN atrocities in the southern prefectures spawn southern liberation movements from bases in the CAR
June 3, 1984	GUNT squads based in the South attack Tandjile and Mayo-Kebbi prefectural offices, killing 14 government troops
September 17, 1984	France and Libya reach an accord for simultaneous withdrawal of troops from Chad
November 1984	French troops complete their withdrawal, but Libya reneges and keeps its forces in Chad surreptitiously
1985	A summit meeting is held in Benin at which seven major antigovernment factions loyal to Gukuni unite to form the Conseil Supreme de la Révolution (CSR)
1986	Habre announces release of 122 political prisoners; Libyan-backed GUNT forces resume hostilities by attacking government positions; Habre appeals for and receives increased French military aid and intervention
February 1986	Gukuni and Libyan Islamic Legion forces cross south of parallel 16 but are repulsed by Habre's forces north of N'Djamena
February 1986	After the resumption of hostilities, France deploys air and ground forces once again to N'Djamena in Operation Epervier.
1986–Sept. 1987	Habre launches a successful campaign against Libyan and remnant Gukuni rebel forces, driving them to the northwestern part of the Aouzou Strip
December 1986	Habre's guerrilla campaign in the Tibesti begins
January 2, 1987	Libyans defeated at Fada
March 19–20, 1987	Libyan Fada recovery force defeated at Bir-Kora
March 23, 1987	Libyan base at Ouadi-Doum falls, causing a strategic withdrawal from northern Chad
August 8, 1987	Chadian forces seize Aouzou village
August 28, 1987	Libyans recapture Aouzou village on third try
September 5, 1987	Chad attacks Matan es Sarra, a base 60 miles inside Libya
1987	OAU mediation culminates in cease-fire between Chad and Libya on September 11; fighting breaks out again in

	November, and UN General Assembly declares OAU responsible for resolving the dispute
October 1987	Chad and Libya restore diplomatic relations severed in 1982
August 31, 1989	Libya and Chad sign an accord, agreeing to submit their border dispute over the Aouzou Strip to the International Court of Justice
December 1, 1990	Idris Deby ousts Habre, who flees to Cameroon and settles in Senegal
January–April 1993	National Democratic Conference held in N'Djamena
August 4, 1993	Disturbances in Abeche, leaving close to a hundred people dead
August 8, 1993	At least 10 people killed in N'Djamena in ethnic clashes during which security forces open fire
February 1994	The International Court of Justice's decision on Aouzou rebuffs Libya's claim
May 1994	Libya completes withdrawal from Aouzou
Early December, 1994	Deby grants amnesty to political prisoners and opposition abroad (except Habre)
April 8, 1995	Djimasta Koibla appointed premier
May 1995	Amnesty International accuses government forces (ANT) of massacres in the South and violations of human rights
March 1996	The government and 13 opposition parties sign a cease-fire and create a special security force to oversee the presidential elections
June 2, 1996	Presidential elections: Deby receives 47.8 percent of the vote and General Kamougue, of the Union Pour le Renouveau et la Democratie, 11.1 percent, out of a total of 15 candidates
June 11, 1996	Second round of presidential elections: Deby gets 69.1 percent and Kamougue 30 percent of the vote
August 8, 1996	Deby inaugurated as first democratically elected president of Chad
January 2, 1997	Legislative elections (first round)
February 5, 1997	Second round of legislative elections: the MPS is declared winner of the majority of the seats

Selected Bibliography

Due to space limitations, we simply list in this paragraph the titles of the periodicals the reader will find quite helpful in understanding Chad: *Africa Confidential, Africa Research Bulletin, Africa News, Afrique Contemporaine, Africa Report, Bulletin de l'Afrique Noire, Jeune Afrique, West Africa, Country Background Notes, Le Figaro, Journal Officiel de l'Afrique Equatoriale Française, Marchés Tropicaux et Méditerranéens, Le Monde, New York Times, Washington Post, Washington Times,* archival materials, and dozens of contemporary sources obtained from Chad and its embassies, *the* Banque des États de l'Afrique Centrale (BEAC), the World Bank, the International Monetary Fund, and the United Nations, and several prominent journals in English and French. Interviews with Chadians were also part of the sources for the chapter on Chad's history.

General Works

Africa: South of the Sahara. London: Europa, 1994.

Collelo, Thomas, ed. *Chad: A Country Study.* Washington, D.C.: U.S. Government Printing Office, 1990.

Decalo, Samuel. *Historical Dictionary of Chad.* Metuchen, N.J.: Scarecrow Press, 1987.

Legum, Colin. *Africa Contemporary Record.* New York: Africana, 1985–1990.

Nelson, Harold, et al. *Area Handbook for Chad.* Washington, D.C.: U.S. Government Printing Office, 1972.

Thompson, Virginia, and Richard Adloff. *Emerging States of French Equatorial Africa.* Oxford: Oxford University Press, 1960.

Geo-economics

Ahmad, Moid U. "Ground Water Resources: The Key to Combatting Drought in Africa." *Desertification Control Bulletin* 16 (1988): 2–6.

Asante, S.K.B. *The Political Economy of Regionalism in Africa: A Decade of the Economic Community of West African States (ECOWAS).* New York: Praeger, 1986.

Azevedo, S., and J. Hervieu. *Mils et sorghos du Tchad.* N'Djamena: ORSTOM, 1975.

Cabot, Jean. *Atlas practique du Tchad.* Paris: Presses Universitaires de France, 1973.

Cabot, Jean, and Christian Bouquet. *Le Tchad.* Paris: Presses Universitaires de France, 1973.

Conac, Gerard. *Les politiques de l'eau en Afrique: Développement agricole et participation paysanne.* Paris: Économica, 1985.

Dadi, Abdelrahman. *Tchad: L'état retrouvé.* Paris: Harmattan, 1987.

Hare, F. Kenneth, Robert W. Kates, and Andrew Warren. "The Making of Deserts: Climate, Ecology, and Society." *Economic Geography* 53, no. 4 (October 1977): 332–346.

Lavy, Victor. "Alleviating Transitory Food Crises in Sub-Saharan Africa: International Altruism and Trade." *World Bank Economic Revue* 6, no. 1 (January 1992): 125–138.

Nnadozie, Emmanuel U. "Regional Organization and the New World Order." In Luis Serapiao, ed., *Africa and the New World Order*. New York: Edwin Mellen Press, forthcoming.

Osterfeld, David. *Prosperity Versus Planning: How Government Stifles Economic Growth.* New York: Oxford University Press, 1992.

Van Chi-Bonnardel, Regine. *The Atlas of Africa.* New York: Free Press, 1973.

History

Amegbo, Joseph. *Rabah conquerant des pays tchadiens.* Paris: ABC, 1976.

Azevedo, Mario Joaquim. "Sara Demographic Instability as a Consequence of French Colonial Policy in Chad (1890–1940)." Unpublished Ph.D. Dissertation, Duke University, 1975.

Barth, Henri. *Voyages et découvertes dans l'Afrique septentrionale et centrale,* vol. 3. Paris: A. Bohne Librairie, 1861.

Bernard, Lanne. "Les deux guerres civiles." Pp. 53–62 in T*chad: Anthologie de la guerre civile.* N'Djamena: Yamoko Koulro-Bezo, 1981.

Brenner, Louis. *The Shehus of Kukawa.* Oxford: Oxford University Press, 1973.

Cohen, Ronald. *The Kanuri of Bornu.* New York: Holt, Rinehart and Winston, 1967.

Collier, John. "Historical Setting." Pp. 1–32 in Thomas Collelo, ed., *Chad: A Country Study.* Washington, D.C.: U.S. Government Printing Office, 1990.

Fisher, Allen, and Humphrey Fisher. *Slavery and Muslim Society in Africa.* New York: Doubleday, 1972.

Gentil, Émile. *La chute de l'empire de Rabah.* Paris: Hachette, 1902.

Kalck, Pierre. *Central African Republic.* New York: Praeger, 1971.

Lange, D. "The Kingdoms and Peoples of Chad." Pp. 238–265 in D. T. Niane, ed., *General History of Africa. IV.* Paris: UNESCO, 1992.

Lapie, Pierre. *My Travels Through Chad.* London: John Murray, 1943.

Manot, Michel. *L'aventure de l'or et du Congo-Ocean.* Paris: Libraire Sécretan, 1946.

Meillassoux, Claude. *L'Esclavage en Afrique precoloniale.* Paris: Maspero, 1975.

Meynier, Octave F. *La Mission Joalland-Meynier.* Paris: Éditions de l'Empire Français, 1947.

Moran, Denise. *Tchad.* Paris: Gallimard, 1934.

Nachtigal, Gustav. *Sahara und Sudan.* Berlin: Weidmannsche Buchhandlung, 1879–1889.

Palmer, H. R. *The Bornu, Sahara, and Sudan.* London: J. Murray, 1936.

Reyna, S. P. *Wars Without End: The Political Economy of a Precolonial State.* Hanover: University Press of New England, 1990.

Weinstein, Brian. *Gabon: Nation-Building on the Ogooue.* Cambridge: Cambridge University Press, 1966.

Wright, John. *Libya: A Modern History.* Baltimore: Johns Hopkins University Press, 1982.

Politics, Government, and International Relations

Arlinghaus, Bruce, ed. *African Security Issues: Sovereignty, Stability, and Solidarity.* Boulder, Colo: Westview Press, 1984.

Blundy, David, and Andrew Lycett. *Qaddafi and the Libyan Revolution.* Boston: Little, Brown, 1987.

Buijenthuijs, Robert. *Le FROLINAT et les révoltes populaires du Tchad.* Paris: Mouton, 1978.

_____. *Le FROLINAT et les guerres civiles du Tchad (1978-1984).* Paris: Karthala, 1987.

Byrnes, Rita M. "Government and Politics." Pp. 135–168 in Thomas Collelo, ed., *Chad: Country Study.* Washington, D.C.: U.S. Government Printing Office, 1990.

Cornet, Jacques Le. *Histoire politique du Tchad de 1900 à 1960.* Paris: Pichon et Duran, 1963.

Decalo, Samuel. "The Process, Prospects, and Constraints of Democratization in Africa." *African Affairs* 91, no. 362 (January 1992): 7–35.

Eboue, Felix. *Politique indigène de l'A. E. F.* Brazzaville: Imprimérie Officielle, 1941.

Foltz, William. "Chad's Third Republic." Pp. 1–8 in *CSIS Africa Notes.* Washington, D.C.: Center for Strategic and International Studies, 1977.

Foltz, William, and Henry Bienen, eds. *Arms and the African.* New Haven: Yale University Press, 1985.

Grundy, K. W. *Guerrilla Struggle in Africa: An Analysis and Preview.* New York: Grassman, 1971.

Hooder, B. W., and D. R. Harris. *Africa in Transition.* London: Methuen, 1967.

Kelley, Michael. *A State in Disarray: Conditions of Chad's Survival.* Boulder, Colo.: Westview Press, 1986.

Lanne, Bernard. *Tchad-Libye: Querelles des frontières.* Paris: Karthala, 1982.

_____. "Les deux guerres civiles." Pp. 53–63 in *Tchad: Anthologie de la guerre civile.* N'Djamena: Yamoko Koulro-Bezo, 1981.

Lemarchand, René. "The Politics of Sara Ethnicity: A Note on the Origins of the Civil War in Chad." *Cahiers d'Études Africaines* 20, no. 4 (1980): 449–471.

_____. "The Crisis in Chad." Pp. 239–256 in Gerald Bender, James Coleman, and Richard Sklar, eds., *African Crisis Areas.* Berkeley: University of California Press, 1985.

_____. "The Case of Chad." Pp. 106–124 in René Lemarchand, ed., *The Green and the Black.* Bloomington: Indiana University Press, 1988.

Moose, George E. "French Military Policy in Africa." Pp. 59–98 in William Foltz and Henry Bienen, eds., *Arms and the African.* New Haven: Yale University Press, 1985.

Mun-Koefod, Captain. "Routing the Libyans." *Marine Corps Gazette* 71, no. 8 (August 1987): 26–27.

Ndive, Koefele-Kale. "Cameroon and Its Foreign Policy." *African Affairs* 319, no. 80 (April 1981): 197–217.

N'Gangbet, Michel. *Peut-on sauver le Tchad?* Paris: Karthala, 1984.

Neuberger, Benjamyn. *Involvement, Invasion, and Withdrawal: Quadhdhafi's Libya and Chad, 1969–1981.* Tel Aviv: Tel Aviv University, 1982.

Somerville, Keith. *Foreign Military Intervention in Africa.* New York: St. Martin's Press, 1990.

Spartacus, Colonel (pseud.). *Operation Manta: Tchad 1983-1984.* Paris: Plon, 1985.

Tartter, Jean. "National Security." Pp. 172–208 in Thomas Collelo, ed., *Chad: A Country Study.* Washington, D.C.: U.S. Government Printing Office, 1990.

Thompson, Virginia, and Richard Adloff. *Conflict in Chad.* Berkeley: Institute of International Studies, 1981.

Zartman, William. "Africa and the West: The French Connection." Pp. 39–58 in Bruce Arlinghaus, ed., *African Security: Sovereignty, Stability, and Solidarity.* Boulder, Colo.: Westview Press, 1984.

_____. *International Relations in the New Africa.* Englewood Cliffs, N.J.: Prentice-Hall, 1986.

Society, Culture, and Demography

Adler, Alfred. *Le pays de Bouna: Notes sur la vie sociale et religieuse d'une population du Moyen-Chari.* Fort-Lamy: Institut National Tchadien pour les Sciences Humaines, 1966.

Bassis, Henri. *Des mîtres pour une autre école: Former ou transformer.* Brussels: Casterman, 1978.

Buck, Alfred, Robert Anderson, Tom Sasaki, and Kawata Kazuyishi. *Health and Disease in Chad.* Baltimore: Johns Hopkins University, 1970.

Chapelle, Jean. *Le peuple tchadien.* Paris: Harmattan, 1980.

_____. *Nomades noirs du Sahara.* Paris: Harmattan, 1982.

Cohen, Ronald, et al. *Quelques populations de la République du Tchad: Les arabes du Tchad.* Paris: Centre des Hautes Études Administratives d'Afrique et d'Asie Modernes, 1971.

Cordell, Dennis. *Dar al-Kuti and the Last Years of the Transaharan Slave Trade.* Madison: University of Wisconsin Press, 1985.

_____. "Society and Environment." Pp. 33–86 in Barbara Grimes, ed., *Chad: A Country Study: Ethnologue, 1.* Austin, Tex.: Summer Language Institute, 1992.

Jaulin, Robert. *La mort sara.* Paris: Plon, 1971.

Khayar, Issa H. *Les refus de l'école.* Paris: Librairie d' Amérique et d'Ouest, 1976.

Lapidus, Ira. *A History of Islamic Societies.* Cambridge: Cambridge University Press, 1988.

Ledentu, Colonel. "La méningite cérebro-spinale en Afrique équatoriale française pendant le premier semestre 1938." *Bulletin Mensuel de l'Office International d'Hygiène Publique* 30 (1939): 1–5.

Mbaiosso, Adoum. *L'éducation au Tchad: Bilan, problèmes et perspectives.* Paris: Karthala, 1990.

McKelvey, John. *Man Against Tsetse: Struggle for Africa.* Ithaca: Cornell University Press, 1952.

Milleliri, J. M., and H. N. Tirandibaye. "Historique de la trypanosomiase humaine africaine dans le Moyen-Chari (Tchad)." *Médicine Tropicale* 49, no. 4 (October-December 1989): 381–387.

Milleliri, J. M., H. N. Tirandibaye, and B. Nana-Madjoum. "The Focus of Human African Trypanosomiasis in Moissala (Chad)." *Médicine Tropicale* 49, no. 3 (July-September 1989): 253–258.

Moore, Patrick, John Hierholzer, Walis DeWitt, Koulienga Gouant, Dezoumbe Djore, Theo Lippeveld, Brian Plikayis, and Claire V. Broome. "Respiratory Viruses and Mycloplasma as Cofactors for Epidemic Group A Meningococcal Meningitis." *Journal of the American Medical Association* 264, no. 10 (September 12, 1990): 1271–1273.

Obert, John. *Islam, Continuity and Change in the Modern World.* Boulder, Colo.: Westview Press, 1988.

Spencer, John J. Trimingham. *A History of Islam in West Africa.* Oxford: Oxford University Press, 1970.

Stanghellini, A., P. Catan, N. Tirandibaye, P. Emery, J. M. Milleliri, and G. Cordoliani. "Epidemiological Aspects of Human African Trypanosomiasis in South Chad." *Médicine Tropicale* 49, no. 4 (October-December 1989): 395–400.

Tubiana, Marie-Joseph, and Joseph Tubiana. *The Zaghawa from an Ecological Perspective.* Rotterdam: A. A. Balkema, 1977.

About the Book and Authors

Chad, the fifth largest country in Africa, has experienced great difficulties politically, economically, and socially. During the 1980s and early 1990s, Chad briefly held international attention because of its warring with Libya. This situation underlines Chad's potential for drawing its neighbors—Libya, Sudan, Cameroon, and Nigeria in particular—and to some degree France and the United States into its conflicts. For this reason alone, diplomats and scholars alike should pay close attention to the pivotal position this former French colony occupies in the heart of Africa. Is Chad the sleeping giant of Africa? What role can we expect of a peaceful Chad in Central Africa? What would be the repercussions if Libya annexed Chad? What role has France played in this protracted conflict, and how do the Chadian people deal with it? What is the role of the northern leaders of the country? Are they warlords or committed nationalists? These are some of the questions Mario Azevedo and Emmanuel Nnadozie raise and answer.

The authors analyze and demythologize Chad's complex socioeconomic and political history as background for understanding its contemporary situation. In addition, they examine Chad's attempts at political and economic reforms and the prospects for entrenching democracy following recent elections. The roles and conditions of women are also emphasized. Based on primary and secondary sources, this book is by far the most comprehensive portrayal and evaluation of Chad's past and present currently available.

Mario J. Azevedo is chair of the Department of African-American and African Studies and Frank Graham Porter Professor at the University of North Carolina at Charlotte. **Emmanuel U. Nnadozie** is associate professor of economics at Truman State University.

Index